NEW LIGHT ON THE YOUTH OF DANT

D0498231

NEW LIGHT
ON THE YOUTH OF
DANTE

NEW LIGHT
ON THE YOUTH OF
DANTE

THE COURSE OF DANTE'S LIFE
PRIOR TO 1290
TRACED IN THE *INFERNO*
CANTOS 3-13

BY

GERTRUDE LEIGH

KENNIKAT PRESS
Port Washington, N. Y./London

NEW LIGHT ON THE YOUTH OF DANTE

First published in 1929
Reissued in 1969 by Kennikat Press
Library of Congress Catalog Card No: 78-101028
SBN 8046-0695-1

Manufactured by Taylor Publishing Company   Dallas, Texas

CONTENTS

CONTENTS

CONTENTS

INTRODUCTION

To ADD to the vast conglomeration of comment and interpretation reared over the *Divina Commedia* demands solid justification. The following work is the outcome of discoveries made during an examination into its allegorical purpose, pursued for over thirty years.

The first step towards the elucidation of the hidden theme was the identification of the journey through the infernal regions with Dante's own journey through life; his entry of the Gateway of Life (*Inferno*, III, 1-21) at conception, shortly followed by his Birth (*Inferno*, III, 130-136); his progress through various phases of mortal existence and its final close with the figure of Death.[1] The immediate purpose of the following pages is to unfold that part of the autobiography of Dante which extends over the first twenty-four years of his life, and can be discerned underlying Cantos III to XIII of the *Inferno*.

Remarkable implications are involved in the recognition of a contemporary narrative of historical events underlying that tale of damned and tortured souls which has hitherto been accepted as a sample of Dante's religious convictions.

Further discoveries tending to elucidate the inner purport of the *Commedia* followed. Long investigation into all the works of Dante, considered in the light thrown upon them by writers contemporary with him, made it evident that in countless passages of the *New Life*, the *Banquet*, the *Purgatorio*, and the *Paradiso* Dante had disclosed himself to be deeply imbued with the religious principles enunciated by Joachim de Flore, further developed by Olivi, and carried to their logical outcome by the influential anti-Papal party of the Spirituals in the early fourteenth century. The Spirituals aimed at nothing short of a complete re-statement of Christianity. According to their doctrine the entire Catholic hierarchy with its wealth, temporal dominion, all-embracing punitive system, and notorious abuses was destined to be

---

[1] *Dante's Inferno an Autobiography. Quarterly Review*, August 1909.

superseded. The central pivot on which Christianity turned they proclaimed to be the Love of the Father, revealed once for all by the Son, communicated to the heart of all mankind by manifestation of the Holy Spirit.

These tenets are wholly incompatible with belief in the kind of Hell which Dante seems to set before his readers. They are compatible, however, with the theory that the surface aspect of the *Inferno* is a satire on the age in which Dante lived, and on the debased religious system enforced by law. We have been led to the conclusion that the satiric or allegorical form of writing was forced upon him by the repressive powers of the Inquisition Courts which during his entire life debarred him from the open utterance of his convictions; that the conception of Divine Justice implicit in the literal subject of the *Inferno*, already repugnant to the spirit of his age, was definitely repudiated by Dante; that the allegorical theme of the *Inferno* was designed to expose the errors of the Papal administration, and to vindicate his own conduct by affording a secret history of his life and times.

The life of Dante Alighieri, which ended in the year 1321, was spent in a prolonged struggle against the spiritual and temporal forces of the Papacy. He wrote chiefly in Italian. His works in this tongue which have survived include the *New Life*, composed of a mystic sequence of sonnets and songs with prose interludes; many lyrics, ballads, and short poems; and the *Banquet*, a comment on some of them, left incomplete. His masterpiece, the *Divine Comedy*, is a trilogy which purports to present his survey as an eyewitness of Hell, Purgatory, and Paradise. His most conspicuous work in Latin was a treatise on Monarchy designed to expose the hollowness of the Papal claims to universal dominion over the minds and bodies of mankind. There remain also an unfinished Latin treatise on language, one on physical science, and several Latin epistles.

Of facts attested by documents there is but a scanty series to throw light on Dante's life. He was born in Florence in the year 1265. On his father's side he came of an old Guelf stock; there is reason to believe that his mother, Bella, belonged to a Ghibelline family. His father and mother both died before, at the age of eighteen, he came legally of age. In 1288 he took arms under the Guelfic League against the Ghibelline forces led by Guido da Montefeltro, and in the following year he took part in the battle of Campaldino, at which the Ghibellines suffered a severe defeat. Shortly after this he produced the *Vita Nuova*, being then already known as a lyric writer. A little later he married Gemma Donati, and four children were born to him before 1301, Pietro, Jacopo, Antonia, and Beatrice. About the time of his marriage he was admitted to the Guild of Physicians and Druggists in Florence, and began to take part in municipal affairs as a member of the Florentine Council. He was elected Prior in 1300 and passed at once into strong opposition to Boniface VIII. In 1302, while absent from Florence, he was condemned with others who resisted Papal encroachments on the liberty of the citizens to the confiscation of all his property and to perpetual exile. To this sentence was added within a short time another, decreeing him to be burnt alive should he ever again venture within the confines of the city. Very little is known of his after life. He took part for a short time with other exiles in attempting to overthrow the dominant Guelf faction which held Florence. He is heard of in various parts of Italy. He wrote letters welcoming the Emperor, Henry of Luxemburg, to Italy, on his abortive mission of pacification in 1310. His last refuge was at the Court of Guido Novello da Polenta in Ravenna, where he died at the age of fifty-six years and four months. The Latin eclogues which he exchanged with Giovanni del Virgilio shed light upon this period of his life. Generally speaking, it is through the allusions to his own doings and interests, the reflections on contemporary affairs, which are to be found interspersed in his writings, that the best illustrations of his life and mind are afforded.

During the last seventy years a flood of light has been thrown on the period covered by Dante's life and the figures of his contemporaries. The oppressive conditions under which he lived and worked, together with the rising tide of enlightened aspiration which carried his generation immeasurably far from the strange dogmas of the dark ages, have been explored by many scholars of repute. The facts thus laid bare form the basis of the following pages, and are not in dispute. But their significance in relation to the greatest figure of that (perhaps of any) age seems to have missed full appreciation. The way of access to the mind and purpose of Dante has remained barred. And the reason is not far to seek. It lies in his

3

apparent crass acceptance of belief in a realm wherein God torments to all eternity the myriad races of mankind, created it would seem solely for this end. A recent writer on Dante maintains, and there are few who will be disposed to contradict him, that ' the literal meaning of the *Inferno* is the most abominable superstition that has ever pestered humanity '. It stands like an iron curtain before the stage on which Dante lived his unfettered intellectual life and gave to the world his inspired visions of a God eternally manifested to *all* His creatures throughout the universe in Love. Once this curtain is raised a new Dante emerges, one in whom was centred all the wisdom of his own age, including that of the preceding ages so far as it was then accessible to students. A politician? yes—with a vision of European unity only now approaching consummation. A theologian? far more—one whose dominating passion was a thirst for the Absolute; one imbued, moreover, with constructive ideals for the regeneration of Christendom. Yet a man of the world, familiar with court life, on terms of intimacy with Popes and Cardinals, Emperors, Kings and princes, statesmen of various countries, philosophers, poets, historians, and ladies of high degree; a skilled psychologist, able to read the hearts and thoughts of all who came under his observation; a master of language such as the world has rarely seen before or since; in his own chosen genre of satire peerless; a subtle dialectician, learned in the arts of the Schoolmen and on occasion using with conspicuous felicity their methods of cloaking plain statements; not always solemn; apt to display a classical relish for a *paranoia*, or expose with a daring quip some absurdity of the orthodox; an ardent investigator into the physical secrets of the universe; the first to open up to his generation in the vulgar tongue the wonders of Ptolemaic astronomy. And with all this we get indications of an even rarer gift, the power to discern and rejoice in whatever rings true in the utterance of every seeker after truth, whether pagan, orthodox Churchman, mystic, bigot, heretic, or sceptic; able to recognize that every facet of truth, wherever visible, is as the hall-mark of Divine inspiration—a witness to the indwelling presence of the Holy Spirit; able, moreover, to pass temperate judgment on conclusions which his own intellect rejected.

We venture to entreat—it is much to ask—that the reader

will keep an open mind for a short space, admitting the possibility that such a Hell as Dante seems to picture may have been no less antagonistic to the ideals of Christianity framed by his mighty intellect than to those of our own day.

There is no escape from the dilemma that the ostensible literal meaning of the *Inferno*, as crystallized in men's minds for the past six hundred years, is wholly irreconcilable with the profound religious philosophy which Dante set himself to teach his generation.

Literally accepted the *Inferno* quite plainly committed its author to a very definite scheme of the universe. It predicates the constitution by Divine command of a supreme Papal hierarchy, infallible, impeccable, from whose judgment is no appeal here or hereafter, to be the exclusive instrument for the instruction and salvation of all mankind. Through this channel alone can grace flow down from God to man. Owing to Adam's disobedience every member of the human race is born guilty—an outcast from God, and unless rescued from God's wrath by the authoritative ministers of the Church must without doubt perish everlastingly. The possession of those qualities defined by Aristotle as moral and intellectual virtues is of no avail in God's sight. All men, however irreproachable in morals and conduct—heroes, philosophers, poets, holy and humble men of heart, whose lives have been dedicated without reserve to the service of God and their fellows—if from the time and place of their birth they have been deprived of the Sacraments, are doomed to expiate this lack of opportunity for evermore in hell, excluded from the light of God's Presence and tortured, in body by everlasting flames, in mind by a sense of undying despair. All who received the Sacraments and conformed to the decrees of the Church were assured of salvation, but even so a heavy penalty for sin, it was taught, awaited them in a future state. The fiery torments of Purgatory, measurable by hundreds of thousands of years, could be mitigated, however, by various devices, by earning indulgences, by undertaking pilgrimages, by payments to the Church in money and land, by Masses bought by survivors for their dead friends. Material proofs of penitence such as these would be accepted as forming a title to absolution if not to remission of penalties. All, however, who had incurred sentence of excommunication were eternally lost. All who died without knowledge of the Christian faith, either in the ages preceding the Atonement or in regions where no Christian priest had penetrated, had their portion in hell torment. Endless torment awaited likewise all babes who died without baptism, and this was the fate even of those who died in the womb.

It is essential to scrutinize Dante's other writings in order to ascertain whether he really believed the infinite love, wisdom, and power of the Creator to have been displayed in a curse laid on the entire race after the first man's foreknown transgression; in a Redemption effected after thousands of years during which even the forerunners of Christianity among the chosen people were swept into hell; and in the institution of a system of salvation which can operate solely for the benefit of a minute fraction of mankind. Such is the basis underlying the structure of the literally accepted *Inferno*.

These doctrines were widely criticized in philosophic circles and constantly rejected during Dante's lifetime. They were repudiated more particularly by those philosophic and learned Ghibellines who found themselves at every turn in the wheel of events liable to be cut off by excommunication from all means of grace. Every one of these tenets, implied though with ambiguity in the *Inferno*, is refuted in Dante's other writings. It can be shown that he was vehemently antagonistic to the false conception of the Deity on which it has been supposed he laid the seal of his genius, and that far from being one of the adroit jugglers who claimed that what was false according to philosophy could yet be true according to faith, he daringly set himself to satirize in the *Inferno* the notions of Hell taught to and accepted by the multitude.

The hostility displayed by Dante towards the rulers of the Church has never been in dispute. He denounced their policy, their morals, their evil influence upon Italy and the world at large, in language which cannot be misunderstood. But it has been less clearly recognized that he also with equal determination, though more obliquely, rejected and denounced many of their cardinal doctrines. Boldly before the face of all he repudiated their claim to deliver such as resisted their authority to eternal perdition; for he depicted many excommunicates peacefully undergoing purification in Purgatory, released from the curses of the Church, and he clearly

6

demonstrated that penitent sinners even when cut off from the rites of the Church, may yet find pardon and acceptance in their last hour through the channel of their faith and love. He denounced as false the instruments granted under the name of indulgences by Papal authority for the mitigation of Purgatorial penalties, and denied the efficacy of Masses and prayers for the dead offered by venal priests—a source of enormous revenue to the Church. The dead, he declared, could only be aided here below by the prayers of those who live in grace.[1] Passionately and more than once at some length[2] he vindicated Greeks and Romans from the doom of God's eternal wrath stamped on them during the Dark Ages. He spurned indignantly the notion that God was at enmity with His creatures, and he demonstrated in opposition to this theory that, by the foreordained Sacrifice of His Son, God had reconciled to Himself before ever the world was made the entire human race, and redeemed it from the guilt though not from all the consequences of Adam's foreseen fall. In the mirror of Divine Justice presented in the *Paradiso* he brought into prominence the fact that, spite of short-sighted ecclesiastical dogmas on the nature of Divine judgments, the virtuous heathen have their place in Heaven.

All these and many more of Dante's utterances directly controvert the theory, presented ironically on the surface of the *Inferno*, that the Creator is compelled, by laws He made and cannot break, to take vengeance on all mankind for the sin of Adam, and that there is no way of escape from His wrath save through the rites of the Church received in unquestioning submission to Papal authority.

If it be indeed true, as we aspire to prove, that Dante rejected with scorn the notion of Hell by which the medieval mind was hag-ridden, we should expect to find that he would take pains to assure his readers that he did not really mean what he seemed to mean in the *Divina Commedia*, that the outer narrative was fictitious and not to be accepted as real. His own testimony in this respect is remarkably precise, and it is borne out in all particulars by the discourses which he introduced as a comment on the Hell framework.

In the unfinished preface to the *Paradiso*, contained in Epistle X, he revealed that there were two ways of regarding

---

[1] *Purg.*, IV, 133-135.   [2] *Mon.*, Bk. II; *Banquet*, Bk. IV.

7

the entire *Divina Commedia*, and that it contained two principal subjects, the one entirely different from the other. The literal and obvious theme was the 'State of the Soul after Death'. But this he insisted was not the real theme. He plainly declared that under the literal theme he had hidden 'an allegorical and true meaning', and thus implied that the obvious literal meaning of the poem was false or fictitious. He went on to explain that the true subject was not confined to 'souls after death'. It was concerned with 'man exercising free will, liable by good or bad conduct to the reward or punishment of justice'—man, therefore, still in a state of probation in this world. Thus he would have us know that rightly understood his vision of hell was a study, not of the dead, but of the living.

He was not without misgivings that the existence of a secret meaning hidden below the surface of his masterpiece might possibly by many be overlooked. He spurred his readers to hunt for the doctrines he disguised under a veil, and we may realize from this the existence of an inner band of disciples who understood his mode of expression.[1] He bade them sharpen their eyes to the truth when on occasion he had spun the veil he cast over his meaning so thin that he was assured it was quasi transparent.[2]

It was not it seems until he was living in comparative safety towards the end of his life, under the protection of Count Guido of Novello, with the Papal Curia at Avignon, and the Emperor Louis of Bavaria in strong opposition to it, that he could openly declare his true subject to be the presentation not of damned souls but of living persons who, though erring, were still open to repentance. The gist of this explanation is to manifest the *Inferno* as a satire. Among all the forms of literary composition this alone admits of a secret meaning being conveyed under the veil of a fictitious narrative.

---

[1] *Inf.*, IX, 61-63:
> O ye that have sane intellects, admire
> The doctrine which is hid under the veil
> Of these strained verses.

[2] *Purg.*, VIII, 19-21:
> Here Reader fix thine eyes keen on the truth
> For verily the veil is now so thin
> 'Tis a light task to penetrate beyond.

Cf. also *Para.*, X, 22-27.

8

The art of writing in such manner that the meaning is contrary to what appears on the surface was of high repute among the ancients under the name of Irony. Cicero, rendering the Greek *eironeia* as *dissimulatio*, calls this figure ' when we say one thing and mean another ', ' the most effective of all means of stealing into the minds of men '; and again, ' the speaker will desire his words to be taken in a different sense from their literal meaning ': ' his meaning will frequently be deeper than his words seem to indicate '.

Irony is a species of Allegory but differs from it in that, while in the case of allegory the words have one meaning and the sense another, in irony the meaning may be altogether contrary to what it appears.[1] From the example of Socrates, whom Cicero extols as the great master of irony, the notion of criticism has always been considered implicit in the use of irony. But it implies also ' the use of language that has an inner meaning for the persons addressed or concerned '.

Dante expressed a high opinion of the value of irony or dissimulation, declaring this figure in rhetoric to be worthy of much praise and, indeed, indispensable, especially in the case of admonitions addressed to a superior. He says, moreover: ' when a friend's shame would be increased or his honour depressed were he to be openly admonished, or when the friend is not patient under admonition but wrathful, this figure which may be called Dissimulation (irony) is specially beautiful and profitable. And it resembles the action of the skilful warrior who attacks the fortress on one side in order to draw off the defence from the other, for then the succour is not directed against the part where the (real) battle is taking place '.[2]

This profitable device for giving utterance to invidious truths has been the resource of poets, prophets, and reformers in every age when writing under political or ecclesiastical constraint, but examples of continuous irony are rare. The ironic allegory demands for its success a subject of universal interest and a combination of circumstances which at once justify a great writer in passionate remonstrance, and cut him off from any possibility of making direct appeal. There were,

[1] *Quintilian*, Bk. IX. The works of Quintilian formed the groundwork of medieval instruction in the art of speaking and writing.

[2] *Banquet*, Bk. III, c. 10.

9

however, two conspicuous examples of imaginative irony which accustomed readers to the use of satire in exposing current abuses. Reynard the Fox, universally popular in the twelfth and thirteenth centuries, was in essence a deliberate attack on the misgovernment of the Roman Church, veiled under the image of the crafty beast. The *Roman de la Rose*, widely circulated in the early fourteenth century, if it did not begin on this note, turned in the hands of Jean de Meung into an ironic allegory which enabled many passages of measured invective against the Inquisition to see the light. Thus people were perfectly familiar with the literary device of setting a fictitious narrative to hide opinions banned by the authorities. It was in the mode of the times.

Notwithstanding its obvious drawbacks Dante adopted the allegorical form for all three of the more important works he wrote in the vulgar tongue. He was fully alive to the danger he ran of being misunderstood, and seems to have become aware as time went on that his surface meaning had reacted too vividly on the minds of his readers. This is certainly suggested in the eclogues which passed between himself and Giovanni del Virgilio near the end of his life. The disciple deplored his master's unfortunate choice of the vulgar tongue for his 'ambiguous' poem, to which he alluded as 'the riddles of the equivocating sphinx'. Had he written his masterpiece in Latin the learned would have thought it worth while to find out his real meaning, while the ignorant would at least have been saved from interpreting it amiss. And there is this to be said for Del Virgilio's opinion, that the inner meaning of Dante's Latin eclogues has received in modern days a far closer verbal scrutiny than that accorded to some cryptic passages in the *Inferno*.[1]

It was surely not without imperative reason that Dante was moved to adopt the allegorical and ambiguous form of writing. It brought misunderstanding and obloquy upon him from the outset of his career when he related in the *New Life* the story of his early love for Beatrice, her premature death, and the consolation to which he afterwards attained—a tale so shrouded in mystery, if regarded as a mere romance, that it lent his enemies a ready handle against him. Later, when he became

[1] See *Dante and Giovanni del Virgilio*, by Philip Wicksteed and Edmund G. Gardner.

aware of this, he wrote the *Banquet*, itself charged with mystic currents of thought and avowedly containing more than one meaning, in order to expose the fact that the *New Life* was not to be taken literally but as a mystic allegory.

With these partial failures in view, for neither the *New Life* nor the *Banquet* could be regarded as successful in exposing with lucidity the author's true purpose, nothing but sheer necessity could have impelled him to act once more in the *Divine Comedy* the part of the 'equivocating Sphinx'.

It is tolerably clear, however, that the use of allegory was forced upon him by his determination from the beginning to write in the language understood by his fellow-countrymen. Two publics were open to him. The one was the comparatively small and exclusive set who were conversant with Latin; professors, doctors, lawyers, ecclesiastics, and other officials, all deriving their income directly or indirectly from the existing form of Church Government, and thus pledged to its support. Among these Dante reckoned there was but one in a thousand capable of receiving his message. He turned from them to address the rest: 'Princes, barons, knights, and many other noble folk, both men and women'—the multitude which had command of their own tongue, had been educated in some degree, but were not Latin scholars.

The opening Book of the *Banquet*[1] is mainly taken up with an impassioned defence of the Italian language, in which Dante examines and tears to pieces the arguments used by the ecclesiastical censors to justify their embargo on all serious works written in the language understood by the people. Their main contention was that Italian was not a proper medium for expressing truth, and this contention was used to support the rigid ecclesiastical ban against translating any part of the Scriptures or Church Offices. All versions of the Bible in the vulgar tongue were declared to be of necessity erroneous; hence they were all mischievous, and to read them or hear them read was heretical depravity. Dante will be found echoing the cry that no translation is ever perfect[2] but in the same breath calling attention to the fact that the verses of the Psalter, 'translated from the Hebrew into Greek and from Greek into Latin', labour under this very defect and lack the music of the original. He left his readers to infer for them-

[1] *Banquet*, Bk. i, c. 5-13.   [2] *Ibid.*, Bk. i, c. 7.

selves how absurd it would have been had the Church decreed
that none but Hebrew scholars were to be allowed access to
the Psalms. In defending his own tongue he advanced step by
step to expose the abominable motives which prompted the
ban on all Italian translations or expositions. It seems clear
enough that he aimed his rebukes directly at the Inquisition
officials, for they alone had power to prohibit the use of the
vernacular. He rebukes their blind stupidity, their dishonest
subterfuges, their ignorance, envy, and abjectness or cowardice. Nay, he does not scruple to denounce them as ' detestable
wretches '. ' If the vernacular be ever vile it is when it sounds
upon the prostitute lips of these adulterers.' Having determined in spite of all obstacles to persist in the use of the vernacular he is compelled to ask his readers to pardon him if
they find even his most painstaking explanations ' a little
difficult ' to understand. Wilful obscurity was the price he had
to pay for writing in Italian. Would it had pleased God that
the cause of this defect in his works had never arisen. It was
the same cause which had driven him into exile and poverty.

To enquire what things Dante was desirous of setting before his chosen public is to open the door to a bewildering
wealth of new ideas, so drastic was the embargo laid on their
discussion in the vulgar tongue.

The impediments to the spread of knowledge imposed by
the Church in this preliminary stage of the Renaissance have
long been familiar to students, but their reaction on the life
and works of Dante has hardly yet been fully realized. They
pressed severely on all men of letters at a time when new
sources of learning had introduced a ferment of speculation
into stagnant medieval theories of the universe.

The thirteenth century witnessed an awakening in every
department of knowledge to which there is no parallel in
history. The introduction of Aristotle to Europe, through
Latin versions based on Arabian commentators, had already
brought about a revolution in the realm of the intellect. To
minds long tolerant of authority in matters of faith, unaccustomed to the exercise of private judgment or, as Dante
called it, ' discrimination,' there was presented an enticing
system of the universe which seemed wholly inconsistent with
orthodox religion. All the best minds of the day were irresistibly drawn to the task of blending the new philosophy into one

12

homogeneous system which would harmonize with received doctrines. Unthinking acquiescence in the dogmas pronounced by successive Roman Bishops gave place to fearless research into the foundations of belief. Albertus Magnus and Thomas Aquinas among great divines assimilated the philosophy of Aristotle, and tried to show its accord with Roman theology. The works of Roger Bacon testify to an awakening of the spirit of experiment, in the face of which monkish theories set current in the darkest ages were exposed as ludicrously mistaken. Ardent investigators were exploring the surface of the earth and the mystery of the heavenly bodies. Marco Polo was discovering the existence of vast empires subsisting in placid remoteness from the sway of Rome. Sailors were pushing into unexplored regions, using the compass to correct old blunders, and map-making was becoming a science. Experimenters in physics and astronomy were making discoveries about which they dared only speak in whispers behind locked doors. For every new fact about the universe had the effect of upsetting some theory upheld as a religious truth. Hence in the eyes of the rulers of the Church all discovery, all research, was regarded as the work of the devil. The result was a violent conflict between the old and the new in matters alike of religious and secular knowledge.

In the period covered by Dante's lifetime the Catholic Church had need of the highest wisdom in order to direct with moderation the passage of men's minds out of age-long ignorance and error. But it is an unhappy fact, attested by unimpeachable contemporary evidence, that the direction of its affairs had passed into the hands of worldly-minded men, better fitted to enlarge its wealth and temporal powers than to advance the Kingdom of Christ. There was no lack of intellect in the Church. In no age was there ever a more brilliant display of zeal, piety, and learning among her sons. But all was nullified, and many of her saints persecuted to the death by the policy of the reactionary minority who had captured the ecclesiastical ' machine '.

The stupendous crime of inaugurating the Inquisition system, and devising its atrocious mode of procedure, had been committed in the previous century. But it was in the thirteenth century that its powers were fostered until its stranglehold threatened to extinguish the very life of the Church. It was an even greater blunder than crime. By the end of the thirteenth century Inquisitors, usurping powers of control hitherto vested in the Bishops, had shown themselves able to trample under foot all civil and religious liberties, and turn the Church into an instrument for involving all Christian people in confusion and terror. A vehement antagonism was set stirring against the Papal instruments in every part of the world to which their powers extended.

By the institution of these Courts, whose judges functioned continuously, irrespective of changes in the Papal Chair, the Church fell under the dominion of a secret and ambitious body of men, possessing unique opportunities for securing wealth, and for turning the vast powers of the Curia into an instrument for evil. The agents of the Inquisition penetrated into every city and diocese, every religious order and secular administration, every Court in Europe, and many distant parts of the world where their long arm brought retribution on political or religious refugees. The permanent control of religion, art, literature, and every branch of knowledge, gradually came under the control of these tribunals. Their baneful influence is apparent in every direction throughout the centuries during which Christendom lay in subjection to their tyranny.

It was largely for the purpose of controlling the output and circulation of all manuscripts that the Inquisition had been founded; the energy of their agents was exerted to the utmost for the suppression of free opinion, and the limitation of every branch of knowledge to a privileged few. In respect to Latin works their powers appear to have been to some extent restricted. The universities, jealous of their own privileges and supported by powerful charters, struggled intermittently to keep a certain current of progressive thought stirring in the theses put forth under their ægis. In the monastic orders, too, were monks who used their infinite leisure for the advancement of learning, and turned to good account the unrivalled opportunities at their disposal for the transcription of manuscripts. Their superiors guarded the output from any too subversive a tendency, and on occasion the over enthusiastic monk would be called on like Olivi, with his treatise on the Virgin, to commit his manuscript with his own hands to the flames, or like Roger Bacon to endure long imprisonment deprived of books and writing materials. Generally speaking, works in Latin could command but a narrow circle of readers, most of whom were impervious to new ideas. Being thus practically innocuous they were less closely scrutinized for subversive theories, and had some small chance of eluding censorship.

It was far otherwise with works in the vernacular. It was the settled policy of the Inquisition to exclude by force and fear the great body of the unlearned from any contact with works in their own tongue on religion, philosophy, or morals, and to suppress every kind of investigation into natural phenomena. All the new knowledge about the world which was the common property of learned men, and not in dispute, was rigorously withheld from the 'people'. Nothing whatever seems to have been allowed to circulate in the language of the country, in this age of enticing awakening, except stale and incredible legends of the saints, a few well-worn tales of ancient heroes, and certain songs of love and war which wandering troubadours were accustomed to recite. Romances were accordingly a recognized vehicle for diffusing secret doctrines, and when, in his youth, Dante set himself to communicate invidious truths to his fellow-countrymen in their own tongue, he found the simplest way to disarm suspicion was to present his experiences in the form of a romantic love-story. In this, he explained, he followed the example of his great predecessor in the New Style, Guido Guinicelli, and that of his comrade, Guido Cavalcanti.

In the dawn of knowledge which succeeded the long slumber of the Dark Ages, men found it an intolerable wrong to be shut off from discussion in their own tongue of the matters which seethed within them. The hungry flock looked up and were not fed. The demand for enlightenment was growing till it threatened to break down all barriers. In the eyes of the men to whose mercies the people had been committed, the thirst for knowledge, whether of God or of the world, was pure contumacy, and was treated as such. It was the aim of Inquisitors to stamp out resistance by striking terror into the minds of the people—a method which in the long run has never proved successful. Boundless powers were committed to them; astonishing ingenuity and resource lay at their command. Yet it is impossible not to be struck by their stupidity in the spiritual domain they had usurped. Vast numbers of simple folk were being drawn from allegiance to the Church by preachers who relied solely on the words of Christ and His Apostles for their persuasive arguments. To reclaim the flock, as St. Bernard had urged, by diligent catholic teaching in their own tongue, was a policy rejected and denounced by the authorities. Their agents were trained for other purposes than to instruct men in the faith of Christ. Punishment, agonizing, long drawn out, in this world; threats of punishment, agonizing and extending to all eternity in the next; these were the means employed to rekindle the love of Holy Church in the hearts of the people. The spirit of terror invoked by the Inquisition system has left its sinister shadow on every fair fruit of the human intellect, not excepting art itself. While architecture and the plastic arts attained to a glory which seems to suggest that few other outlets for genius were left open, the art of painting became fouled with a taint of horror. In every Church the vision of lost souls, damned and tortured by the God of Love, was the first to meet the eyes of the worshipper. Ecclesiastics were the principal patrons of the arts, and it was they undoubtedly who smirched by their commissions the dawning glories of Italian art with the horrible scenes of torture, meant to overawe the ignorant, which move the modern with disgust.

In the light of modernity, and under the influence of Aristotle and his Christian commentators, the vulgar superstitions of the Dark Ages had long been rejected by educated men, and much monkish lore had been thrown into the melting-pot. But under the sway of the Inquisition no terrifying concept of the Deity was allowed to fade. Preachers were admonished to fill their discourses in the vernacular with threats of perdition, and were warned that it savoured of heresy to rehearse the promises of the Saviour.

By long continued stress laid on damnation and its concomitants here and hereafter, the Inquisition, unhappily identified with the Church whose highest doctrines it was undermining, became inextricably associated in men's minds with the conception of hell-fire. Flames were the sign manual of the Courts, burning their worst torture and last doom. The threat of an eternal burning was rendered appallingly vivid to the popular imagination by the scenes of horror staged from time to time when all were gathered to watch a heretic burn.

Thus it came about that no conceivable screen could have been more efficacious for Dante's purpose of revealing Gospel truths to his generation than the one which he adopted. In feigning to set before the world a vision of eternal perdition he ensured the favour of the Inquisition, and license to say practically what he would. If some small part of the cryptic message within the semi-transparent veil did, indeed, penetrate (as seems likely) to the Inquisitors who controlled publication, it would seem that these persons astutely guessed that the lively images of perdition evoked by the genius of Dante would serve their purpose, and hide his own. To stress the odious theme of God's impending penalties could but aid in reducing the ignorant to cowed submission. And thus Dante's surface theme was entirely to their mind. Let who would peer into it for the dangerous implications it undoubtedly contained. Such investigations and discoveries were not for the vulgar.

The early commentators were fully as much under the control of the Inquisition as Dante himself. They were debarred from unfolding the truth about him. Was it not perhaps for this reason that only a fragment of Boccaccio's comment on the *Inferno* was achieved, or has at any rate been preserved? Later when the shadow of the great dread begun to be shifted from the Church Dante had become established as the medieval poet, credulous, superstitious, implacable. The Renaissance had blotted out the memory of all the daring speculations of his age, and what we may venture to call the Dante myth had crystallized round his figure.

The horrible conception that the minds and bodies of all save a narrow remnant of the souls born into the world will be reconstructed after death in such a manner that they will be exposed to torture and despair, had been already hotly disputed in the highly sceptical thirteenth century. It was a legacy from the darkest ages, a phantom shadowing the Christian's imagination, a political weapon ostentatiously brandished to intimidate the rebellious. There is much to suggest that secretly it was widely discredited. It was notoriously an acceptable jest among the rabble. It was the gravest count of the freethinker against popular theology. The universality of its application was doubted by more than one doctor of the Church. Thomas Aquinas, for instance, had suggested the possibility of exceptions, quoting with approval the dictum that ' if anyone in barbarous nations do what lieth in him God will reveal to him that which is necessary for salvation, either by inspiration or by sending him a teacher '.[1] Duns Scotus, who was lecturing in Paris at the time when, according to Boccaccio, Dante was there also writing the *Banquet* under a powerful impulse to declare philosophic truths, defined for his students the nature of eternal fire and its action on the damned. But it is significant to find him declaring the essential penalty of lost souls to be ' not the penalty of the senses but of damnation itself—the lack of the Divine vision and fruition in which their essential beatitude consists '. He could even conceive that God could assign a penalty which should punish intensively ' without annihilating the sinner and without resorting to an eternity of pain '. Ramon Lull, contemporary with Dante, dared also to maintain that ' God hath such love for His people that *almost* all men in the world shall be saved '. Dante appears to have believed with Duns Scotus and Ramon that some who deliberately reject the good of the intellect can make evil their eternal choice, and thus be cut off for ever from the Divine vision. But this solemn realization of a possible condition in which no place for repentance may be found, is quite distinct from the theory of excruciating ' penalties of the senses ' for all outside the Church presented in the *Inferno*. Here, in some passages, we are in the burlesque atmosphere of the Miracle Plays, then just coming into vogue, wherein devils with horns and tails, scourges or prongs, pursue the damned who jest amid their tortures. Such passages (*Inferno* XXI and XXII) compel attention to the ironic nature of the penalties, and forcibly suggest the existence of a basis of contemporary history disguised under allegorical language.

[1] S. Thomas was one of the most advanced thinkers of his day, and himself narrowly escaped post-mortem condemnation on the score of heresy. His dicta on the punishment and ultimate fate of heretics, as those on some other matters, were suspect in the eyes of Ghibellines who imagined that his manuscripts had been tampered with by the Dominicans, much as those of Duns Scotus were, in later years, by the Franciscans, though more adroitly. Dante certainly put it on record that Thomas Aquinas had been assassinated by Charles of Anjou, official champion of the Curia.

As a satire on current events, veiled under such a distorted theology as filtered through in that age to vulgar minds, the *Inferno*, though full of mysteries, is intelligible. Taking it at its surface value, it is a bewildering anachronism, presenting notions poles asunder from any theory of the Deity or the universe which could be held by a fourteenth-century Ghibelline and philosopher.

The two conflicting points of view are irreconcilable. Either the Papacy was the divinely-appointed arbiter of truth, unique dispenser of salvation, or it had become an unjustifiable usurpation, an instrument for deluding and oppressing mankind. The surface aspect of the *Inferno* employs the horrors of eternal damnation to emphasize the former view. Yet Dante made no secret (in later years) that it was the latter point of view he really held, and he dared to bring St. Peter himself on the stage to declare that there was now no Vicar of Christ on earth, his place was void, the Holy See vacant. He branded the existing Pope as an usurper, and inveighed against his abuse of the Keys, and the lying privileges (indulgences for sin) bartered for money to Christian people.[1]

From first to last the *Inferno* presents a terrible indictment of the Papal system, in its political, moral, and spiritual effect upon the world. There was justification for attributing the evils of the times to the Papacy. It claimed at this period in the world's history entire jurisdiction over the thoughts, words, and deeds of all men. It denied to civil rulers the most necessary exercise of their powers. It put down one Prince and raised up another. It left no domain of public or private life unregulated by its prescriptions, ordained originally with wisdom, but long perverted by venal agents. From the hour of birth to the day of death and beyond, in the realm of eternity, men found no way of escape from its discipline and threats. Had the result been a world at peace, a race of men generally schooled to virtue through the influence of their stern shepherds, the Church would have had a strong case for depriving men of liberty. But at the time when Dante wrote, and for generations before and after, the failure of the Papacy to carry out its programme, to promote public peace and justice, or to influence men's private conduct in the right direction, was conspicuous and damning.

[1] *Para.*, xxvii, 19 ff.

The *Inferno* presents the summing-up, by perhaps the keenest observer the world has ever seen, of the Papal system judged by results. To behold in the entire region traversed by Virgil and Dante a picture of the world, not as God made it, but as Rome and her allies had distorted it, is gradually to become aware that every single feature in it reflects some aspect of ecclesiastical authority. It is the officers of the Inquisition who threaten and inflict retribution; it is they who call down hell fire, scourge, torture, imprison in loathsome dungeons, maim and burn their fellow men after the fashion exhibited in the *Inferno*. Contemporary comment on these shameful deeds was effectually repressed. Dante had the art to make men tremble six centuries afterwards at their recital. This, he would have us understand, is a picture of life under a system which degrades law and extinguishes liberty. What worse thing can be pictured of hell? This is life as lived under the officials who dominated Church and State—a living death in which men groan in anguish for that ' second death ' which shall liberate them from their woes. It was all too easy so to construct the framework that what seemed like the eternal torture of the damned should be in reality a reflection of the horrible ills endured by mankind under ecclesiastical control. Yet with all the indignation which breathes in the *Inferno* it is smirched by no trace of *odium theologicum*. Not on account of dogmas from which his intellect dissented, but as a protest against deeds committed under his eyes, did Dante bring so formidable an indictment against the rulers of the Church.

The Hell theme looms more large in men's estimate of Dante's work than we can believe it to have done in his own mind. It provided a vehicle for the vindication of himself from calumny, and it enabled him to throw light on many obscure events in the history of the times. But it did not embody the vital truths he aspired to reveal to his own generation. There is much in the *Purgatorio* and *Paradiso*, even more in the *Banquet* and the treatise on Monarchy, to indicate that Dante was closely allied with the powerful body of advanced thinkers who repudiated as unscriptural many Roman tenets, and took their stand on the doctrines of Joachim de Flore, as subsequently developed by Petrus Johannis Olivi and the Spiritual Franciscans. Examined in the light of Joachist and Franciscan speculations it may prove that Dante's preoccupation about political affairs has been somewhat over accentuated, and that the pivot on which his life turned was more purely spiritual than has been suspected. There is room for a re-examination of his life based on the theory that his intellect was sensitive to the influences which inspired some of his noblest contemporaries, and that even his Imperialistic principles took a second place among the forces which dominated his life. The secret which we believe to lie hidden below the surface aspect of his writings is his adhesion to a very pure and spiritual mysticism, which had become to the very last degree obnoxious to ecclesiastical authority.

The natural refuge of faith betrayed by unworthy ecclesiasticism lies in mysticism. The course of Dante's life synchronized with a great revival of mystic fervour which thrust rites and dogmas into the background, and recognized in the heart of man the temple of the Holy Ghost.

Of the Blessed Francis and his influence on thirteenth-century religion there is no need to speak at length. He stirred the hearts of his generation with a fervour which brought about a bewildering perception of the gulf which separated the pure ideals of Christ from the morals of conspicuous Churchmen. In adopting a rule of poverty admitting of no exception for himself and the brethren of the Order, who were forbidden to touch money or even to mention it, he set stirring the belief that abuses in the Church could only be reformed by her return to pristine poverty. In the succeeding century this doctrine, extolled by Dante, was to become an anti-Papal weapon of unexampled force. The Gospel teaching of the early Friars, freely preaching to the people at first in their own language, roused a natural desire among the laity to study the Gospels for themselves, and although this was strictly forbidden, a great impetus was given to the study of the Bible. The mystic fervour of the Franciscan movement insensibly lessened the reliance of the devout on rites and ceremonies, and their asceticism made them impatient of the worldly-minded superiors set over them by Papal authority. They became still further detached from rigid orthodoxy by the Joachist theories long cherished in their Order.

Joachim de Flore, a saintly monk who died in 1202, had attained, after long meditation on the evils of official Christianity, to a conviction that the Catholic Church in its existing framework was a merely temporary dispensation, answering in some respects to the Jewish Synagogue, doomed to be superseded, as this had been in the fullness of time, by a pure and spiritual revelation. Joachim taught specifically that mankind was on the brink of a New Age in which the existing hierarchy—Popes, Cardinals, Bishops, Priests—would disappear. Just as the First Age of the Father, figured in the Old Testament and governed by the Jewish Church had passed, so the Second Age of the Son, figured in the New Testament and governed by the Catholic Church, was also, he declared, nearing its end. The Third Age of the Holy Spirit, in which the Old and New Testaments were to yield up their secrets, and reveal the Eternal Gospel of the Divine Love through the exercise of contemplation, was at hand. It would begin in the year 1260.

The mystic theology of Joachim had a widespread influence on the minds of Churchmen throughout the thirteenth century, and was held in high esteem until the time approached which he had unfortunately fixed for the fulfilment of his central prophecy. Then with disconcerting suddenness the Curia assumed an attitude of determined hostility towards Joachist doctrines. A book in which they were embodied, known as the *Introduction of the Eternal Gospel*, was publicly burnt in 1255. All copies of it were confiscated, and a taint of heresy rested ever after on his theories. They continued, nevertheless, to be held in great reverence throughout Christendom.

During the time when Dante as a young student was passing through the experiences he recounted in the *New Life*, it became evident that the mantle of Joachim had fallen on Petrus Johannis Olivi, a Franciscan monk of deep learning and magnetic eloquence, who fired the Church anew with the ardour for reform. Under Olivi, the theories which had appeared in the likeness of rather disconnected prophecies developed apparently into a body of evangelistic doctrine. The Spirituals who owned his leadership grew rapidly in number and influence. It was not long before their power in the Church was demonstrated by the election of a Spiritual Pope, Celestine V, of unhappy memory. In the early fourteenth century their political power in France and in Italy was able to awake tremors in the Curia. Intensely loyal to their conception of the Holy Catholic Church as the spotless Bride of Christ, they opposed determined resistance to the evils of the ' Carnal Church ', with its unhallowed wealth, its unrighteous tribunals, and its laxity of morals. The new current of thought set stirring by Olivi and his followers profoundly affected the Church during this and the following century. It would seem that they only just failed in bringing about that reformation by consent which might have drawn all Christendom to unity.

Dante openly acclaimed Joachim as a prophet, and set the recognition of his divine inspiration in the mouth of Thomas Aquinas. He adopted many of his well-known doctrines which, as will be shown later, he incorporated in his works. It was from Joachim apparently that he took the central idea of the *Inferno*. For Joachim in his exposition of the Apocalypse had said: ' *Infernus superior est iste mundus presens,*' and the logical outcome of this dictum was the presentation of the misgoverned world under an image of hell. Dante shadowed forth vividly in the *Purgatory* the distinction drawn by Joachim, and even more clearly by Olivi, between the Carnal Church and the Church of the Holy Spirit. In his dream of the Siren (*Purgatorio*, XIX, 7 ff.) he presents the former under the figure of the *antica strega*, stuttering in utterance, squint-eyed, crooked in the feet, maimed in the hands, in the act of weaving enchantments to beguile men from the right path, till the Lady, holy and eager, figuring the Spiritual Church, calling on Reason for aid, unveils the other's shame and puts her to confusion.

During the entire lifetime of Dante, Italy lay in subjection to Angevin rulers, Charles of Anjou, his son Charles II, and his grandson Robert. It was one purpose of the *Inferno* to expose the evils which had ensued from the alliance of these Princes with the Papacy. Each of these rulers held his dominions at the price of setting an armed force at the disposition of the Curia. Dante regarded their ascendancy as an intolerable humiliation for the ancient Roman people. It was round Imperial doctrines that he and his compeers rallied in their revolt against political and intellectual bondage. In this direction lay boundless hopes, on occasion some measure of effectual protection, in short, the only outlet towards freedom of thought. Thus it came about that alike as an Italian patriot, a philosophic statesman, a poet and a mystic, Dante was impelled into the path of resistance to Rome. The phrase which he set in the mouth of Virgil sums up the purpose of his life: ' *Libertà va cercando* '[1]—The quest of this man is freedom.

There is no way of escape from the fact that the entire trend of Dante's philosophy was directed to give the lie to that doctrine of eternal torture for all outside the Church which hits men in the face on opening the *Inferno*. Hell-fire was a bludgeon astonishingly effective when reinforced by all the civil and religious apparatus which the Curia then held at its disposition. To their unique powers of stifling opinion and smirching the reputation of their opponents was added the awful terror inspired by the supernatural threat. It was this more than all else which sapped the vitality of the Imperialists. Sooner or later, the reformers, however truly pacifist in intention, were compelled to do battle for the cause of liberty. Again and again, from the days of Manfred to those of Henry VII and Louis of Bavaria, they must bear to see their supporters quail and melt away before the thunders of Rome awaking in them a blind and contagious terror.

Against this terror Dante stands out a figure of incomparable grandeur in stern unyielding protest. Never in one single instance, we aspire to prove, did he bow the knee before the threats of the avaricious and degraded men who had usurped sway over the Church of Christ. It would seem a thing incredible, were it not a rooted principle of Dante interpretation, that the ' fictitious ' aspect of the *Inferno*, emphasizing all the deadly assumptions which were employed to drive such men as Dante and his chosen comrades to ruin and despair, should ever have been accepted as reflecting his own beliefs and forming part of his design to set before the world.

L'AMOR CHE MOVE IL SOLE E L'ALTRE STELLE.

[1] *Purg.*, I, 71.

24

CHAPTER I

THE PRELUDE

[*Inferno I*]

Symbolic narrative of the events which led up to the final rupture of
Dante with the Papal Curia in 1301.

IN THE year 1301 the entire course of Dante's life underwent
a sudden change. Within the course of a few weeks he found
himself abruptly severed from high place in the service of his
country, from wealth, family ties, friendship, and ardent
literary labours, reduced to beggary and exile, under sentence of death. A dense cloud of obloquy tarnished his fair
name. He was deprived of all opportunity openly to defend
his honour. Reluctant to break the unwritten law which
prohibits the orator or poet from speaking of himself, he yet
felt the circumstances fully justified him in following the
example of his favourite authors, Boethius and Augustine, and
unfolding the secret of his life.[1]

Under its superficial aspect the *Inferno* is not concerned
with Dante's own actions. It seems to present him to view as
a mere passive spectator of crime and punishment. But to
follow closely in his footsteps is to perceive with increasing
clearness how deeply he was involved in the scenes enacted
before his eyes. It was against him personally that certain
damned souls, certain demoniac figures, displayed their malice.
He was hampered in his journey by personal difficulties and
experienced personal triumphs. He shows himself throughout
an intensely individual figure, identified personally with the
fortunes of many with whom he lingered on his way. In continual subtle ways he introduced an autobiographical note
into his adventures.

In the Prologue to the *Inferno* he laid great stress on the
autobiographical character of the world narrative. In accordance with classical usage, he took pains in his opening canto

---

[1] *Banquet*, Bk. I, 2.

25

to make 'a preliminary statement of what he was about to say so as to prepare the mind of the listener.[1] It is therefore of the utmost importance to examine first of all the import of his prologue and make it the basis of interpretation for all that follows. The Prologue, however, consists of two parts. Canto I recounts the events which brought him to ruin and the influence which rescued him; it is in particular the Prelude to the *Inferno*. Canto II is more mystic, or as Dante called it 'anagogical', in character. It is largely taken up with the interplay of the mental and spiritual forces in his being, more elaborately presented in the *Purgatorio* and *Paradiso*. It seems better therefore to concentrate attention for the time being on Canto I and to regard it, as it was surely intended to be regarded, from the historical point of view. Thus regarded it becomes a record of actual happenings.

Although the aim of the present work is to carry the story of Dante's life no farther than to the year 1289, when he was in his twenty-fifth year, it is necessary to follow the order he prescribed and begin by furnishing a brief narrative of the events which led up to the crisis of 1301.

In the opening line of the poem Dante related that this crisis occurred in the middle of his life journey. According to his own estimate, based on that of the Psalmist, of about seventy years for a normal lifetime, this would indicate either the year 1300 or 1301. Half-way through the journey a definite date was mentioned by Malacoda, the Master-Demon,[2] in a somewhat cryptic statement about the time of day when the earthquake after the death of Christ took place. ' Lately (ier) there were completed, five hours later than this hour, one thousand two hundred *one* with sixty-six years since this road was broken up.' Adding to the 1267 years above specified thirty-four years for the age of Christ from conception to Crucifixion, the date becomes 1301. This reading was adopted by the Italian Lana, based on the authority of two very important (probably the two oldest dated) manuscripts, dated respectively 1336 and 1337. Most other manuscripts read '*mille dugento con sessanta sei*', instead of '*mille dugento uno con sessanta sei*' and thus assign to the crisis in Dante's life the date 1300. Very strong evidence for the later date is afforded by the sequence of events narrated in the Prologue when

[1] Epistle x. [2] *Inf.*, xxi, 112-114.

26

elucidated by the known facts. During the year 1300 Dante was living in high honour and security. It was in 1301 that Boniface VIII began the series of manœuvres against him which drove him down to ruin.

The mental aspect of Dante's struggle with the Papacy must not be suffered to distract attention from the bitter injuries inflicted on him by the Church. The nature of these injuries, related in quasi-allegorical fashion, can hardly be apprehended unless the Prologue be studied line by line in close comparison with the history of the period. At every turn it is imperative to recognize that Dante is relating things which actually happened to him at the time indicated. He presented the forces with which he came in contact under symbols not difficult of interpretation, and it will be found that their general significance is hardly in dispute. The extent to which these forces altered the entire current of his life has received less attention than their abstract meaning. To consider them from the historic point of view is to open up a peculiarly poignant chapter of Dante's life.

THE TRUE THEME

When half-way through the journey of our life   *Inf.*, 1, 1-9.
I came unto myself in a dark wood[1]
Where the direct road had been turned awry.   Prelude
Alas, a heavy task to tell what like it was,   declaring the
This savage, dangerous and stubborn wood.   purport of
So bitter is it death were itself scarce less.   the poem.
Yet that I may describe the good I found in it
I will relate the other things I there went through.

In the first line of the *Divina Commedia*, with all the emphasis lent by this position, Dante set before his readers the idea of his own journey through life under the image of a passage through a dark wood, an image to which he recurred later and even more clearly. It happened, he says, that when he was half-way through the wood of this life, he found that the direct road had been broken up and that he was lost in a

[1] The dark Wood typifies material things, the Greek word Hyle being highly charged with esoteric meaning. Cf. *Banquet*, IV, 24. The young man who enters the misleading Wood of this life would not be able to keep the good road unless he had been shown it by his elders.

dark and dangerous place. At this point, however, in his journey he came to himself or found himself again, and resolved to tell the world what had happened. He shrank with horror from recalling the unspeakably bitter things he had encountered on his pilgrimage, yet he nerved himself to the task on account of the Good which he had discovered, *i.e.* the right path through the thicket, the road which leads to peace and union with God. These nine lines of prelude indicate quite clearly that the subject of the poem is the story of his own experiences in life.

After this declaration of his general purpose he proceeded to give a brief résumé of his life up to that half-way point alluded to in the first line when its whole course was changed by the discovery of the right road.

EARLY YEARS

Inf., I, 10-12.
Birth and
Infancy.

> I cannot tell
> How first I came into the Wood (of life)[1]
> So steeped was I in Slumber[2] till that point
> When I began to stray from the true path.

The sleep of infantile unconsciousness enwrapped him on his first entrance into the Wood of life and for some time after. No sooner was he endowed with conscious power to exercise his will than he began to go astray, and how this came about he was afterwards to express in a beautiful refutation of the orthodox doctrine that all infants are born ' in the wrath of God'. ' The simple tender soul of the new born knows only that it springs from a Creator inspired by joy and gladly grasps whatever pleases it. At first if guide or curb turn not its love aright it takes delight in trifling pleasures, deceives itself and runs a backward course.'[3] This was the period then of childish temptations and transgressions which

[1] Cf. *Inf.*, IV, 65, 66:
  We went on, passing through the *Wood*
  The *Wood*, I emphasize, crowded with souls.

[2] Cf. *Inf.*, IV, 67, 68:
  Our way had still not far proceeded on
  Beyond the *Slumber*.

[3] *Purg.*, XVI, 85 ff .

gradually as he grew older filled him with discouragement
and led him by a downward track from the Light.

BACKSLIDING AND RECALL BY BEATRICE

Down in that vale my heart was filled with fear

Until it ended; then before me rose

A hill, and on it, at the foot, I stood.

I looked aloft and saw its sides illumined

Already by the glory of that Sun

Which guides us through all tracks to the true path.

Then was the fear a little quieted

Which in my inmost soul had lasted long

Throughout the night I had passed so piteously.

Like one who comes forth panting to the shore

From the deep sea and turns him back to gaze

Over the perilous waters—so my mind

Still fugitive, turned back to contemplate

The Pass that living person never left.

Inf., I, 13-14.

The period described in the New Life. This lasted from about 1283 to 1288.

He writes the story of the New Life.

In his nineteenth year Dante was visited by the second
vision of Beatrice, and from now onwards, after much sorrow
and many doubts he set his feet on the upward path of study
and purification. Here are summed up the experiences more
elaborately described in the New Life. The extreme danger
in which he stood from the Inquisition during these years
will be demonstrated in a later chapter. Meantime it is
enough to note his own conviction that he escaped with his
life as by a miracle.

The introduction passes to outline the events of his early
manhood after a pause which preluded a change of scene.

This seems to be the season after the death of Beatrice when,
so she was later to remind him, high achievement lay in his
power.[1] He indicates, however, that he did not devote his
whole mind to the ascent. His course swerved, though still
upward, and he suffered himself to be distracted from the
ascent by less worthy preoccupations.

[1] *Purg.*, XXX, 115-117:
> Questi fu tal nella sua vita nuova
> Virtualmente, ch' ogni abito destro
> Fatto avrebbe in lui mirabil prova.

FLORENCE

Inf., i, 28-30.
End of
military
service.
Marriage.

A season of
intense ab-
sorption in
the affairs of
Florence.

Youthful en-
thusiasm and
high wrought
hopes of
public service.

> When my tired body had awhile reposed
> I took my way up the forsaken strand
> Swerving, my right foot lower, towards the left.
> And lo, near the beginning of the rise
> A Leopard, lightly moving, very swift,
> Covered with spotted skin.
> I ne'er was rid of it before my face;
> It blocked my path so constantly, I turned
> Many a time as though to retrace my steps.
>
> The time was morning dawn; the sun
> Moved up the sky surrounded by those stars
> Which stood about it when the Love Divine
> First summoned these fair creatures into being.
> So that the time of day and the sweet season
> Were my excuse for setting such good hope
> On the wild creature with the variegated skin.

Commentators unanimously identify the Leopard with the city of Florence. Among the known facts of Dante's life is his intimate connection with the Florentine Government for a period of some seven years from about 1295 to 1301. While devoting a large part of his time to the philosophic studies figured by the ascent of the Mount, he interested himself deeply in the affairs of state, became a member of the Guild of Doctors and Druggists and was elected to the Council of One Hundred from which the Priors were chosen. Nothing could be more distracting to a studious man than the claims of municipal affairs. As the leading free city of Tuscany, Florence was involved in many important negotiations with the Pope and came in course of time to be reckoned by Boniface VIII the principal obstacle to his design of securing the domain of Tuscany for the Church. The good hope which Dante cherished of the Leopard, when he devoted so much time to the fickle and captivating creature, may be best understood through the medium of Villani's early impressions.[1]

' At this time in the year of Christ 1300 our city of Florence was in the greatest and happiest state it had ever been in since it was rebuilt, or even before, as well in size and power as in

[1] Villani, Bk. viii, c. 39.

the number of her people, for there were more than 30,000 citizens in the city, and more than 70,000 fit to bear arms in the districts belonging to her territory. And by reason of the nobility of her brave knights and of *her free people*, as well as her great riches, she was mistress of almost the whole of Tuscany.'

It is no matter for wonder that Dante should have admired the many-sided beauty of this free state ; he allowed it to entice him from his ardent pursuit of abstract truth, and was drawn more deeply into the current of its affairs than he could afterwards justify to himself. He has perhaps not received due credit for the state of prosperity to which the city was raised as the consequence of his devoted labours.

So matters stood when in the year 1300 Boniface VIII in his lust for temporal dominion appointed as his champion Charles of Valois, brother to the French King, under the flaming title of ' Captain of the whole earth, subject to the jurisdiction of the Roman Mother Church'.

THE ANGEVIN EXPEDITION

Not such my confidence that unafraid
I could endure the appearing of a Lion.
It seemed expressly against *me* he came,
Rearing its head with ravenous desire
So that the very air was terror struck.

Inf., I, 44-48. Entry into Italy of Charles of Valois with an army of mercenaries.

It is tolerably clear that resistance to Papal encroachment on the liberties of Tuscany centred round the figure of Dante. When Boniface demanded an armed contingent from Florence to aid in deposing the King of Sicily in favour of the Angevin Charles of Naples it was Dante who moved emphatically in the Senate that ' in the matter referred to them by the Pope nothing be done ' (*nihil fiat, nihil fiat*). It was in his presence that the Senate passed the notable resolution exhorting the Signory to enforce the Enactments of Justice, and guard ' the ancient, customary and continued independence of the Florentine Commune and people, in present danger of being changed to servitude by many perilous innovations coming no less from within than without'. There could be no mistake about the allusion to the Papal designs and the hand of Dante may clearly be traced in this energetic declaration of Florentine liberty founded on Imperial law. He was the chosen ambassador to San Gemignano when the Senate determined on summoning a Parliament for all the cities of the Tuscan League for the election of their new Captain—a definite step towards federation. He was one of the Priors elected to govern the city in the fateful months 15th June–15th Aug. 1300, and directed his energy to rendering the governing body strictly impartial and strong enough to resist outside aggression or internal treachery. He was the outstanding figure in Florence, righteous and inflexible, one who could neither be bullied nor bribed.

But the appearing of the Lion did, he confessed, awake his fears—not without cause. The French force bearing down on Florence, to subdue the city by force of arms to the Papal will, was formidable because of the powerful party of Blacks within the city, vociferating against their own government and urging the Valois to come to their rescue. This group of malcontents, to whom nothing was less acceptable than firm municipal control, was dominated by Corso Donati, a dangerous conspirator, in the pay of Rome, and the bitter personal antagonist of Dante. Through the agency of Corso Donati, and with the support of French soldiers, the Pope planned to break up effectually the Florentine government, which under Dante's influence had become the principal obstacle to his scheme of dominating all Tuscany.

PAPAL USURPATION

Inf., 1, 49-60.

The Papal Curia as usurper of temporal dominion.

Ruin awaited Dante.

A She Wolf, too, seemingly weighted down
By every craving which its leanness shows—
That many folk hath brought to live in woe—
So sore oppressed me with embarrassment
Of dread which oozed from the mere sight of her
I lost the hope of mounting the ascent.
As one who hath gained much by force of will
The time was come when I was made to lose;
Thus in my every thought I wept and mourned.
The creature void of peace so dealt with me
That as she came against me, step by step,
She drove me back to where the Sun was hid.

These words are no mere allegorical representation of abstract sentiments; they are a highly condensed but accurate account of the manner in which Boniface VIII dealt with Dante.

With the Valois threatening the city at close quarters the Leopard displayed a more than common fickleness and uncertainty of humour. The Signory was hastily re-elected before its time had expired, and from the new governing body Dante was excluded. It is as certain as anything that is related of him that he undertook the dangerous office of ambassador to the Papal Court, two minor persons also being sent to entreat the protection of Boniface for the doomed city. Of what happened after he left it seems that Dante was for some months unaware, a condition of affairs which points to his detention under close surveillance if not actual imprisonment. No one remained in Florence capable of guiding the course of events. Blind and terrified intrigues among nobles and burghers alike were succeeded by the entry of the Valois with his band of foreign troops early in November 1301. Thereafter all proceeded 'according to plan'. The 'Captain of the whole earth', obsequiously obedient to his Lord and Master the Pope, gave up the city with the rich country-side for miles around to fire, slaughter, and pillage during six days, in the course of which, as Dino Compagni records, many shameful deeds were done. It was no common outburst of disorder. It bore the marks of a deliberately-plotted campaign, instituted in a spirit of vengeance. The design was to extinguish the grandeur of the city and bring to ruin all who had dared to guard its ancient and accustomed liberties. The subsequent enslavement of the free city, the corruption of its municipal government, and the ruin of its inhabitants, exposed to incessant outrages at the hands of successive tyrants and completely at the mercy of Papal intrigues, were a direct consequence of the conspiracy into which Boniface entered between the Blacks and the Valois. It was another exhibition of the wrathful spirit which had dictated his so-called Crusade against the Colonna Cardinals when their city was razed to the ground and its site sown with salt.

It is needless to recall the long list of proscriptions and forfeitures which succeeded the first days of horror in Florence.

D

Dante was in the power of the Pope and his execution was expected. But a delay occurred. The Wolf drove him *a poco a poco*, he records, down to despair. It was not till early in the following year, when the notorious Conte de' Gabrielli had been appointed Podestà in Florence, that proceedings against him were instigated. Boniface desired a more complete revenge than the mere death of one who stood so high in honour, so unapproachable in intellect, the one man able to withstand him to his face and reduce his temporal pretensions to ridicule. Dante was to be degraded in the eyes of all the world, to be stripped of every shred of reputation and exposed to posterity as one whose word counted for naught. In a proclamation read in every quarter of the city he was branded as a dishonest administrator who had used his official position to exact money under false pretences, had conspired against the Pope and his champion, and had destroyed the peace of Florence. The accusations were hurled against him in his absence, and there is a tradition that for many weeks he knew nothing of the sentence passed upon him. First he was fined five thousand florins and ordered to repay the sum he was accused of embezzling. Next, failing payment, all his goods, including his manuscripts and the entire contents of his house, were forfeited and destroyed. Further he was banished for two years from Tuscany and declared unfit ever to hold office again. His name was recorded in the Book of the Statutes of the People as that of a common thief and a traitor to his trust. The vengeance was not yet complete. On 10th March a second sentence condemned him to be burnt alive should he ever at any time come within the boundaries of the Commonwealth.

To follow the sequence of these events is to realize in some small degree the depth of despair into which Dante was plunged by the exercise of that usurping and iniquitous authority he veiled under the symbol of the Wolf. There is no direct information about his movements immediately after the sentences were promulgated. A likely tradition has it that he joined the other exiles at Arezzo shortly afterwards. But for the purposes of his life story the light thrown on what was passing in his mind at this period by the first and second cantos of the *Inferno* is worth far more than a mere itinerary of his movements.

34

In these cantos[1] he confessed that the dread which over-powered him turned him back in his quest for truth; that he was driven so far from the right road as to be in acute danger of never recovering it; that in that hour he fought with death itself, of the Intellect surely, but may be also of the body.

Homeless, beggared, parted from his wife, children, and friends, all his disinterested labours discredited, his name a byword for vituperation, his native city reduced in great part to ruins, with vile thieves and tyrants triumphing in cruel insolence, what prospect lay before the poet, the philosopher, the mystic? The Papal Curia had so ordered it that his influ-ence, already great, had vanished, his rising fame had been extinguished, so it seemed, for ever. No word of his was henceforth to gain credence. The smirch of dishonour, set ineradicably on his name, was to nullify alike his rebukes of vice in high places, his proclamation of the truth.

Up to the point now reached the Prelude has been mani-festly autobiographical. It has led by successive stages to the great crisis of Dante's life and presents a condensed account, highly charged with emotion but strictly accurate, of his per-secution at the hands of the Papal Curia in 1301-2. He was absolutely ruined in mind and spirit by the anguish and despair which swept over his soul and seemed to shut him out for ever from the presence of God. The crisis in his life was no sudden ' conviction of sin ', such as might be thought to make a glimpse of Hell expedient for his salvation. It was an actual disaster deliberately plotted by the usurping Curia which he had dared to challenge.

---

[1] *Inf.*, II, 62 ff.:
> He who not by mere accident is my friend
> Has met impediment on the barren shore
> So grave that fear hath turned him from the road;
> I dread he may have gone so far astray
> I may be roused too late to rescue him—
> I speak what I have heard of him in Heaven.

. . . .

Inf., II, 103 ff.:
> ' Beatrice, true praise of God,
> ' Wilt thou not rescue him who loved thee so
> ' That for thy sake he left the common crowd?
> ' Dost thou not hear the piety of his plaint
> ' Upon that stream which flows not out to sea? '

35

VIRGIL SYMBOL OF REASON

Inf., 1, 61-78.

The voice of Reason long silenced by Authority, made itself heard in the person of Virgil, poet and prophet of Imperial Rome.

Whilst in vile place I had been brought to ruin,
One who by his long silence seemed to grow weak
Appeared and claimed attention.
When I beheld him in the wilderness
I cried:—' Have pity on me, be thou shade,
' Or veritable man, or aught beside;'
He answered:—' Not a man. Man was I once;
' Lombards my parents were, and Mantua
' The native country of them both.
' Born under Julius though his rule came late,
' I dwelt at Rome under the good Augustus;
' Lying and false the gods we worshipped then.
' I was a Poet, and sang Anchises' son,
' The just Aeneas, who went forth from Troy
' After proud Ilion had been burnt.
' But thou, why to such torment seek return?
' Why not ascend the Mount delectable
' The beginning and the cause of every joy?'

Virgil, the dominant figure of the *Inferno*, has been universally recognized as the symbol for Reason. His is a complex personality and reflects the several aspects under which Reason may be envisaged.

Objectively Virgil stands for the reasoning faculty which differentiates man from brutes. Most conspicuous among the functions of Reason is that displayed in civil government; it is man's innate ability to rule himself and others. Hence, since in Dante's philosophy the only true form of government is that which ensures unity and tends to promote universal peace, Reason is identified with the theory of universal monarchy. The Imperial principle, which preceded revelation and prepared the way for it, is identified with Virgil.

Subjectively, Virgil is Reason revealed as the higher strand in Dante's own being, the faculty which enabled him to discriminate good from evil, in short his conscience.

Lastly and continually, Virgil is himself, the veritable Virgil, the author revered by Dante, the poet on whose style he largely modelled his own, the philosopher in whose works he had with much labour, so he himself relates, discovered an

36

esoteric philosophy of life hidden under the fictitious narrative.[1] In the Middle Ages the life of Virgil was the subject of
an extraordinary series of legends known to modern scholar-
ships as the Virgilian myth[2] and there are several passages in
the *Divina Commedia* which display Dante's intent to expose
the falsity of these vulgar tales. It has been conjectured that
his mother's name, Magia, may have suggested the fable
which turned Virgil into a magician. Certainly some of the
wildest features of the legend gathered round his parentage
and places of birth and burial.[3] Hence the significance of
Virgil's simple declaration at his first appearance on the scene,
that he was once a man, and that his parents were natives of
Lombardy and dwelt at Mantua, the date being fixed by
reference to the reigning Emperor.

In more senses than one his voice might sound hollow from
disuse. The place of Reason in the sphere of government
had long been usurped by Authority. In this as in other
matters to appeal to Reason was to incur suspicion of heretical depravity. Imperial principles, too, could not but suffer
eclipse during the unsatisfactory reigns of German Albert
and his predecessor at the close of the century. The voice
of the Empire was practically silent. Moreover, from the
personal aspect, Virgil as a reputed magician had long
ago lost status; his influence, just beginning to revive, was
still weak.

In stating that he was ' born under Julius although he came
late in time ', Virgil brought to light his rôle as the symbol
of Universal Monarchy, a principle finally evolved by the
Roman people in this epoch after many preparatory years.
He added significantly that at this time the gods were
false and erroneous, the inference being that the principle
of right government had nothing to do with revelation
or Divine authority, but was synonymous with Reason
itself.

Dante was clearly convinced that Virgil had veiled a deep
philosophical intention under the story of Aeneas, who, as the

[1] Canto IV, 26.
[2] See Comparetti: Virgilio nel Medio Evo.
[3] The exact spot where he was born is carefully defined in *Inf.*, xx, and
his burial place in *Purg.*, III, 25-27. These matter of fact statements
effectually swept away the legends.

son of Venus[1] (Divine Love) and Anchises (material things), was a type of human nature. In this allegory, as generally understood, Troy stood for the pains and pleasures of mortal life, and Italy for the goal of Contemplation or Union with God, while the long perilous journey from Troy to Italy typified the life of purgation.

Virgil made a direct application of this allegory to Dante's case, when, recalling how Aeneas departed from Troy after its destruction, he demanded : ' But thou, why dost *thou* turn back again to such torment? ' Dante's material existence corresponded with that of Aeneas when Troy was in ruins; like Aeneas he had lost home, wealth, fame. He has put it on record that in that hour of utmost desolation it was the voice of Virgil which summoned him to gather the forces of his mind together, as Aeneas did with his comrades in the burning city, and, abandoning all hope of worldly rehabilitation, to set out anew on that ascent of the Mount from which he had been deterred by the machinations of the Wolf.

Under this apparently visionary encounter with a ghostly Virgil is disguised a momentous change in Dante's mental outlook, dating from this time. Like Paul appealing to Caesar from Pharisaic condemnation, Dante turned to Virgil, voice of Reason, as to a court of appeal against Papal persecution:

VIRGIL INSPIRES HIS TREATISE ON MONARCHY

Inf., I, 79-90.

The appeal from Papal Authority to Reason as enunciated by Virgil.

' Art thou indeed that Virgil, fountain-head
' Whence issues such rich streams of eloquence? '
I answered him with shame-encompassed brow.
' O glory of other poets and their light,
' Let the long ardour and the love profound
' Which set me searching in thy works avail:
' My Master art thou, my own author too.
' Thou art he alone from whom I have derived
' The noble style whose honour rests on me.
' Behold the Beast, on whose account I have turned;
' From her deliver me, illustrious sage.
' She sends a shudder through my veins and pulse.'

[1] A secondary meaning attached to Venus as human love, and Paris following this lower aspect of the goddess, was led to destruction. Anchises refused to leave Troy and a contest ensued between father and son (flesh and spirit) which ended in Anchises being forcibly carried off.

38

At this point in the story of the crisis, the Prologue begins to exhibit a curious parallel with the Latin work which Dante put forth about this time in daring opposition to Papal policy. In this work Dante demonstrated (Book I) that Imperial rule is absolutely necessary for the well being of the human race; (Book II) that the Roman Empire was ordained to exercise this overlordship; (Book III) that Imperial rule derives its authority from God and is not in any degree dependent on the Papacy.

It is difficult in easy modern days to realize the immense sensation created by this work, in every country to which it penetrated. It effectually pricked the bubble of universal Papal dominion. It swept away in a blast of ridicule the puerile arguments on which ecclesiastical lawyers had built such an imposing structure of Papal temporal rights. It prepared the way for some, on whom the yoke of Rome was pressing hard, to assert their freedom. It opened up a new and truly inspiring Imperial philosophy. If, as seems very probable from allusions in the text to the machinations of the Black faction in Florence, this work were secretly put forth by Dante in the year 1300, then the brutal determination of Boniface to degrade him in the eyes of the world by every possible means is easy to understand.

Virgil's response above quoted to Dante's appeal for help shows a remarkable correspondence with passages in the *Monarchy*.[1] It was 'to the light of human Reason' that he resorted, so he tells us, when he undertook to demolish the Papal claim to dominate the world. Moreover it was Virgil,[2] divine poet and sage, typical voice of Reason, whom he elected to follow in this matter; it was Virgil's testimony in the *Aeneid* on which he grounded the divine origin of the Roman Empire. The reply of Virgil to Dante's appeal is identical in argument and anticipation with the final chapter of the *Monarchy*.

IMPERIAL IDEALS OF JUSTICE

'Thou needs must start forth on a different course,'   *Inf.*, I, 91-111.
He answered, after he had seen me weeping,

---

[1] *Mon.*, Bk. II, c. 1.   [2] *Loc. cit.*, c. 3.

' If from this rugged region thou wouldst be saved:
' Because this Beast 'gainst whom thou clamourest,
' Permits not any to pass along her road
' But circumvents them till they are put to death.
' And so perverse and vicious is her nature
' She never satiates her ravenous will—
' After her glut more ravenous than before.
' She mates herself with many animals
' And shall do yet until the Greyhound come,
' He who shall make her die in agony.
' Not land nor pelf shall this one feed upon,
' But wisdom, love and virile qualities.
' Twixt Feltro shall his nation be and Feltro.
' Healing will he be to lowly Italy
' For which the wounded maid Camilla died
' Like Turnus, Nisus, and Euryalus.
' This one shall drive the Beast from every city
' Till he hath set her once more back in Hell
' Whence envy in the beginning set her loose.'

Dante must renounce allegiance to the usurping Curia.

Its unholy alliance with ambitious rulers. The temporal power of the Church will in the end be broken by the establishment of universal Monarchy.

The theme is precisely similar to that of the *Monarchy*: it denounces Papal civil rule as usurpation; it demonstrates Universal Monarchy as ordained by God for the security of all mankind. Both in the poem and in the treatise Virgil is held up to view as a prophet, divinely inspired, whose utterances are authoritative and indisputable. In both, great stress is laid on the iniquitous alliances of the Curia with usurping rulers and the essential malignity of the forces set in motion by the Curia is forcibly indicated. In both, stress is laid on the personal danger incurred by Dante and on his overpowering dread of the punitive measures at the service of the Beast. In both, there is the declaration of deliverance at some undetermined time by means of a disinterested Power, ruling by consent and thus restoring mankind to freedom and peace. The spirit of high-strung emotional resolve exhibited in the *Monarchy* is echoed in the Prologue, and it is hardly possible to believe that on two separate occasions in his life Dante was wrought up to a defiance so unprecedented in this age, so deadly in its consequences.

In the year 1301, and hardly before or after within Dante's lifetime, all the circumstances concurred which are exposed in the Prologue and the *Monarchy*. Boniface VIII, by his settled policy of bartering his sanction to lawless usurpers in exchange for the overlordship of the territory involved, had made the Curia a world danger. His allies in this very year were filling Italy, Sicily, and Flanders with slaughter and desolation. The whole weight of the Catholic religion was being invoked to sweep away ancient rights by the expedient of converting allegiance to Imperial law into the crime of heretical depravity. Dante, too hopefully believed that once he had established the truth 'all mortals will recognize that they are free from the yoke of these usurpers'.[1] But he had no illusions about the danger he ran.

It was in a white heat of resolution that in his Prelude to the third book he stepped into 'the present wrestling ground', dreading most the defamation of his character yet referring the issue to God: 'By the arm of Him who delivered us from the power of darkness by His Blood, in the sight of all the world I will hurl the impious liar 'impium atque mendacem' out of the ring. What should I fear since the Spirit, co-eternal with the Son, says by the mouth of David: 'The just shall be had in everlasting remembrance'; 'He shall not be afraid of any evil report.'

The result was amazing. When in the course of two years only from the time when he had driven Dante down in utter ruin to 'a low place', Boniface himself collapsed at the touch of an unsuspected foe, and died in helpless imbecility, self-confessed in his last hours, so it was whispered, a creature of the devil, what could his opponents think but that 'the impious liar' who had boasted 'I, I am Caesar', had indeed met the fate foretold, and had been driven in single combat ignominiously from the arena?

THE LOST ROAD REGAINED

Both in the *Monarchy* and in the Prologue to the *Inferno* Dante proclaimed that the Church had no mandate to interfere with man's actions or the forms of civil government. In his momentous resolve to turn his back on the Beast and follow Virgil, Dante definitely abjured ecclesiastical authority in all save the inner mysteries of the faith, and followed unre-

[1] *Mon.*, Bk. II, 1.

servedly the dictates of Reason. The goal of human existence, so he declared in the beautiful final chapter of the *Monarchy*, is happiness. To find happiness converts this life into an earthly Paradise, and the only road to this state of felicity is to use the gift of Reason which God has bestowed on man for this very purpose. Man's blessedness in this life, he reiterated, is to be found only by the use of his own directive power of Reason, brought completely to knowledge by the philosophers and therefore not dependent on ecclesiastics.

By the exercise of Reason, the Roman people, though ignorant about God, ensured the peace of the world through the Imperial system and thus paved the way for revelation. The path followed by the Romans in the use of their own directive powers was the right path. Men have wandered from it in these latter days of misery, but one day a Hound will once again guard the sheep-fold, not for himself, but under the Master of the universe. The only way to attain this consummation is for men once again to enthrone Reason as their guide. In accordance with these conclusions Dante perceived that he must turn his back on Papal authority and trust to his own intellectual powers.

DEFINITE REJECTION OF PAPAL AUTHORITY

Inf., I, 112-129.

   ' Wherefore deliberating, I decide
' That for thy future good thou follow me
' And I will be thy Guide. For place eternal
' I will deliver thee *from hence wherein*
' *Thou wilt hear the clamour desperate* of souls
' Of antique valour, suffering, who invoke
' Each one, (to end his pain) the second death.
' And then within the fire thou wilt behold
' Those who are yet at peace hoping to reach,
' Whensoever that may be, the folk in bliss.
' Then if thou wouldst ascend to be with these
' There is a soul more fit for this than I;
' With her I will leave thee when I part from thee.
' Because that Emperor Who reigns above
' For that I was rebellious to His laws
' Wills not that man through me enter His city.
' In all parts He commands; there is His rule obeyed;

' There is His city; there is His high Throne.
' O happy he elected to that spot.'
I answered: 'Poet, I implore of thee
' By that Divinity thou knowest not
' Thou bring me forth thither where thou hast said,
' That from this evil and worse I may escape:
' So I may see the Portal of Saint Peter
' And those who are made sorrowful by thee.'
Then set he forth. And I held on behind.

The grand climax to which the rest of the canto is intro-
ductory is reached when Dante surrenders himself whole-
heartedly to the guidance of Reason as opposed to Usurped
Papal Authority. This was the re-discovery of himself foreshadowed in the opening line of the *Divina Commedia*. This
way of Reason was the road through the Wood of Life, long
lost to mankind. From now on Dante knew himself to be
completely emancipated.

It was an age in which every action of a man's life from
birth to death was regulated by ecclesiastical authority.
From the oppressive penalties by which he was kept in subjection, civil law offered no appeal and no protection. Attempts to establish a more stable form of government and
amend faulty laws reckoned as rebellion, and those who made
them were liable to be treated as heretics, outside the pale of
laws human or divine. With this daring declaration that the
authority exercised by the Papal Curia in civil matters is
contrary to Reason and must be abjured it is impossible to
reconcile the popular notion of a Dante scrupulously orthodox, pledged to implicit belief in the utter damnation of the
Roman people—nay of that very Virgil who was to lead him
to peace and freedom. He was not content with demonstrat-
ing his change of allegiance as a mere academic principle.
He exhibited himself in his Prologue dramatically in the act
of yielding unreserved obedience to the heathen philosopher
he had chosen for the symbol of Reason. ' Then he set forth
and I held on behind.'

It remains to determine in what direction their steps
tended. Whither will Reason lead mankind? Boniface would
have no hesitation in answering ' Down to Hell ', and even
more modern theologians can be found to echo the verdict.

But in the *Monarchy* Dante declared with no uncertain voice that the end for which men (all men, not merely Christians) were created was an earthly Paradise of blessedness. To follow Reason and lead a virtuous life is to attain happiness—always provided that the human race be left to govern itself wisely and rest in the tranquillity of peace.[1]

The reader is left to determine for himself whether with such a purpose in view for all mankind *in this life*, the merciful Creator have prepared for the virtuous, the free, the blessed an eternity of torment. The exact words which Virgil used about their destination are of the utmost importance. It will be seen that they contain no mention of Hell, no hint even that it was necessary for Dante's salvation that he should visit the infernal regions. But they do clearly *suggest* Hell, and were obviously intended to do so, because the *Inferno* could never have seen the light had it not presented a surface air of conformity with orthodox notions about Hell and Purgatory. Virgil's promise was to deliver Dante *from here*—the ' *basse loco* ' to which he had been driven by the Wolf—the impasse to which usurped authority had reduced the world. It was *here*, under the misrule of the Wolf, that he would hear ' the despairing cries of those suffering souls of ancient lineage who invoke each one the second death'; these were exiles, dead in the eyes of the law, eternally dead according to the verdict of the Church, outlawed, excommunicated, imprisoned, whose only hope and consolation lay in future liberation from their tortured bodies at the hands of death. The eternal place for which he was to set out was the Earthly Paradise of peace and freedom ordained by Divine Providence

---

[1] Cf. *Purg.*, XXVII, 130. Virgil had brought Dante through the flame of the seventh Cornice in Purgatory to the garden which typified the state of natural happiness for which man was foreordained by his Creator. When they reached this place of blessedness ' thither where thou hast said ', Virgil declared: 'Thou hast seen *temporal* fire and the eternal, and thou art come into a region beyond which of mine own self I can see no further. I have brought thee hither with genius (inborn) and art (acquired). Take now for guide thy pleasure. . . . Over thyself I crown and mitre thee'. It is here if anywhere we might expect an allusion to Hell. We find instead an allusion first to purely *temporal* fire, the fire of this world's agony, reinforced by the literal flames of the Inquisition, and secondly, the Eternal purifying flames which extinguished sin, the flames through which they had themselves just passed in Purgatory, but no mention whatever of Hell or lost souls.

for men who accepted the guidance of Reason. The language
which *seems* to indicate clearly enough that he was bound for
a journey through Hell under Virgil's guidance was so framed
as to be applicable in all respects to a new survey of this life
with Reason instead of ecclesiastical authority for guide. Such
a survey must embrace the whole extent of his own life and
take in the most important events in the world at large of
which he had been witness. Under how changed an aspect
must life present itself to him when viewed in the cold light of
Reason. All his own errors, his weakness, his pride, his passions must be laid bare. That was much. But more exacting
still must be the task of subjecting the rulers of cities and
nations to the judgment of Reason; Charles of Anjou, his
sons, his grandsons, James of Aragon, Frederic of Sicily, Philip
of France, how would these notable men of the day look when
surveyed by Reason? Finally, more dangerous, more terrible,
Reason was to regard with impartial eyes the men who wore
the livery of Christ, scrutinize their motives, examine (for
Reason was competent to do that) the character of the agents
employed, and pass judgment on the influence they exercised over men's morals and well being.

Such a survey of his life and times demanded the entire
dedication of his genius and art. The aim was no mere
literary achievement, still less revenge for past persecution. It
was the good of humanity which drove him to attempt this
mighty task. First he would show up the evils resulting from
the Papal usurpation of civil power and so paint the misery of
the times that all men should shudder as at a tale of Hell.
Next, he would inaugurate sound principles of world government, pointing out in the history of the past both the failures
and successes of former statesmen, linking the historical
episodes with a vision of God's dealings with sinners through
successive stages in the Way of Purgation. Lastly he would
attempt to set out the pure tenets of the Christian faith, corrupted in recent times by avaricious ecclesiastics, and would
essay to depict in immortal verse the joys of the interior life, joys
which even in this life have power to suggest an echo of Paradise.

Virgil's words seem to point unmistakably to a bliss beyond
his own reach. Only through intuitive perception, an intellectual height inspired by Christ, and imaged in the person of
Beatrice, we are to understand that the Beatific Vision of the
Triune Godhead can be attained.

CHAPTER II

THE *INFERNO* AS A PARABLE OF BIRTH, LIFE, AND DEATH

[*Inferno III*, 1-21, 70-136 ; *Inferno XXXIV*, 1-69.]

The normal life of man in general, and of Dante in particular, presented under the image of a twenty-four hours' journey, the duration of one hour being allotted to each three years of life.

THE THEME of damned souls and their retribution is overwhelmingly conspicuous at the outset of the journey. Hell as a place of torment and despair deriving from an implacable Deity is brought to view with unparalleled vigour and vehemence. No words before or since have held such power to impress on the imagination the awful implication of eternal perdition. Whether it were the poet's design to enforce the authority of the priesthood and compel men to submission and repentance by the road of fear, or whether he aimed at painting in its true colours a doctrine of Divine Justice too horrible to be credited by any able to realize what conception of the Deity it actually involved, there can be no question that the note of terror is accentuated. Dante was conducted into the Inferno through a gateway which proclaimed itself as the first creative act of Divine Power, Wisdom and Goodness, and the words suggest that the most urgent preoccupation of the Deity in creating the universe was to make provision for the eternal torment of a still uncreated race. We venture to maintain that the stupendous horror of the outer Hell meaning was but the orthodox curtain under cover of which Dante designed to unfold to the world the Gospel of Divine Love.

The essential point in 'the art of disguising' was to possess the mind of possibly suspicious readers so forcibly at the very outset with a fixed idea, that they would go on unconsciously colouring all that followed for themselves. Once present to the imagination a strong fictitious impression, the more violent the better, and the author can say almost anything he pleases without risk of discovery.

46

Passages quite inconsistent with the literal meaning will then be readily adapted by readers to the one theme they have in mind. Clues to the inner and true meaning may be fearlessly supplied. Once completely possessed by the dominating literal theme, the acutest intellects will uncritically ascribe to the author's obscurity whatever in the text may point to the cryptic meaning he is trying to convey.

THE LITERAL INFERNAL REGIONS

When Dante began in the *Banquet* to explain the allegory which he had hidden under the story of the New Life, he declared that in all cryptic writings the literal narrative must be dealt with and made clear, first in order, since it forms the foundation of the whole structure. Although fairly simple in its broad outlines, the literal plan of the *Inferno*, closely regarded, is exceedingly complicated. It opens up a map of the infernal regions, delineated, not once for all but according to the experience of the two pilgrims, hour by hour, and the task of the commentators resembles that of the geographers during the war who laboured to furnish a working itinerary for the troops in regions never before surveyed, by aid of data gleaned from casual accounts of travel. There is no general description of Hell. Virgil furnished, it is true, in his synopsis of sin a clear scheme of the several types of transgressors undergoing retribution, from which it may be computed that there were in all twenty-four distinct places of torment. But the actual localities prove on close inspection far removed from the regularity of a clear-cut design. On stepping from one to another the whole atmosphere, background, and accessories undergo a startling transformation, comparable only to a new scene of life. Dante represents himself in the act of acquiring knowledge about the Inferno only as he passed through successive stages of experience, and the few definite facts he mentions about the region have to be pieced together to form a coherent whole. He seems to have adopted the general framework expressly with a view to suggesting the crude monkish traditions current in the Dark Ages:

' When Lucifer was ejected from Heaven he fell to the earth on the side of the Southern Hemisphere. The velocity of his descent and the weight of sin which he bore caused him to strike the globe so violently as to invert its conditions, the land of the Southern Hemisphere being forced to the North and the waters changing in their turn to the South. For, to avoid so grievous a sinner, the very earth recoiled in horror; and the matter displaced by his passage through the Southern Hemisphere rushed upwards and became the mountain of Purgatory. In the void thus caused in the bowels of the earth was Hell—situated beneath the surface of the Northern Hemisphere—in an immense empty space in the form of an inverted cone. The apex of this cone is supposed to be the relatively small sphere of ice called the Giudecca, into the centre of which Lucifer is frozen; some have maintained that his navel was the centre of the Universe.' [1]

These general conclusions have been built up out of vague suggestions in the text rather than definite statements. The Cosmography exposed in the *Banquet* is entirely alien from such monkish speculations as also that of the little treatise on *Water and Land* commonly attributed to Dante. Incidentally we are given to understand that the Inferno was divided into concentric rings of varying breadth which formed a succession of zones or terraces containing many subdivisions, all gradually decreasing in size towards the central point. Dante passed through every Zone and witnessed the retribution assigned to a long series of transgressions arranged in sequence from lesser manifestations of Incontinence or Profligacy to the basest crimes of Violence, Fraud, and Inhumanity or Brutality.

He gave a few careful indications of the length of time he took over different stages of the journey which was timed to occupy about twenty-four hours altogether.

Entering as twilight came on, about 7 p.m., he occupied five hours in traversing the early zones until at midnight he was on the banks of the Styx. He spent about three hours in crossing this river with its outlying swamp and securing entrance to the city of Dis. Soon after 3 a.m. he approached the River Phlegethon, and for the next three hours went through so many adventures that the events crowded into this time occupy nine cantos, a third of the space allotted to the whole journey. From 6 a.m. to 7 a.m. he spent all his

[1] W. W. Vernon, *Readings on the Inferno of Dante*, vol. 1: 'The Cosmography of Dante'.

time among Barrators or dishonest politicians, incurring grave danger from the Demons who persecuted them. After 7 a.m. the direct references to time fail. There is only one more ambiguous allusion to the hour, resting on the fact that the moon was now below his feet, and, towards the end, an indication that night was approaching. At an indeterminate moment he passed out of Hell, ostensibly by the odd expedient of climbing down the gigantic leg of Satan to the other side of the world where he found himself in the Realm of Purgatory.

From beginning to end, with one or two notable exceptions, this literal narrative of a journey through Hell suggests in uncompromising realism a picture of bodily torments such as were invented for the vulgar by priests hardly less ignorant than their flock. It suggests an image of judgment in which all but a tiny fraction of mankind, and they not the worthiest, do without doubt endure everlasting torture. Such was the story of Hell which being an allegory Dante warned his readers *not* to accept at its surface meaning, but to regard as a 'menzogna', a falsehood hiding a truth he was not at liberty to express.

Once the strong Hell suggestion has been withdrawn from the mind the beautiful fabric of Dante's philosophy of human life lies open to view:

> 'Like perspectives which, rightly gazed upon
> Show nothing but confusion; eyed awry
> Distinguish form.'

Neither code nor cipher is needed to apprehend the allegorical subject of the *Inferno*. All that is needed is to alter the point of view.

Under the image of Hell a picture of the world, darkened by ignorance, oppressed by evil rulers, lies hid. Under the imagery appropriate to Hell and as such 'horrible and fetid', various painful aspects of the medieval world are realistically brought into view. Under the framework of a night and a day spent in the infernal regions, we are to recognize the day's journey of human existence.

The names by which Dante described the region of Hell are full of significance. Rarely is the word Hell used, but the terms men commonly use about the world and mortal existence continually recur. He alludes to the region for instance as: the mournful vale of the abyss, the blind world; a place where no light shines; sorrowful hostel; disconsolate land; base world; dwellings of woe; blind prison; evil world; eternal exile; gloomy world; groundwork of all evil; sorrowful kingdom; eternal prison; profound night; infernal valley; sad place; valley wherein none can exculpate himself; defunct world; vale of sorrow; bitter life. Virgil definitely mentioned Hell as the ultimate destination of the Wolf.

Immeasurably wide, baffling all attempts at computation of its extent, as this infernal region is depicted, the travellers passed through it in the course of a day and a night typifying the normal life of a man. There are two chapters in the *Banquet* [1] in which Dante explained how life may be regarded under several images. Here he compares life to an arch which rises towards its summit and then declines; to a year, in that its four ages, youth or adolescence, manhood, ripe age, and old age are as spring, summer, autumn, and winter; to a day, since the passing of its hours is marked by temporal divisions *which vary in length* just as the Church's hours vary according to the position of the sun. A similar image of life underlies the day's labour in the Parable of the Vineyard and none is more familiar. Taking the normal life of man at about seventy years, according to his own estimate, and compressing it within the compass of a twenty-four hours' journey, it is obvious that each year will stand for twenty minutes. Each hour that passes will embrace a period of three years in the traveller's life, so that starting at 7 p.m. it must be estimated that by midnight he would have reached the age of fifteen. Once the date is known at which the traveller entered upon the secret things of this life, every subsequent mention of the passing of the hours supplies a further date. [2]

[1] *Banquet*, Bk. IV, 23, 24.
[2] It is interesting to find this computation of years by days recurring, according to Dr. Garnett (*Eng. Lit. Illust.*, vol. ii, p. 251 *n.*) in *The Tempest*:

' In Act 1, Scene 2, Prospero enquires from Ariel the time of day, and is told that it is " past the mid-season." He replies:

" At least two glasses: The time twixt six and now
" Must by us both be spent most preciously."

Why should the hour be two in the afternoon? The average day of

In the plan of the *Inferno* the scale of transgressions is graduated to fit the successive temptations of life. Children are not alive to great transgressions; they can neither perceive nor commit them. So the earlier examples of the seven deadly sins all (as Virgil significantly brought to notice) partake of the nature of those errors described by Aristotle as childish sins of *Akrasia*. Here are examples of greediness, anger, extravagance and stinginess, lustful impulses and the like. Then come examples of intellectual error, such as men are most likely to encounter in their student days. The hot violent impulses of unbridled adolescence are next treated in some detail. Later on, in Malebolge, the malice of hardened sinners meets its retribution, and, lastly, the frozen inhumanity or *brutality* of a wicked old age. This rough classification of offences which man in every age is liable to commit constitutes the moral allegory which, so Dante declared, made part of his plan. It marks out a kind of general itinerary from birth to death, along which, encountering many temptations and sinners of every description, it was ordained for Dante to walk.

THE INFERNO AS A RECORD OF DANTE'S LIFE

It was not only the life of man in the abstract but the course of Dante's own life which was to be described. The track he followed was the track of his individual freewill. He was guided and governed in it by Reason, a trustworthy but not altogether infallible guide. Together they were sometimes baulked by obstacles, made serious mistakes, took long détours, and once or twice narrowly failed of losing their path irretrievably. Attention is continually directed to the condition of the road, and it may be inferred from the

twelve hours represents what, slightly departing from the letter of Scripture to suit the duodecimal system by which diurnal time is measured, should be the normal term of human existence, seventy-two years. Allowing six years to the hour, two in the afternoon answers to forty-eight years, Shakespeare's precise age when he wrote *The Tempest*, if this was written for the Princess Elizabeth's marriage. Prospero's admonition to himself that his remaining time must be spent most preciously, corresponds to his concluding declaration that henceforth " Every third thought shall be my grave." '

hints in the text that a smooth bit of track indicates a peaceful period in Dante's life and that its ruggedness marks temptation and difficulty.

Great importance attaches throughout to the intercourse between Dante and Virgil, and from the autobiographical point of view these passages are of the highest value. Recording as they do his recollections of the motives which actuated him at the moment indicated, they constitute an apologia for his actions.

The main allegorical theme, as defined by Dante himself, is throughout kept clearly in view, viz., *to display man subject to reward or punishment according to his actions*, therefore (by implication) man in the world of the living. But it was no Divine order of justice which Dante beheld meting out retribution in the various zones. The penalties imposed were often such as reflected the tyranny and injustice which Dante had beheld and himself experienced in life. The design was to reveal through what errors men have drifted into this deplorable condition, with a view ' to remove those living in this life from the state of misery and lead them to the state of felicity '.[1]

Often the Hell atmosphere disappears altogether. Dante drops his rôle as spectator of souls to become absorbed in subjects wholly disconnected with the torments of the damned, but bearing very closely on the particular religious and political problems of the period in life at which he had arrived.

THE MYTHOLOGICAL ENIGMAS

The apparent mystification which Dante practised on his readers in lending his poem three distinct meanings (the fourth or mystic meaning seems to be much in abeyance in the *Inferno*) can most readily be reduced to logical consistency by concentrating attention on the mythological figures scattered throughout the *Inferno*. They are all described with a care which suggests that they hold an important part in the structure of the poem. They are unmistakably enigmas and from the outset they betray a three-sided meaning. The Beasts in the Prologue afford an

[1] Epistle x.

admirable illustration of the method adopted throughout. Taking the narrative literally we have to believe that on his way up a mountain Dante came across first a Leopard, next a Lion, and lastly a Wolf, all of which were aggressive and blocked his path. But no reader ever believed in these actual Beasts. They plainly stand for something quite different which Dante for good reasons could not express without a disguise. Their moral significance leaps to the eye ; the Leopard as youthful desire or sexual impulse, the Lion as pride or ambition, the Wolf as avarice. There seems no call for allegory to hide these harmless implications.

But commentators have long recognized in the Leopard an image of the gay and fickle city of Florence; in the Lion with its threatening violence the country of France or Anjou; in the Wolf a symbol of the Papal Curia with its never sated lust for usurping temporal power. These dangerous political comparisons were safely secreted under the more obvious moral significance of the Beasts, for no ecclesiastic would venture to bring a writer to book because the Papal Court appeared to correspond in every particular with the figure which Avarice presented under the image of a Wolf. In the art of disguising, which Dante admittedly employed, a secondary harmless meaning was indispensable. Under the stalking-horse of human influences or passions it was possible to pillory officials and world powers with impunity, notwithstanding the fact that every breath of criticism reckoned as heretical depravity.

Following the analogy of the Leopard, Lion, and Wolf, each mythological figure encountered in the Inferno will be found to conceal under its fairly prominent moral significance an ironic intent. And because under the domination of the Papal Curia, all power, and thus inevitably all abuses, centred in the ecclesiastical administration, it will be discovered that the mythological figures which presided over the several zones all exhibit under their mantle of morality some aspect of ecclesiastical constraint obnoxious to the intellect.

The *Inferno* falls into a succession of scenes, each distinct with its own atmosphere, setting, and *dramatis personæ*. But a connected purpose runs through it from end to end, combining it into a reasoned protest against the debased ecclesiastical administration.

The enigmatical mythological figures or images encountered by the traveller at irregular intervals in the journey were incredibly out of place in Hell proper, being but profane inventions of a heathen poet, but they fall into their right place in Dante's autobiography as various aspects of the clerical interference with civil rights and liberties, which he encountered through life. It is these figures which make Hell what it is; they are the ministers of Dis, and are actively responsible for the wretchedness portrayed in the region which Dis controlled from the centre. Representing in a long series the chief instruments employed by the Carnal Church to subjugate mankind, they unite the action which would otherwise fall into a mere succession of painful episodes.

Dante seems to have underrated the difficulties which his chosen readers would have to overcome, but this was partly, it may be surmised, because it was all very clear in his own mind, and partly because the danger he tried most to avoid was that of being too well understood by the wrong people. Looking back over his own life he found ample material for a survey of ecclesiastical misrule sufficiently horrible to pass for a vision of Hell. He had only to describe what he had seen. But in writing the truth he must inevitably expose the iniquity of men who had it in their power to commit both him and his poem to the flames. The extraordinary feat he attempted in the *Inferno* was to show up principalities and powers, the rulers of the darkness of this world, spiritual wickedness in high places—to let the light of uncensored criticism play on their dark manœuvres—while actually incorporating this exposure in a work which could be reckoned strictly orthodox, nay, even a powerful auxiliary in keeping men subject to Roman dogma. If he could do this he was sure of a world-wide audience. Among the readers thus secured he believed he could count on myriad ' intelletti sani ', well versed in symbolic language, who would read below his words the truths he panted to unfold.

Once the region through which Dante travelled is regarded not as Hell but as mortal existence, the Gateway which confronted him at the beginning proclaims itself as Life.

THE GATEWAY

Through me man passes to the city dolorous:
Through me man passes to eternal woe:
Through me man passes through the lost folk.
Justice inspired my sublime Creator;
Power Divine created me,
Wisdom, most high and Love without beginning.
Before me were not any things created
Excepting the eternal,
And I eternally endure.
Lay aside, ye who enter, hope.

Inf., III, I.
Entrance to
mortal exist-
ence.

Before all created things, eternal among the eternal, is
Life. When the Spirit of God walked upon the face of the
waters, this was not for the building of Hell but for the out-
pouring of Life. At the entrance of Life man passes to a
region wherein Divine Power, Wisdom, and Love co-operate
for his well-being. Of man himself, imbued with life, it was
declared that Justice inspired his Creator.[1] Impregnated with
that fruitful germ which Dante terms 'Nobility', man in-
herits the Divine Nature which formed him in order that he
might be a partaker of the eternal Kingdom.

What then of the ' città dolente ', the ' eterno dolore ', the
' perduta gente '? They are echoes of language used in all
ages about mortality and the world of living men. The ' città
dolente ' is that ' civitas terrena ' where man is born to
trouble as the sparks fly upward. Some, alas, who pass
through the Gate of Life will lose the good of their intellect.
Life for such is the road to the ' eterno dolore ' of exclusion
from God's Presence. *All* who pass through the Gate will find
themselves among a lost people, but the word ' lost ' holds
no message of despair. The prophets repeatedly used the
word *lost* to describe the people of Jerusalem, led astray by
evil government.[2] It is to be understood that the nations of
the world who have gone astray are as the lost sheep for whom
the Good Shepherd gave His Life.—They are lost because like
Dante himself in the Wood they forsook the guidance of
Reason and followed the wrong track.

[1] Is., xlv, 12. I made the earth and created man upon it ... I have
raised him up in justice (ad justitiam).
[2] *Cf.* Ezekiel, xxxiv, 16. I will seek that which was lost.

Lasciate ogni speranza voi che entrate. The words more than any in the literature of the world spell the language of despair. Yet spite of their *duro senso* they hold a natural meaning. When Job declared that his days were consumed without hope he was merely expressing the familiar conviction that all earthly hopes are vain, that the happiness of this world is an illusion.

The Vestibule to which Dante gained access through the great Gateway presents some remarkable features. It was a dark and mysterious place. Its occupants had 'never been alive' and had 'no hope of death'. They were in fact compared to abortions, and as such were fit to cloak the identity of the cowards who surrendered Sicily to the French on the eve of Dante's birth. Considerable light is thrown on the condition of these 'captive souls' by a study of the momentous events which preceded the birth of Dante, a train of circumstances which is examined in the ensuing chapter. Confining the present theme to the broad outline of the *Inferno* as a figure of human existence, it must suffice to indicate that some preliminary sojourn in a hidden place 'without stars' (described as the truest microcosm, the obscure world, the womb of our mother, by Sir Thomas Browne) must of necessity precede the moment of actual birth, seeing that according to Florentine usage a man's age was reckoned from the date of conception.[1] It was believed that the soul descended on the 24th day into the foetus, after which moment it was presumed that it became capable of incurring eternal damnation on account of the inherited taint of Adam's guilt. In the Decretals of Gratian incorporated in Canon Law it is laid down on the dictum of Augustine 'that not only men of rational age but even babes who having *begun to live* in the mother's womb either die there or already born die without the sacrament of Baptism in the Name of the Father, Son and Holy Spirit, pass from this world *to be punished with eternal fire*'.

The passage through the Vestibule during which Dante showed himself endowed with prophetic insight to discern the fateful débâcle of Manfred's army, ended with a swift change of scene. He moved on obedient to the impulse which

[1] *Banquet*, Bk. IV, c. 24. Adolescence does not start at the beginning of life but some eight months after.

drives souls forward to the act of birth, an impulse not to be
understood until he himself made one of the throng.

ANTENATAL EXISTENCE

Inf., III, 70-
136.

Then, farther on, as I began to look,
I saw folk on the bank of a great stream
Whereat I said: 'Master, now grant it me
'To know what like are these, what instinct drives,
'Seeming to make them eager to pass over
'As by the faint light I discern.'

> Unborn souls
> pressing on
> to the hour
> of birth.

And he: 'The things shall be made known to thee
'When we shall stay our steps upon the stream,
'The melancholy stream of Acheron.'
Then with my eyes ashamed and lowered lids
Fearing my words displeased him,
I kept myself from speaking till the stream.

> Dante would
> feel the im-
> pulse when
> the moment
> came.

And, behold, there came by boat towards us
An old man, white, with ancient head of hair,
Proclaiming: 'Woe upon you, guilty souls.
'Expect not ever to behold the Heaven;
'I come to bear you to the other bank
'Into eternal darkness, heat and ice.

> The Church's
> message of
> despair to the
> unbaptized.

'And thou, O soul alive, that stayest there,
'Depart thou from among those who are dead.'
But when he saw that I departed not
He said: 'By other road, by other ferry,
'Not here, shalt *thou* come to pass on to shore.
'A boat more glad must carry thee across.'
To him my Guide: 'Charon, vex not thyself;
'Thus it is willed where power is one with will.
'Therefore demand no more.'
Whereon the woolly cheeks were quieted
The pilot bore—he of the livid swamp
That all around his eyes had wheels of flame.

> Dante must
> be safe-
> guarded in
> the Ship of
> the Church
> through
> Baptism.
>
> Reason re-
> bukes the
> judge.

But those souls that were naked and foreworn
Altered their colour, gnashing with their teeth,
The instant they had heard the bitter words.
God they blasphemed, their parents and the race

> Unborn souls
> becoming
> aware of
> their doom
> to eternal
> torment.

57

Of all mankind—the place, the time, the seed
Of their engendering and of their Birth.
Then all of them together, weeping sore,
They drew them to that unpropitious bank
Which every man awaits who fears not God.
Charon, the demon, with his glowing eyes,
Beckons them and gathers all together,
Smites with his oar any who seek delay.

Birth of man
apparently
haphazard
but in
reality con-
trolled by
Providence.

As when in autumn one by one the leaves
Rise up in air until the bough beholds
Its spoils all scattered on the ground below:
In such a fashion, Adam's evil seed
Cast themselves one by one from off that shore,
At signals, as the bird comes at its call.
Thus they depart over the gloomy wave;
And ere they land upon the farther side
A fresh band gathers upon this anew.

All whether
their lives
are to be ill
or well spent
are born
alike athirst
for life.

' My son,' thus spake my Master courteous,
' Those all who die under the wrath of God
' Gather together here from every land.
' And they are eager to pass o'er the stream
' Because justice Divine so spurs them on
' That fear turns to desire.
' This way there passes never a good soul.
' And therefore if against *you* Charon rails
' Now mayest thou know well what his words impart.'

The act of
birth.

This ended, the dark plain shook violently
So that the memory of my fright even yet
Bathes me with sweat.
The ground all tear-bedewed sent forth a blast
Which flashed a crimson glare; this overcame
Every sensation.
Like one whom slumber seizes, thus I fell.

The scene on the banks of Acheron gains immeasurable
force when regarded, not as a gathering of damned souls,
but as a presentation of the unborn hovering on the brink of

a world whose spiritual rulers had condemned them in advance to eternal torment.

There is a scene in *l'Oiseau Bleu* which throws some light on the psychology of this vision of birth. Maeterlinck's unborn souls crowd impatiently, they also, waiting the appointed moment, fully conscious that it is big with fate. They are keyed to the highest pitch of expectation, in alternate hope and fear as they near the unknown future. But in the vision of the modern the awful figure proclaiming a doom of horror before they have begun their probation is absent.

Charon stands first among the enigmatic figures which hold sway in the realm of the *Inferno*. It must be remembered that it is presented as a realm in which the Love of God is altogether ignored. Truth and justice found no place in it. Dis was the Emperor and his was a law of falsehood and wrong. His ministers were perfidious. They condoned vice and threatened virtue. Virgil never lost an opportunity to rebuke and refute them. Deriving their authority from Dis they were yet subject to a higher power and quailed before Reason. By many apparent clues they are revealed as the corrupt instruments of the Carnal Church—Dis or the Wolf—which had usurped dominion over the world and was responsible in Dante's judgment for the manifold wretchedness of mankind.

In Virgil's picture of the lower regions in the *Aeneid* Charon was carrier of souls over the Styx to eternal torment. The suggestion that Dante's Charon holds a similar office is therefore irresistibly conveyed to the reader. In the moral sense of the Image Charon as Time does indeed bear souls to encounter the vicissitudes of this life. But his figure differs widely from that of Virgil's Charon, who was a creature of disgusting squalor in person and attire. The Charon of the text is a reverend and awe-inspiring personage. Round about his eyes were *wheels of flame* and his beard was *like wool*, features which seem meant to recall Daniel's vision[1] of the Ancient of Days, whose hair was like the pure wool and his wheels as burning fire, ' ten thousand times ten thousand stood before him, the judgment was set and the books were opened '. It was the office of the Judge of all mankind that Charon had usurped. Myriad souls flocked to hear their doom from his lips. No

[1] Daniel, vii, 9.

59

reader was ever so dull or unimaginative as to hear his fatal
words without a shudder:

> 'Woe upon you, souls depraved.
> Never may ye hope to see the Heavens
> I come to drive you to the other bank:—
> Into eternal darkness, heat and ice.'

The full horror of the scene does not dawn upon the mind
until the beings on the shores of Acheron throw off their
disguise as ghosts and stand revealed as the souls of the
unborn generation assured in the moment preceding birth
that an eternity of torture awaits them.   Such in effect was
the sentence passed by the Church upon the great mass of
unbaptized mankind.   And the figure of Charon, robed in
attributes of Divine Justice, typifies the Catholic Priesthood
beckoning hellwards each successive generation as though it
had been created for this and this alone.

Myriads were hastening to begin their earthly pilgrimage—
male and female, ready to be born in those immense Kingdoms
of the East, whose existence, now in the late thirteenth century, had been revealed by travellers; Greeks, Turks, infidels,
heretics; heathen who would never hear of Christ; babes
of Christian parents fated to die unbaptized; all sentenced
irrespective of future conduct to eternal perdition and all
in that moment made aware of their doom.   Their attitude
towards the future was suggested by the passage in which
Job cursed the day of his birth: ' Let the day perish wherein
I was born, and the night in which it was said " There is a
man child conceived "; let that day be darkness'.   They
cursed God and their progenitors, the human race (for beasts
have no future retribution to dread), the time, the seed of
their engendering, and their BIRTH.   This was but rational, for
according to the orthodox doctrine of Original Sin, it was
these accidents and not their own sins which procured them
their eternal doom.

Charon did not include Dante among the number of those
eternally dead before the hour of birth.   Among the countless
crowds pressing forward to enter this world, a few were pre-
destined to escape perdition by baptism and priestly absolution.   Dante was recognized as a ' live soul', and without

much cordiality on the part of Charon was referred to another Way, the Narrow in contradistinction to the Broad Way; to another Portal, that of Baptism;[1] a happier Boat, the Ship of the Church was to be his safeguard.

It was part of Dante's scheme in the *Inferno* to endow all its occupants, including the Guardians of the Zones, with prescience of the future, though but indistinctly. By this device he was able to introduce into his work, ostensibly confined to a survey of events preceding the year 1301, criticism on the politics and leading figures of the years in which his interests were most deeply involved. The hostility towards him exhibited by Charon and the other Guardians is meant, it may be surmised, to indicate their perception that under the escort of Reason Dante was to prove a formidable foe to the Papal Curia.

Not without cause was the epithet ' courteous ' bestowed on Virgil in his exposition of the scene. He was himself numbered among the wretches whom Charon denounced. Yet he put the orthodox point of view with calmness and restraint.

Some, he explained, of those awaiting the beginning of their earthly pilgrimage, would actually die in the wrath of God, not, it may be presumed, for lack of ecclesiastical privileges, for they are from *every* country, but because with or without such privileges they chose to surrender their lives to evil. No human soul can be pronounced wholly good. All are liable to follow false notions of good in the gratification of their desires and fall a prey to evil leadership. Charon's cause of complaint against Dante even in the womb was not difficult to surmise.

BIRTH

The scene upon the banks of Acheron is presented with amazing animation, in spite of the ghastly atmosphere which hangs over it like a pall. The flight of the souls to the hour of birth went on unceasingly, with breathless haste and impetus. Two beautiful similes which gain fresh illumination from the allegorical subject illustrate the scene. In the first, the birth of men, falling unnumbered on the earth like showers of leaves, is figured collectively. In the second, the birth of man as an individual is presented, and the souls are beheld

[1] Cf. *Inf.*, IV, 36. Baptism, the portal of the faith that thou believest.

responding one by one as a falcon to the voice of the fowler, each settling on the spot for which it has been fore-ordained.

Sir Thomas Browne has conjectured that it is probably more painful to be born than to die. Dante carried the sensations of birth a step farther; a violent upheaval, a sickening sense of dread, a rush of air, a flash of dazzling crimson light, and then all senses lulled into the unconscious slumber of the new-born infant, unstirred until the first perception of sound startled like thunder the inexpert ear.

THE END OF LIFE'S JOURNEY

In this preliminary survey of the *Inferno* as an image of human existence it is necessary to turn abruptly from the opening passages which figure man's entrance to life through the blind world of the womb, to consider the manner of exit. If the beginning be Birth, assuredly the ending will prove to be Death.

None can ever have failed to wonder at the monstrous medieval phantasy depicted at the close of the *Inferno*. That Satan's body should be discovered corporeally in the exact centre of the world gnawing selected sinners with triple head in the lowest pit of perdition, that the leg of the devil should be the appointed ladder by which Dante was to rise to realms of light, surely these are fragments of lumber borrowed from the puerile monkish inventions of the darkest ages; they ill accord with the mind of the learned Aristotelian, close disciple of Reason.

THE IMAGE OF DEATH

Inf., xxxiv, 1.   ' The banners of the King of Hell move on
' Towards us; therefore look in front of thee ',
My Master said, ' if thou canst make him out '.
As when a heavy fog suspires, or when
Our hemisphere grows dusk at night
Appears a Mill, far off, turned by the wind,
Now such an edifice I seemed to see.
Then as a shelter from the Wind I turned
Behind my Master; no other lair was there.
Now I had reached, with dread I write the verse,
The place wherein the shades were quite enclosed—
Transparent as it were a straw in glass.

Some there were lying; others stood erect,
One on his head, another on his soles;
Another like a bow turned head to feet.

When so far forward we had come, it pleased
My Master to display to me the Creature
Which (once) had outward semblance beautiful;
He moved him from in front and made me stop,
Saying ' Lo, (there is) Dis, and lo the place
' Where thou must arm thyself with fortitude '.

How icy chill, how faint I then became
Enquire not Reader, or I write it not;
All words would fail to utter it.
I did not die, nor did I stay alive;
Bethink thee then if thou hast flower of wit
What I became, mulcted of Life and Death
                    (of one and the other)

The Emperor of the Kingdom Dolorous
From mid-breast issued forth out of the ice;
And I myself am more like to a Giant
Than are the Giants, contrasted with his arms.
Mark now what that must be in its whole size
Which corresponds to such constructed parts.
If he were once as beautiful, as now
Repellent, and he lifted up his brows
Against his Maker, well might there proceed
All anguish from him.
O what great marvel did it seem to me
When I perceived three faces on his head.
One was in front; that was vermilion red.
Other two were there that were joined to this
Over the very middle of each shoulder;
Meeting together at the point of the crest.
The right-hand one seemed between white and yellow;
The left was such to look upon as they
Who come from Egypt where the Nile descends.
Beneath each one there issued two great wings
Wide stretching as befits a mighty Bird.
No feathers had they but after a bat
The wings were fashioned. And he was flapping them

63

So that three winds proceeded out from him.
Cocytus from this cause is wholly frozen.
With six eyes he was weeping; down three chins
The tears were gushing and the blood-stained foam.
In each mouth he was champing with his teeth
A sinner—even as a brake might do—
Thus in such torment he kept three of them.

Regarded as a symbol of Death the grandeur of the dread
figure flashes at once into view. Not Satan but Death marks
the close of the theme, the end of the pilgrimage. It is Death,
not Satan, that stretches sable wings, stealthy and soft as the
wings of a bat, over the nether region, and it throws some
light on contemporary understanding of Dante's inner meaning that, as Professor Platt has pointed out, Death is represented with the wings of a *vipistrello* in the fresco at Pisa which
used to be attributed to Orcagna. It is Death who is Emperor
of the sorrowful realm of human existence—it is he who is
King of Hades or the grave. From Death proceeds the icy
blast which chills all who approach the dread presence. It
is Death which devours the sons of men and Dante was
strictly Scriptural when he called up the spectacle of writhing
forms in the very *jaws of Death*, for he founded it on the words
of the Psalmist: ' They lie in the Hell like sheep; Death
gnaweth upon them '.[1]

Prophetically Dante beheld himself *in articulo mortis*—that
dying state concerning which Augustine in the City of God
(Bk. XIII) lengthily argues whether it be death or life.

It should be noted that the Hebrew word ' Sheol ', which
originally meant the grave, was commonly rendered as
' infernus ' in the Vulgate; and there are many passages in
the Psalms, Proverbs, and Book of Job in which the word
' infernus ' can only be understood of death. In the Apocalypse death and hell are spoken of as one conception; as, for
instance, ' Et mors et infernus dederunt mortuos suos qui in
ipsis erant '.[2] The words with which Dante described the
nethermost Hell all reflect Biblical images of Death: ' il
punto dell universo '; ' il Fondo '; ' il Pozzo ' are sugges-

[1] *Cf.* Job, xviii, 15. Devoret pulchritudinim entis ejus; consumet
bracchia illius primogenita Mors.
[2] Rev., xx, 13.

tive of the Pit. And the image of a lake can be traced to Psalm lxxxviii, 6, ' Possuerunt me in lacu inferiori: in tenebrosis et in umbra mortis '.

There then was the end of the long journey. By this appointed Stair of Death, and certainly without aid from Satan, Dante was to make his way undismayed in the arms of Reason to the realm of Purgatory, ultimately to behold the Beatific Vision.

LUCIFER THE GREAT USURPER

In approaching the final great symbol of his *Inferno*, Dante drew together all the scattered threads of his complicated design. Literal, allegorical, moral, each meaning has its part in the mystic figure which closes the scene. In no place is the symbol called directly by name. ' The creature which had [used to have] the beauteous aspect'; 'the Emperor of the dolorous kingdom'; Dis or Lucifer; these are the expressions used about the monster with three heads whose influence was paramount in the *Inferno*. Thus the way was left clear for weaving the threefold strand of meaning which the poet embedded in his narrative throughout, and miraculous indeed was the skill which could assign to one symbol so great diversity of intention.

The figure is but vaguely indicated. For instance there is mention of arms: yet a few lines farther on the monster is called a bird, and three sets of wings are described which are incompatible with the notion of arms. It has to be regarded as an assemblage of various images, an enigma, rather than as a Giant whose proportions are indicated and whose form could be drawn. Under all three aspects of the allegory the image is to be regarded as the usurping Emperor of the dolorous kingdom. As Satan, as Death, as Papal Temporal Power it holds its place in open rebellion against the Most High. All wretchedness flows from the Usurper. From sin, from death, from the misrule of usurpation, proceed all the woes of mankind.

The daring symbolism which has made of the usurper a trinity in unity cannot escape notice. Every principle of good has its counterpart of evil; Power, Love, Wisdom have their opposites in Impotence, Hatred, Ignorance. The flaming vermilion of the centre is perhaps hatred manifest in bloodshed; black is the hue of ignorance, for black is the negation of Light; the colour between white and yellow is ' livid ',[1]

[1] Lividus—pale and wan, Cicero classes together ' Lividi et timidi '.

and stands for cowardice, which is the offspring of impotence, for only the weak are cowardly. This is the colour assigned in the Apocalypse[1] to the horse on which Death rode, for fear bears death to men.

Dante displayed extreme caution in indicating the Papal aspect of the Emperor of the dolorous kingdom. From the very beginning of the poem, however, he had been leading his readers to this inevitable conclusion. The Papal Curia aspiring to govern the world had turned it to an inferno of dark despair. On the Papal Curia must rest full responsibility for its misgovernment. Enthroned in ghastly mockery of Divine authority sat the central power whence all the mischief proceeded. In place of the minister of Divine Justice is exposed a fallen Lucifer, a minister once divinely gifted, who had lifted up his brows against his Maker, the Hound transformed to Wolf, preying upon those he had been set to guard. From Dante's standpoint no other explanation of the wretchedness of mankind was possible. Here is the kernel of the problem, the ultimate discovery of the voyage, the secret which justified all his elaborate precautions.

'O fair beginning!' cried St. Peter; 'to what vile end must thou needs fall!'[2]

A few years after Dante's death the following epistle ascribed to a pious monk, was addressed to Clement VI and his Cardinals in the name of Lucifer, Prince of Darkness. It was signed by 'Beelzebub, your special friend, Farfarellus and Catabriga, secretary', and was dated 'From the centre of the earth and the place of darkness':

'We yield you hearty thanks'; it commences, 'persevere, and by 'your precious assistance we shall soon have reconquered the whole 'world. However in order to second your effort we send you from here 'some of our most skilled satraps who, admitted into our counsels, will 'work to assure you the victory. Powerful and adroit as you are, cease 'not to negociate in appearance for peace between the kings of the earth, 'doing all you can at the same time to divide and destroy them. We 'recommend you also our very dear daughters, Pride, Avarice, Fraud, 'Luxury and the others, but above all Dame Simony, who gave you to 'the world and has nourished you with her milk.'

---

[1] Rev., vi, 8. Et ecce equus pallidus, et qui sedebat super cum, nomen illi mors. *Cf.* Zech., vi, 2-3. In the first chariot were red horses; and in the second chariot black horses; and in the third chariot white horses; and in the fourth chariot grisled and bay horses. (Lat., varrii at fortes.)

[2] *Para.*, xxvii, 59, 60.

CHAPTER III

THE VESTIBULE

[*Inferno III*, 22-69]

A shadow of the events which were taking place in Tuscany during Dante's pre-natal period. Cowards and captives from Manfred's army displayed in a blind world as men who had never been alive.

Period covered : from September 1264 onwards—the time of Dante's conception.

Corresponding hour : 7 to 7.20 p.m.

DANTE ALIGHIERI was born in Florence towards the end of May or beginning of June, 1265. Like many facts relating to him the month of his birth is known only through an allusion to it in the *Divina Commedia*. Describing the rising and setting of the constellation Gemini (within which sign of the Zodiac the Sun enters 17th May) Dante hailed them as the glorious stars which were in ascendancy when he first felt the air of Tuscany and ascribed to their power[1] whatever genius he possessed. The Twins, mightiest of all the signs of the Zodiac, stood according to familiar allegory for the Twin Luminaries, Church and Empire, which God had appointed for the governance of this world, and it so happened that the year of Dante's birth was the last for generations to come in which Italians could claim that they were born directly under the ægis both of Church and Empire.

There can be no understanding of Dante or of the times in which he lived without some perception of the functions of these two world powers, almost continuously at war during his entire life. Each power represented a great ideal and was able to inspire many noble adherents with enthusiasm and self-sacrifice. The Ghibellines upheld the authority of the Holy Roman Empire, ruled by an Emperor intended to perform his functions as head of a confederation of nations,

---

[1] *Para.*, XXII, 112.

united under one Imperial Law. The Guelfs recognized the dominion of the Pope as supreme, not only in spiritual things, but likewise in the realm of politics. Empire and Church alike stretched back in their origin to the beginning of the Christian era. Alike they founded their civil authority on the Roman law and the possession of ancient charters. Each had lawyers, expert in the interpretation of the law, Civil and Canonical; officials great and small in abundance; courts and officers of justice to enforce a multiplicity of penalties. Theoretically, every Emperor and every Pope was divinely appointed to fill his sacred office. The Emperor was chosen in solemn assembly by the seven great officials of the Empire known as Electors, and the result of the election was made public by the sounding of a silver horn. The Pope was chosen by Cardinals, varying in number, assembled in solemn conclave. Alike in the election of Emperor and Pope votes were notoriously bought and sold. Yet, in spite of such abuses and the frequent intervention of armed forces to influence the result, the tradition that the ultimate choice was divinely directed was kept alive. Neither Pope nor Emperor could exercise complete world jurisdiction. A vast Empire had its seat at Constantinople and maintained its independence in the East; while the existence of the Greek Church, practically independent since the sixth century, severed definitely from allegiance to Rome in 1054, rendered abortive the Papal claim to direct Christendom in its entirety.

The Church had several great advantages over the Empire which tended to increase as the centuries rolled on. In particular the Pope had established the right to confirm the election of the Emperor by bestowing on him the title of King of the Romans and inviting him to Rome for the ceremony of consecration. Without this formal assent to his election on the part of the Church, the Emperor was shorn of much dignity and his claim to universal authority could hardly be maintained. In order to obtain it, important concessions were made to the reigning Pope by successive Emperors, all tending to extend the temporal dominions of the Papacy and restrict the area within which the Emperor exercised the right of investiture, with revenues according.

It must be realized that both Empire and Church were badly organized at this time for the gigantic tasks they undertook. The actual business part of the world control was quite beyond their powers of administration. The Church, by means of its complete hierarchy of Bishops and parish priests, supplemented by the monastic orders, was immeasurably the better equipped for exercising valid control, but in practice this elaborate organization was heavily handicapped by the ignorance and greed of the inferior ill-paid agents and the personal ambitions of the higher ecclesiastics. Rome, usurping to itself authority as a court of appeal for the whole world, became the most incompetent and iniquitous, because the most widely-acknowledged, tribunal known to history.

In the Imperial government there were perhaps fewer abuses only because less was attempted. A strange lack of organization is apparent. There was no acknowledged capital to the Western Empire nor fixed seat of government. The Diets or assemblies, by assent of which the Emperor alone had power to issue edicts, were irregularly convoked and the central government was so inadequately supported that their decrees were frequently disregarded. The subsidies which the Emperor could legally claim from every territory owning allegiance to him were often denied, and, in this particular, the Church, which had a most efficient system of collecting its dues, had an overwhelming advantage. To balance this, however, the Pope had no army and was compelled to rely on a foreign prince to enforce his commands, while the Emperor could usually count on support from some of the warlike nations in Central Europe.

As the Church gained in wealth and authority, ambitious Pontiffs were enabled more successfully to encroach on the civil rights of nations. A violent reaction against the excessive spiritual and temporal prerogative claimed by the Popes was set stirring. Nothing, absolutely nothing, in the life of man was exempt from clerical regulation. From the moment of birth to the hour of death and beyond into the far stretches of eternity he was to be kept in subjection to priestly authority, liable, if disobedient, to hideous penalties. From the mere fact of its inferior powers the Empire aspired to interfere little with individual rights, and thus gradually, and as it were in spite of itself, it became identified with the idea of liberty. While it could afford some slight material protection to men who had fallen under the ban of the Church, its moral influence was stronger, for the effect produced by continual and often successful defiance helped to undermine the terror inspired by the Papal curses. Yet, alas, when the visible sign of Imperial liberty became a horde of unpaid and ill-disciplined German soldiers overrunning the country, the most ardent disciples of theoretical freedom might be excused for preferring the old ecclesiastical yoke which habit, coupled with adroit financial concessions, had adjusted to their necks.

It can easily be perceived that the dual system of world control had practically broken down altogether. Acute dissension existed between the two powers pledged to uphold the peace of mankind, and in no place did their strife produce more tragic consequences than in Italy. Guelfs and Ghibellines began to find it impossible to live side by side in the same city. Each party conspired ceaselessly to banish the other, and savage vendettas were maintained with bloodthirsty ferocity for generations.

The date of Dante's birth synchronized with events which determined the ascendancy of the Guelf party in Italy during his entire lifetime. The representative of the Empire at this time was Manfred, crowned King of the Two Sicilies in 1258, son of the late Emperor Frederic II, whose hereditary rights over Sicily extended back some centuries. There were flaws in Manfred's title, for his mother Bianca had not been the wife of Frederic, though he married her it seems on his deathbed and thus legitimized his son. Moreover, strictly speaking, Conradin, Manfred's young nephew was the heir. But the Italian Ghibellines under Guido Novello had universally accepted Manfred as their chief.

Urban IV (1261-1264), greatly perturbed by Manfred's influence in Italy, had applied to Charles of Anjou, brother of Louis IX, to turn the Imperialists out of Sicily and hold the territory himself as the vassal of the Church. The Kingdom of Sicily at that time included the southern part of Italy with Naples as its capital, and bordered on the Papal territory, with the result that the Imperialist army could directly threaten the Pope. It was to obviate this danger that Urban sought to introduce the house of Anjou into Italy, and thus began the long quarrel between the Empire and the Church over the right of investiture to the Kingdom of Sicily. To this foreign invasion and the alliance cemented between the

Angevin adventurers and successive Popes, Dante ascribed all the misfortunes which befell his native country. Under the tyrannous rule of the invaders he was to spend twenty-one years of his life in poverty and exile.

During the months preceding Dante's birth, Charles of Anjou was fighting out his fateful duel with Manfred, who was bastard, infidel, and excommunicate in the eyes of the Guelfs, but to Dante the 'well born' whose simple prayer for pardon at the end outweighed the curses of four Popes and won him admission to Purgatory.[1]

It was natural that Dante should come to regard with intense interest the struggle for the liberties of Italy which marked his own arrival in the 'lower world'. Out of the bewildering series of impressions conveyed to him by eye-witnesses he could reconstruct in after years each phase of the conflict with a vividness to which the third canto of the *Purgatorio* bears witness.

Alighiero dei Alighieri, father of Dante, was a notary belonging to an old Guelf family in Florence. It was a learned profession demanding of all who entered it a special term of study at the Bologna University and it was certainly the most lucrative and secure career open at that time to the laity. The number and complicated nature of the constantly changing statutes which affected every transaction in civil life made the notary an indispensable personage in the Italian commune. As a class, however, notaries were not very highly esteemed, for it seems the temptation to advance their own interests in the general unrest was not always resisted.

In the year 1264-5 Florence lay in a seething state of excitement and suspense. Only five years before, an army of German mercenaries, supporting the Ghibelline forces of Italy under

---

[1] *Purg.*, III, 118:

> After I had received two mortal strokes
> Which crushed my body, weeping I gave myself
> To him who freely pardons.
> Horrible my transgressions
> But infinite goodness stretcheth such wide arms
> It taketh whomsoever turns to it.
>
> . . . . . .
>
> Through curse of theirs one is not so far lost
> That Love eternal may not come again
> While hope keeps shoot of green.

71

Guido Novello, had achieved a notable victory for Manfred at Montaperti (4th September 1260) 'on which occasion', says the chronicler, 'the ancient Florentine people were annihilated and put to rout'. Hardly any family in the city had escaped loss. Hardly any house belonging to the Guelf nobility but had been pillaged by the exultant Ghibellines. Many had been razed to the ground, the destruction being completed by fire, and displayed years after their charred ruins in the wealthiest quarter of the city. So atrocious was the rancour of the German and Siennese mob which burst into the city on this occasion that the few sane patriots in the victorious army, conspicuous among whom was Farinata degli Uberti, had the greatest difficulty in saving Florence from entire demolition. Amid the universal ruin, Alighiero had known how to secure his own property from confiscation and retain his position as notary. How he succeeded may be partly surmised from the example of lawyers in all ages who have understood the art of facing both ways. A vast deal of useful information would lie in his hands. The Italian Communes were great sticklers for law and precedent. As soon as the orgy of drunken outrage and vengeance, common to every revolution, had died down, the aid of the lawyers was eagerly invoked to find, on the one hand, titles for the new possessors of houses and lands; on the other hand, by the wretched exiles, secretly to secure from confiscation some fragments of their estates. Services which the notary had perhaps been able to render in days gone by, when it was the lot of the Ghibellines themselves to flee from the hostile city, may have been remembered by them on their triumphant return. At any rate Alighiero seems to have remained undisturbed in his substantial house in the quarter of San Martino del Vescovo, and in 1263 or 1264, he had further consolidated his position by bringing hither a wife from among the new masters of the city. For there are grounds for believing that Bella, the first wife of Alighiero and the mother of Dante, was the daughter of one Durante (Dante) of the old Ghibelline family of the Abati.

To visit in imagination the house in Florence where the infant Dante was about to see the light is to understand in what sense, taking the *Inferno* as a reflection of events in chronological order, his head even before the hour of birth was 'begirt with horror'.[1] Every step in the long drawn-out contest between Manfred and Charles echoed fatally in the ears of the Florentine Ghibellines whose rule, surrounded as they were by a hostile majority kept in awe by arms, gradually became in the last degree precarious. The position of Alighiero, Guelf by family and by carefully concealed convictions, was anomalous. He must have kept up communication throughout with banished kinsfolk and friends for his position did not alter for the worse when the crash came. His would be the quasi impartial attitude of the neutral non-party man. Every rumour would reach him. Tidings of the varying fortunes of Guelf and Ghibelline, the wavering allegiance of the Ghibelline troops, and the growing strength of the Guelf interest, would be brought to the house by adherents of both parties, the husband at the beginning quiescent, cautious, submissive, the wife confident in the power of her kinsmen to protect them both with the unborn babe, resting all her hopes on a speedy Ghibelline victory.

Gradually, very gradually, the tables turned. One reverse after another overtook the forces of Manfred. So persistent were his misfortunes that suspicion began to rest upon some who stood high in his confidence, on one in particular in whom the Florentine nobles of the party had trusted implicitly. Guido Novello, Imperial Vicar General of Tuscany and Captain of the Ghibelline army, began to be recognized as conspicuously unfortunate in all his undertakings. He had it in charge to stop the Provençal Crusaders from landing in Italy and to capture Charles should he set foot in Pisa. In both enterprises Guido failed. Charles was suffered to land unopposed, under circumstances which to all appearances had made it easy to capture him and so end the war. It began to be whispered that Guido was lukewarm in the Imperial cause, or, worse, a coward at heart. When the momentous battle took place at Benevento, 26th February 1266, between Charles and Manfred, Guido was absent, and it was repeated at the time that Manfred, beholding the fine forces of Italian Guelfs led by Guido Guerra, exclaimed in sorrow: 'But where are my Ghibellines for whom I have done so much?' It was the coward Ghibellines who sealed the fate of Manfred and secured the triumph of the Church. Long before the final

[1] *Inf.*, III, 31. Ed io, ch'avea d'orror la testa cinta.

débacle at Benevento the *morale* of Manfred's army began to be undermined by a very skilful propaganda carried out at the instigation of Urban IV, and by his successor Clement IV, who dignified the Angevin adventure with the name of a Crusade. Salvation was assured to all who should fall under the banner of Charles, eternal damnation to every supporter of Manfred. Unfortunately a body of Saracen troops formed a conspicuous element among the very mixed forces on which Manfred was forced to depend, and the presence of infidels fighting as their allies became a source of great scandal to Christian soldiers. It was not difficult to persuade Ghibellines, who at heart were orthodox Churchmen, very far from desiring excommunication, though opposing the policy of the Pope in Sicily, that they were fighting against God. A continual stream of deserters began to set in from Manfred's army, while in every part of Italy Ghibellines found excuses for not fulfilling their pledges to the Imperial cause.

Passions ran very high. The lust for plunder possessed the enormous mob of Provençals who had followed Charles to Italy without hope of payment save what their arms could carve out of their opponents. The deserters met with scant mercy from the most Christian army to which they fled. The fugitives were hunted down by both sides, and in the horrible dungeons of medieval days had leisure to realize too late, in a black despair which knew no division of time, their baseness in abandoning without a blow the struggle for liberty.

With this picture of the torments experienced by the cowards who deserted Manfred on the eve of Dante's birth, must be compared the vision of the cowards which stands first among the torments of the *Inferno*, and preceded Dante's formal entrance into the 'lower world'.

VISION OF THE COWARDS AND CAPTIVES

Inf., III, 22-69. Wretched state of Ghibelline prisoners herded together in dungeons.

In this place, sighs, loud wailing and laments
Re-echoed through the air, lit by no star,
So that from the beginning I was weeping.
Diversity of tongues, horrible utterances,
Words of anguish, accents of wrath,
Loud and faint voices, sound of beating hands,

74

Made up a tumult which went whirling on
For ever in that timeless, deep-dyed air,
Like sand when in a cyclone it spins round.

And I, that had my head begirt with horror,
Said: 'Master, what is this I hear, what folk
'Are these that seem so vanquished in their pain?'

And he to me: 'This miserable state
'The wretched souls are tethered to of those
'Who lived without ill fame yet without praise.
'Among that captive band they are included
'Of angels who rebelled not, nor kept faith
'Towards God, but were for nothing save themselves.
'Heaven expelled them, lest it be less fair:
'Nor will the depth infernal take them—for
'No glory would the guilty get from them'.

> They were half-hearted adherents who tried to hold aloof and face both ways.

And I: 'Master, what weighs on them so sore
'To drive them to lament thus bitterly?'

He answered: 'Briefly will I tell it thee;
'These have no hope of death.
'And their blind life is so exceeding base
'They are envious of any other lot.
'No record of them doth the world allow.
'Mercy and justice equally disdain.
'Let us not speak of them.   Look and pass on'.

> Compared to abortions.

And, as I looked forth, I beheld a banner
That whirling round rushed on so rapidly
It seemed to me unfit for any pause.
Behind it straggled such a lengthy troop
Of people that I never would have deemed
Death had undone so many.
Some I could recognize, and after that
I saw and knew the shadow of that man
Who made through cowardice the great surrender.
Instantly I perceived and was assured
This was the *band of captives*
To God unpleasing—to his foes no less.
These wretches, who had never been alive,

> Ensign of Coward Ghibellines fleeing from the enemy.

> (?) Guido Novello the coward Commander-in-chief.

75

Were naked, and were sorely goaded on
By the gad-flies and the wasps that were there by.
Thus were their faces made to stream with blood
Which being mixed with tears fell at their feet
Gathered by loathsome reptiles.

The passage affords a striking illustration of the manner in
which the history of the times has been woven into the autobiographical strand of the *Inferno*. The actual scene by a
few deft strokes is made to suggest the secret place through
which Dante must needs pass to the moment of Birth, followed by the Slumber of infancy. The actors in the scene,
dimly beheld by Reason's aid hereafter, were the men who
decided the fate of Italy in the days immediately preceding
and following his own birth. Many times in after years must
the exiled Ghibellines have reflected bitterly on the defec-
tions which suffered the Angevin invaders to gain so deadly
a grip on the country. These cowards were like men who had
never been alive, of whom fame could take no account, thus
described in the words of the Preacher: ' And some there be
which have no memorial, who are perished as though they
had never been '.

The failure of the Ghibellines to resist Charles of Anjou
set in motion a train of insurrections, tyranny, and anarchy
which spread far beyond the limits of the countries immediately affected, destroyed the liberties of Italy, and reduced to
ignominy the fair city of the poet's birth. These things began
to happen while he was yet in his mother's womb. Their
bitter consequences were only too manifest at the time when
he began the *Divina Commedia*, and we behold him, as he
reviewed his life from its inception, depicting first in chronological order the fate of the cowards in captivity who had betrayed Italy to the French.

In the description of this ' captive crew' in the blind world
of their subterranean prison, there are all the marks of personal observation. The tale of Benevento and the long
struggle preceding it, was told over and over again for many
years to come by the veterans from all parts of Italy who had
taken part in it, and it may have been among Dante's earliest
recollections to listen while the Guelfs who visited his father's
house fought their old battles over again, and supplied links

of all that was happening in the days immediately before and after his birth. The account seems to fall into two parts. First we have a vivid glimpse of the captive deserters supplied by one who had passed by and heard the horrible cries proceeding from the dungeons below, without catching sight of those who were within. The child's quick imagination would hear, as the recital proceeded, the groans, lamentations, and deep sounds of woe which resounded through those dismal caves where hundreds could be packed indiscriminately to linger in semi-starvation, fighting for the scraps thrown to them, envying the better fate of those who had fallen in battle. Strange tongues were audible, for the deserters belonged to many races, horrible outcries, angry reproaches hurled one against another, voices deep and hoarse, sounds of palms beaten in despair; the tumult all heightened in horror by the black darkness which shrouded them from observation and blotted out time. No tears were to be shed over them. This was the result of sacrificing honour for the sake of life. Here they were to long unavailingly for that death they had been afraid to face. The blind life of these captives was so base, so lacking in all which makes life worth living, that there was no lot however hard and bitter that they would not choose in comparison. None pitied them. The friends they had betrayed acquiesced in the justice of their fate. And as for the enemy, there was little glory in the remembrance that it was the cowardice of their opponents which had brought them victory. No form of retribution was more terrible than this. They had become as men who had never been alive.

Then the story of the betrayal is recounted. The cowards are pictured in the act of flight, carrying with them the ensign which in its movement hither and thither witnessed to their inconstancy, fleeing so swiftly that it seemed to disdain a moment's halt. And after it straggled the long train of fugitives, far more in number than had fallen in fair fight, and surely it was again an eye-witness who painted their horrid state. With their clothes in rags, and some who had fallen among camp-followers actually stripped to the skin, they tore along. A cloud of hornets and wasps pursued them. Their faces were streaming with blood and desperate tears stained their cheeks, while, as they pursued their headlong

77

way through woods and marsh, they were exposed to attacks of vipers and poisonous snakes, the ' fastidiosi vermi ' at their feet. Such was the fate of the cowards, and there needed no morbid invention to expose it.

Afterwards, Dante recalls, when he had come to know some of them personally, he saw and actually became acquainted with the shade of him who out of the baseness of his heart made the great surrender. To revert to Florence, where in the Alighieri house the position changed as the husband came once more into his own, and the wife grew sad and silent, is to gain a possible clue to the identity of the coward traitor. The news of Manfred's defeat and death at Benevento spread dismay throughout the Ghibelline interest in Tuscany. Yet even then all was not lost. The dominant nobles, still under the leadership of Guido Novello, held the country with a powerful grip. The exiled Guelf families with rising hopes were plotting to re-possess themselves of their ruined castles and the estates confiscated five years before. They had many friends among the burgher citizens who were desirous to secure peace with the Church, always an essential to trade interests. Yet in the city of Florence the Ghibellines remained unassailable and so long as Florence held out the Guelfs were powerless. Guido Novello was supported by a valiant and well armed force of the territorial nobles, while those who opposed him lacked skill in arms and military leaders. Strongly fortified, Florence was the bulwark of the Ghibelline cause and was deemed impregnable.

Judge then the dismay with which the news was received within as without the city by those who deemed themselves secure under his protection that Guido Novello had basely surrendered Florence to the enemy. His pretext was the outbreak of a street riot in which the populace displayed their discontent. Refusing to listen to remonstrance Guido called for the keys of the city, reluctantly given up by the Podestà, unlocked the old ox-gate and led the unattacked Ghibelline force which he commanded away to inglorious safety at Prato. The occasion on which this memorable surrender of Florentine liberties took place was St. Martin's day, 11th November 1266. There was never the slightest hope that the Ghibelline army would be suffered to return. The great rejection was made once for all and gave the death-blow to Ghibelline supremacy in Tuscany. It put the crowning touch to the ignominy of Manfred's betrayal.

Villani, who gave an animated account of Guido's surrender of the city, strongly emphasized the circumstance that he went without striking a blow, ' moved by great dread and suspicion of the people '. Was it his figure that loomed large among the rest of Manfred's betrayers, when those who witnessed the great surrender discussed the event in years to come?

Guido Novello will be encountered again. At the battle of Campaldino he was again suspected of intriguing with the enemy. His fate was to become an outcast from the city he so lightly surrendered and taste in his own person the bitterness of the ruined coward. Perhaps some feeling which was not all contempt withheld the man who had once fought against him from openly joining with his Guelf detractors to proclaim his shame. Dante left the name of the great Coward, smirched with the ignominy of his notorious ' rifiuto ', to be guessed at by such as bore the story of the times in mind. Whoever it may be that Dante meant to pillory, it is certain that the benefit of a doubt was always to rest upon his identification.

CHAPTER IV

IMPRESSIONS OF EARLY CHILDHOOD

[*Inferno IV, Limbo*]

Dawn of intelligence, succeeding the slumber of unconscious infancy. First impressions of Bible characters. Early notions of the poets. Beginnings of education. The names of authors come within his ken, distinguished by some special attribute.

Period covered : from 1265 to about 1273-4.

Corresponding to hours between 7.20 and 10 p.m.

THE ALIGHIERI family, in the house situated in the Via Bardi, still pointed out as the spot where Dante first saw the light, evidently came well through the terrible period which succeeded their son's birth. After Count Guido Novello had made his ignominious sortie from the city a determined reaction made itself felt against the overlordship of the Ghibelline families who had ruled the city for the past six years. The burghers were Guelf almost to a man. They had proved by long experience that the goodwill of the Church was essential to trade. Imperialism, backed by German troops, had made itself hateful. Even while the noble Guelf families previously expelled from the city came pouring back to claim their houses and property, the wealthy traders were sitting in council to draw up a new constitution which threw all the power into the hands of the seven greater Guilds. The aim was so to stabilize the government of the city that it could never again be overthrown by warring factions of nobles. Every guild was an independent, self-ruling institution, with separate magistrates, laws, and councils. Under the new constitution the Guild-masters formed the most influential element in the Councils which governed the city. By a law which was passed at this time on the authoritative advice of the Pope, they succeeded in perpetuating their hold on the city and rendering any fresh revolution in favour of the Ghibelline nobles impracticable. This was effected by the

80

formation of a trust into which all property confiscated from the exiled Ghibellines was paid. The sums were considerable. Three thousand Ghibellines had been condemned and many heavy sentences of confiscation pronounced. On previous occasions of revolution all the confiscated property of the dispossessed faction had been divided among the victorious nobles returning from exile. But under the new law only one-third of the spoils was made available for purposes of restitution. The remainder was divided equally between the Commune and a Party Fund, laid by under trustees for the purpose of maintaining the Guelfs for ever in power. The wealth thus accumulated was added to from time to time and became a great force in deciding the issue between the rival parties in the state. It facilitated the raising of an armed force whenever required and, more sinister, it provided means for bribing the large section of citizens who sought only their own private gain in every turn of events.

It would have been well for the Florentines had they trusted to their own powers to maintain order in the state. There was a moment after Guido Novello's flight when it seemed that Guelfs and Ghibellines might bring themselves to live peaceably side by side in their own city. Marriages were arranged between the sons of the one party and the daughters of the other. And it was at this time that Guido Cavalcanti, destined to become the closest friend of the unconscious infant in the Via Bardi, was betrothed (he was then about ten or twelve) to Beatrice, daughter of the great Farinata degli Uberti, the Ghibelline who had saved Florence when its destruction by the Germans had been determined on a few years before. But the Guelfs could not feel secure under the new conditions. The old wrongs were too recent; the prowess in arms of the Ghibelline nobles among them had been too fatally exhibited, and their every movement roused suspicion. Secretly the Guelf masters of the city sent word to King Charles, now in the first flush of victory over Manfred, inviting his protection. On Easter Day, 1267, the city gates were opened to receive a troop of French men at arms under the escort of an exiled Englishman, Philip de Montfort, whose father, Earl of Leicester, had been killed at the battle of Evesham two years before. The night before he arrived, the Ghibellines who still remained in the city gathered together whatever they could carry and, silently, with the connivance doubtless of the city authorities, fled never to return. Their departure marked the beginning for Florence of a long period of subjection to French military power. Their loss of freedom was brought home to the citizens when Charles of Anjou visited Florence in person to conduct a campaign against the cities of Pisa and Siena, still holding out in the Ghibelline interest. The burghers were compelled to raise an immense sum to defray the cost of his victories and, when Charles left Tuscany in haste to subdue Conradin, the young Emperor elect who was making powerful headway in Rome, they found themselves in the grip of an English Vicar (Guy de Montfort), backed up by French soldiers and a French Podestà. Conradin was defeated and barbarously executed by Charles the following year to the horror and despair of the Ghibelline Imperialists. Whatever hope of return the Florentine Ghibellines may have nursed ended with his death. Thereafter for the entire period of Dante's life, Florence was a Guelf city, admitting no Ghibelline to its councils, and save for one short and brilliant period, held down under the heel of the Angevin dynasty so fatally invoked in 1267.

Throughout these unquiet years the most influential persons in the city were the judges and notaries whose Guild stood first in order of precedence. They alone had skill to unravel the intricate claims to property which arose on all hands. There can be little doubt that many Guelf applicants for the restitution of their estates remained unsatisfied. In many cases title-deeds had been lost or destroyed by fire. Many noble families were divided in politics, and set up counter-claims against each other. Adventurers who had forced their way to power appropriated estates to which they had no legal claim. Fortunes were lost and gained by the turn of a pen. And, as happens after all restorations, some who had done most for the Commune were left destitute when the time came for distributing rewards. It was a rich harvest for the notaries. Not only were they heavily paid to establish a good case at law by members of the dominant party, they were also appealed to by the banished Ghibellines to secure them, by the finesse in which the medieval Italian was an adept, some small fragment of their former estate in the general débacle.

It was hardly possible that Dante's father should lack opportunities for advancing his own interests at such a time. However upright he may have been in the discharge of his public duties, it is certain that calumnies would be freely circulated against all who had taken part in the great re-distribution of wealth and land which marked the Guelf restoration to power in Florence. This may in part account for the low esteem in which it would appear he was held by some in the city.

To Dante's mother the years of his infancy can have brought little comfort save what he himself contributed. Her marriage kept her from persecution, but many of her rela-tives and intimate friends would be among the destitute exiles ; some in all probability had suffered execution. Every month brought distressful news of the Ghibellines still in Tuscany. Round the unconscious babe the dark tapestry of spoliation, revenge, despair, which made so terrible a back-ground to the joys of family life in the divided city, was ceaselessly weaving.

The first event of which we can be sure in the story of Dante's individual life is his Baptism. This he alludes to in the *Paradiso* (xxv, 1-12) in a passage which lies between his declaration of Faith to St. Peter and of Hope to St. James. It was in Florence, at the Font of his Baptism, he there records, that he entered the Faith which makes men to be aware of God; it was at that spot (by the Baptistery of San Giovanni) that he looked to assume the laurel wreath, should it ever happen that the sacred poem, which for so many years had kept him lean, while both Heaven *and earth* set their hand to it, were at length to overcome the cruelty which barred him from Florence the beauteous sheepfold; there once as a lamb he slept, an enemy to the wolves warring upon it. There is a further allusion, in a cryptic simile (*Inf.*, xix, 16-18) to the Baptistery of ' my beautiful San Giovanni ' in Florence and to the places where the baptizing priests stood to perform their office.

Early commentators affirm that the sacrament of Baptism was at that time administered only twice a year, on the eve of Easter and Whitsunday. If this be so Dante may have had to wait nearly a year for the rite during which time, according to orthodox belief, he lay in deadly peril of losing by accident for all eternity the joys of Heaven. Many a weeping mother, in an age when the rate of infant mortality was surely no less than it is to-day, had to bear the thought of her unbaptized infant exposed to never-ending flames. This then was the first danger in life to which the infant Dante was exposed.

Very early among the recollections of piously brought up children come Bible stories. At his mother's knee Dante would learn about Adam and Eve, about Cain and Abel, the Flood and the Ark, Moses in the bulrushes and how he rose to be Lawgiver, Abraham tending his flocks, and David the shepherd king. And of these in response to eager questioning he had to learn in words suited to his comprehension that though God loved them and favoured them in their lifetime He did not take them to Heaven when they died. He was taught to believe that like the babies, whose death unbaptized he may have heard lamented, they were shut away from God in a sorrowful place, always longing, until one day Christ came and set them free, while others imprisoned with them were left behind still longing but now without hope.

These were days in which education began early. It need not be claimed that Dante's infancy rivalled that of some more modern prodigies, but he may well have been able to read by the age of three or four, and to have mastered the rudiments of Latin, a tongue which at no time presents much difficulty to Italians, sufficiently to enable him very early to read for himself some of the compendiums through which the medieval child was introduced to the glories of literature. A revival of learning, a true Renaissance, was already stirring at the time of his birth. The dreary stereotyped routine of the Dark Ages was giving way. The works of Aristotle were accessible in Latin translations and were conned as a Divine revelation by ardent disciples. Through the medium of passages quoted by Aristotle some inkling of the grandeur of Homer filtered through, and his fame as the greatest poet of the world had already become established. More widely diffused because appealing more readily to Italian readers, and more powerful in their influence, were the works of Virgil, rescued at length from the ban which the monks had long striven to maintain against pagan authors. A peculiarly cruel calumny had long deepened the ecclesiastical prejudice against Virgil as a non-Christian writer. The Virgilian myth, which represented the Roman poet as a sorcerer in league with the devil for the performance of vulgar and discreditable feats, had largely contributed to banish his works from the schools. Its falsity had become apparent to educated men, but it lingered on for another generation or two in popular imagination. At the opening of Dante's life the cult of Virgil was the mark of the most advanced literary opinion, and his works were the source through which the classical spirit could be best imbibed. The belief, grounded on the Second Eclogue, that he had foretold the coming of the Saviour, was eagerly caught up, and as an additional spur to the reverent study of every line he had written or been reputed to write, came the conviction that his works contained, closely hid from the vulgar, a complete esoteric philosophy.

If there were any in the Alighieri family penetrated with the spirit of the ancients, Dante may well have learned to love the name of Virgil before he could pick out the letters composing it. There is a strong presumption that one in his family, possibly the grandfather Durante, was well versed in the poets and took note of the upward soaring of his thoughts. How otherwise, we may ask, could that noble mind have been framed in its perfection of strength and delicacy save in the plastic hours of infancy? In the season when the first dawnings of intelligence colour the horizon, we know from the confessions of other poets that strange visions form in the sensitive mind prepared to harbour them. Weaving dreams as he sat through the long evenings in the family circle by the side of some absorbed figure poring over a manuscript, may not the child Dante have watched in fancy the poets whose names he had been taught to revere beckoning to him to join their company and make a sixth among the immortals?

Virgil, Horace, Ovid, Lucan were the authors, so Comparetti states, through whom the medieval boy first approached the study of literature. Selected extracts from their works were arranged in manuscript compendiums for the use of those learning to read. And thus, early in the journey of life, Dante could catch glimpses of the great shades in the Elysian fields.

Regular education would begin at or before the age of six. Studies were grouped under the heading of the Seven Arts, and were divided into two courses: the Trivium consisting of Grammar, Logic, and Rhetoric; the Quadrivium of Arithmetic, Algebra, Music, and Astrology (Astronomy). From particulars given by Villani [1] of the educational system in Florence a few years later (1336), it appears that there were three grades of scholars. The first included both boys and girls, in number from eight to ten thousand, who were in the stage of learning to read. The second was made up of a thousand or twelve hundred boys who were learning the abacus and algerismus, in six schools. The third and highest grade comprised only about six hundred boys who learned grammar and logic in four schools. One of these Grammar Schools Dante would have attended later on. It would be his lot to pass through all the Seven Gates which guarded the Castle of Learning, skimming lightly, or according to Latin idiom, dry-shod, over the Pierian stream, yet receiving impressions never after effaced. The foundation of the passionate reverence he displayed in his works [2] for the ' almost Divine Roman people ' who derived from Troy was laid, it cannot be doubted, in these impressionable years during which the men, and especially the women who made history of old, took form as he read, walking visible to his imagination before him. In the higher classes he would begin on the study of Aristotle through extracts from an Arabic rendering into Latin. An introduction to the study of Logic and Rhetoric would make him familiar with at least the names of the masters of philosophy and with passages from the works of Cicero and Seneca ; he would dip into Arithmetic, Algebra, and Astronomy through Euclid and Ptolemaeus, while in summaries arranged with dry brevity he might get some faint idea of other authors known to his generation.

In such studies passed his early years. What they lacked in precision was made up out of the working of an imagination boundless in scope, already swift to personify, keen to appropriate for its use whatever material of a live nature was presented to eye or ear.

Inf., iv, 1612.
Dawn of
Consciousness
in the infant.

CHILDHOOD AND EARLY EDUCATION

A sullen thunder broke the Slumber deep
That held my head, so that I started up

[1] Villani, Bk. xi, 94.   [2] See *Banquet*, iv, 5; *Mon.*, Bk. ii, 3.

Even as one may do who is waked by force;
And having stood erect I turned about,
My sight renewed, and looked with fixed intent
To understand the place wherein I was.
In truth I found myself upon the brink
Of the valley of the dolorous Abyss
Which gathers thunder of infinite laments,—
Obscure, profound, and nebulous—
So that fixing my gaze upon its depth
I could not plainly make out anything.

He stands upright, hears, takes notice.

' Now let us go below to the blind world',
Began the poet, with a deathlike hue,
' I will be first and second thou shalt be'.

In depicting human existence under a fictitious narrative Virgil led the way.

And I, that had remarked his colour, said:
' How shall I come if thou displayest fear—
' Thou that are wont to comfort me in doubtings? '

Reason pales before this dogma of eternal damnation for the innocent.

And he to me: ' The anguish of the folk
' That are down here imprints upon my face
' That deep compassion thou mistakest for fear;
' Let us go on; the long road beckons us '.

Thus he set on and thus drew me to enter
The circle which first girdles the Abyss.

Herein, so far as listening could tell,
Was no lament excepting that of sighs
Which caused the air eternal to vibrate—
Sighs stirred by grief devoid of agony
Which the great crowds and numerous possessed
Of infants and of women and of men.

Spake the good Master: ' Thou dost not enquire
' What souls are these thou seest?
' Now would I have thee know, ere thou goest on,
' That these have sinned not, and if they have grace
' 'Tis not enough, because they lack Baptism,
' The portal of the faith that thou believest.
' If living before Christianity
' God they adored not duly.
' And I myself am such an one as these.
' For such defects, for no offence whatever,

The doctrine of the Church.

87

'Are we condemned, solely punished so sore
'That void of hope we live in endless longing'.

Great grief, when I heard this seized on my heart,
Because I knew folk of high excellence
Were there within that Limbo, under suspense.

'Tell me, my Master, tell me, O my Lord',
Thus I began, wishing to be assured
About that Faith which conquers every error,
'Did ever anyone get out from here
'By his own merit or by that of other,
'That afterwards was blest?'

And he, who understood my cryptic speech,
Replied: 'In this condition I was young
'When I saw come among us One in power
'Crowned with a Sign of victory.
'Thence he took the shade of our first parent,
'With that of his son Abel and of Noah,
'Of Moses, Lawgiver and obedient,
'Abraham the Patriarch, and David King,
'Israel with his father and his sons
'And Rachel for whose sake he did so much,
'And many others; and He made them blessed.
'And I would have you know that before these
'There were no human spirits saved'.

We did not cease to go because he spoke
But meanwhile went on passing through the WOOD.
The Wood, I emphasize, of crowded souls.
Our way had still not far proceeded on
Beyond my Slumber, when I saw a Fire
Which vanquished half the circuit of the shadows.

A little distant were we still from it—
Yet not so far I could not partly tell
That honourable folk possessed that spot.

'O thou that honourest all science and art
'Who are these men that stand in such high honour
'It severs them from contact with the rest?'

And he to me: 'The high renown of honour

The living Faith to which, in Hebrews, IX, is ascribed the redemption of Jews and Gentiles.

Below the whole passage lies concealed Dante's repudiation of the notion of Divine Justice exposed.

The WOOD of material things. Cf. *Inf.*, 1, 2.

He learns early to revere the great poets.

The poets he most admired and sought to imitate.

88

'Which echoes of them in your life above
'Gains Grace, which thus in Heaven advances them'.

Meantime a Voice was overheard by me:
'Give honour to the highest poet of all;
'His shade that had departed now returns'.

Revival of Virgil's fame.

When the Voice paused in silence,
I saw four mighty shades coming towards us:
They bore an aspect neither sad nor gay.
Then the good Master thus began to speak:
'Look thou on him that has the sword in hand,
'Who comes before the three, as though their sire:
'That is the sovereign poet Homer.[1]

'Next comes the satirist Horatius,[2]
'Ovidius[3] the third, and Lucan[4] last.
'Because the name fits each of them with me,
'The name the solitary voice acclaimed,
'They do me honour and therein do well.'

[1] The Epic.
[2] Satire (Lat. *Dissimulatio*).
[3] Allegory.
[4] History.

Thus I beheld assemble the fine band
Of those great Lords of loftiest poesy
That soar like eagles above all the rest.
When they had spoken together for a while
They turned to me and beckoned graciously,
So great a thing my Master smiled thereat.
And still more honour yet they did to me;
For they admitted me among their ranks
And I was sixth in this high intellect.

The *Divina Commedia* blends in its composition the epic, satire, allegory, and history.

Thus we were going forward towards the Light,
Talking of things on which to muse in silence
Is just as beautiful as speech itself
In that place where I was.
A Noble Castle[5] at its lowest point
We reached, circled by high walls seven times,
Defended round by a fair Rivulet.[6]
This, as though 't were hard ground we crossed dryfoot.[7]
Through seven doors I entered with those sages;
We came into a meadow[8] with fresh verdure.
People were there with eyes intent and grave.
Of high authority in their demeanour;
They spoke but seldom and with gentle voice.

Intellect awakes.

[5] Parable of Education, figuring the seven arts of the Trivium and Quadrivium.
[6] The Pierian Stream.
[7] Classical metaphor for superficial study. Cf. *Banquet*, IV, 2.
[8] The Elysian fields.

Thus from one of the sides we took our way
Into a place so open, luminous
And high, that one and all were visible.
There right before me on the green enamel
Were pointed out to me the famous spirits
Whom it exalts me in my mind to see.
I saw Electra with much company
Midst whom I knew both Hector and Aeneas;
Caesar all armed, with his (keen) falcon eyes.
I saw Camilla and Penthesilea
On other hand, and saw the Latian King
Who with Lavinia, his daughter, sat.
I saw that Brutus who expelled the Tarquin,
Lucretia, Martia, Julia,
Cornelia, and in part alone
I saw the Saladin.

After I raised my eyelids somewhat higher
I saw the Master of those men who know
Sitting midst philosophic family.
All gazed at him; all rendered him honour;
Here I beheld Plato and Socrates
Who stand before the others, nearer him.
Democritus ascribing the world to chance;
Diogenes, Thales, Anaxagoras,
Empedocles, Zeno and Heraclitus;
I saw the good collector of qualities,
I mean Dioscorides; and I saw
Orpheus, Tullius and Linus.
And Seneca the moralist,
Euclid, geometrician, and Ptolemy,
Hippocrates, Galen, Avicenna,
And him who made the famous commentary,
Averroes. I cannot here recall them all in full,
Because the lengthy theme so drives me on
That many times my words come short of facts.

The company of six shrinks into two.
By other path the wise Guide leads me on;
I come to a place where there is nought that shines

The Roman heroes whom he passionately vindicates in *Monarchy*, Bk. II, and *Banquet*, IV, 5, as Divine rather than human, and moved by Divine inspiration.

He advances in his studies to elementary philosophy and natural sciences.

His early recollections are perforce cut short.

The train of ideas presented to the medieval child on his first entrance to the world of men and books corresponds remarkably with the successive images presented in the Fourth Canto of the *Inferno* which described Dante's progress through the realm of Limbo. In choosing to cast his early recollections into the framework of Limbo it should be marked how deliberately Dante studied to set at naught the orthodox notion of that indefinitely situated abode, where souls expiated their lack of baptism. There is no dispute over the fact that in Roman doctrine Limbo or Abraham's bosom was a spot reserved for the Old Testament Saints awaiting redemption, and for them alone. Thomas Aquinas urged that the unbaptized infants of believers were probably spared the torture of eternal flames, but no theologian had ever gone so far as to suggest that pagan spirits could be thus favoured. The possession of natural righteousness on which Virgil laid stress in the text was absolutely repudiated. It was universally held that ' even should every kind of goodness be accumulated, without baptism all possibility of attaining eternal life is cut off'. To dispute the generally received opinion that the souls of Aristotle, Virgil, and the rest had been delivered over to the devil in hell proper, to suffer the pains of eternal fire for their own sins and for the sin of Adam, was heresy of a particularly obnoxious kind. For it was the aim of ecclesiastics to root out every opinion which could in any way cause men to doubt that salvation was reserved absolutely without exception for Christian infants baptized under proper conditions, and adults who in addition had been absolved by the priest. Dante could hardly guess that his narrative would have so convincing an effect on the imagination of mankind that in time to come the honourable place he assigned to the heroes of old would be accepted without demur. But clearly he meant to make a startling impression, and, writing in the vernacular, to strike a blow at what he believed to be pernicious doctrines.

We find him dealing first with the fate of unbaptized infants, ministering comfort by his assurance of their soft sighings of desire ' without torment', to countless mothers yet unborn. In this he followed Aquinas. Next he boldly transported all the righteous heathens who either lived before Christ or for other reasons had no opportunity of becoming

Christians, to the very place where tradition had it that the holy Saints of the Old Testament had lain awaiting His coming. Virgil denied that he and his fellows in Limbo had sinned. They owed their exclusion from Heaven, he declared, to the decree that any merit they possessed was of no avail because they were not baptized and had not adored God in the prescribed fashion (*debitamente*). He turned pale as death when he explained to Dante how all the generations of mankind preceding the death of the Saviour had been deprived of the Presence of God from no fault of their own. Assuredly we are to understand that he counted it no light sentence to be cut off for all eternity from the hope of the Beatific Vision. But if we are to take his words as an exposition of orthodox doctrine they are an amazing understatement of the case. Nothing was more deeply rooted in the minds of theologians or more incessantly urged upon laymen than the awful condition of the souls who had lived in the days of old. Augustine believed he had polluted his mind by reading Virgil. The monks for centuries deemed it sin to touch a pagan manuscript. Aristotle's works when translated into Latin were long banned by the University. As for Avicenna and Averroes, the followers of Mahomet, whom Dante dared to introduce into the green pastures of the blest, no form of torture was considered too horrible for them. Greek, Roman, Arab, all were alike limbs of Satan, active agents for evil, credited with the worst crimes, worthily punished for all eternity in the depths of hell. Their astounding inclusion in the cloisters of Limbo has passed almost unnoticed in modern days. But in the fourteenth century for far less infringement of ecclesiastical dogma men were being burnt alive.

The classic poets and philosophers find their place naturally at the beginning of the autobiographical scheme of the *Inferno* when the boy Dante first became aware of their existence. His early introduction to them marked a definite and happy stage in his journey through the dolorous valley of this world. The place of honour assigned to them among the Old Testament Saints had the further purpose of vindicating their good fame. Dante's achievement for the philosophers whom he believed to stand very high in sight of God[1] was to trans-

[1] *Banquet,* IV, 6.

form for their benefit the cloudy shades of Limbo into the illumination of the Elysian fields. After reading how the noble company of Greeks and Romans walked on the enamel sward conversing of honour, none should ever dream that any shadow of shame could rest upon them for lack of Baptism. Translucent for all eternity in high serenity and content, in a lofty place, open and luminous, they have their being. After the first outburst of sighs over the blind delusion which conceived them to be cut off from God, Dante found among them no image of despair, no lingering torment or unfulfilled desire, an aspect neither sad nor joyous. To the end of his life he gloried in the visions of the great spirits vouchsafed to him in early youth. As he saw them then he was moved to bring all mankind to see them evermore.

In successive stages of development we can trace the workings of his awakening mind throughout the length and breadth of Limbo.

In his first conscious moments Dante found himself on the prow of the sorrowful valley of this world's bitter experiences. So soon as he was able to stand upright he began to look round in order to gain some idea of where he was. In short, he began ' to take notice '. All was dim and nebulous, and gazing as he might he could yet distinguish nothing. Memory, the eye of the mind, was not yet awake, and the first months of life were wholly obscure.

This exquisite canto gains immeasurably when regarded as the reminiscence of a happy childhood consecrated to the immortals. Here there were no tears. True he could recall the dismay with which he found the curse of the Church resting on whomsoever charmed his fancy, from his favourite Bible characters, inexplicably imprisoned in a place of mystery, to the heroes, poets, and philosophers of Greece and Rome. But, after all, damnation does not seem a very dreadful thing to a child, and Dante seems in this canto to present the figures of the ancients under such a glamour as they wore when first presented to his own imagination—damned certainly, but unspeakably blessed nevertheless.

Very early in life (he was not far removed from the Slumber of infancy) he caught a glimpse of the sacred fire of poesy which was to light him throughout his life. It was in this stage and before education commenced that he came to know the names of the five poets he pictured grouped in high converse. He recalled in after years, with a smile perchance at the soaring ambitions of his baby mind, how they saluted him and how in fancy he sat sixth among them; read in this light the dream becomes reconciled with the deep humility of the poet in his ripe age.

It is plain to see that the boy was nurtured upon honour. The word echoes in line after line and testifies to the high influence exerted upon him. From the first, he could understand, though only to some extent (in parte) that the classical writers were an honourable people. It would seem that he could distinctly remember the admonition first laid upon him by some ardent Virgilian disciple. 'Honour the supreme poet', coupled as it was with rejoicing at the restitution of Virgil's works to fame. Virgil's fine answer, 'Because each agrees with me in the name that solitary voice proclaimed they do me honour and in that do well', brings testimony to the actual beginning in that epoch of the Virgilian cult which was soon to wipe out all memory of the centuries of neglect.

It can be noted of his heroes that they illustrate the quality of 'Highmindedness' as described by Aristotle in the *Ethics*.[1] ' It is Honour with which Highminded men are concerned; it is Honour that great men claim and deserve. The Highminded man exhibits his character especially in the matter of Honour and Dishonour.' Thereupon in that blend of recollection, tempered with ripe culture characteristic of the childish memories of great men, we watch Dante passing dryshod over the sacred river, entering the portals of the Seven Arts, learning to distinguish the principal figures in the drama of Roman History, raising his eyebrows a little higher to get an inkling of the philosophers, walking amidst the company of the Highminded, with their eyes slow and grave; of great authority in their bearing; speaking seldom, with gentle voices, for ' the character of the highminded man seems to require that his gait should be slow, his voice deep, and his speech measured'. There, in some spot consecrated to memory, he was wont to muse while in imagination he watched them in high converse together. Thus he moved forward towards the light, 'speaking things about which it is as beautiful to keep silent as was speech itself in the place

[1] *Ethics*, Bk. IV, 3.

where I was'. 'For the highminded man will neither talk about himself nor about others.'

The classic poets who taught him beauty of diction taught him no less and thus early something of the beauty of restraint. Honour and highmindedness alike, twin stars of his childhood, forbade him from open disclosure of his thoughts.

It is noticeable that a double current of personality is united in the figure of Dante through all the early stages of the journey. He picks out the names and incidents belonging to his infancy which float uppermost in his memory. In this sense he is once more a little child taking half unconsciously the first steps in the long pilgrimage. But as with mature judgment he meditates on his own first impressions of religion and literature he casts them into a sequence which corresponds with the central theme. And thus we watch the child Dante as he goes his way, while the philosopher Dante, under the image of a colloquy with Virgil, makes ripe observations and exercises his reason, as most men are wont to do, over the long past things brought back to him by his vivid memory. From time to time an unmistakable note of irony intrudes; as for example that emphatic declaration 'I would have you know' of Virgil that *before* the first created mortals, Adam, Abel, and the patriarchs, no human spirit was ever saved.

CHAPTER V

STIRRINGS OF DESIRE

[*Inferno V. Second Circle*]

Dante encounters Minos, figuring the Venal Confessor; confession probably preceding First Communion. This was the time when he first saw Beatrice. His mind dwells on the stories of famous lovers and their retribution as recounted by the poets. His imagination is deeply stirred by the tale of Francesca's marriage in this very year, and her fatal passion for Paolo who had wooed her as proxy for his deformed brother.

Period covered : 1274-5.

Corresponding hour: about 10.20 p.m.

IN THE first chapter of the New Life Dante affords a wonderful glimpse into the forces which were consciously moulding him at the age of nine. It is a picture which has always delighted the world. From the moment when he first caught sight of the crimson-robed child and met the truthful look in her timid eyes he surrendered to her as the glorious Lady of his Mind, meet to bear rule over his whole being. All the craving for beauty which possessed his awaking artist soul was satisfied in her, the blessed realization of his visions. All lower desires, as of greed, temper, or impure imaginings which begin to exert power over growing lads, confronted with her pure image, shrank back dismayed. Drawn often to seek her out by a strong impulse of love, he became continually more deeply penetrated with the sense of her nobility in mind and bearing, and grew to liken her, in the few words of Homer which he knew, to the goddess Athenae. All this time some inward sense of dignity, some fear of covering her or himself with ridicule, kept him *reasonable*, even though pure passion ruled his heart. Neither in thought, word or deed did the child Dante incur reproach from his more mature self in days to come.

FIRST THOUGHTS OF LOVE, HUMAN AND DIVINE

' In that part of the book of my memory before which little could be read is found an inscription which says: " Incipit Vita Nuova " (Here beginneth the New Life). Under this inscription I find words written which it is my intent to copy in this book, or if not all at least their meaning.

' Already nine times after my birth had the Heaven of Light returned to about the same point according to its own revolution, when there appeared first to my eyes the glorious Lady of my Intellect who by many who did not know what to call her was called Beatrice.

' She had already been so long in this life that the Heaven of the fixed Stars had moved eastward during her time the twelfth part of a degree. So that she appeared to me at the beginning of her ninth year and I beheld her at about the end of my ninth year. She appeared to me clad in a most noble crimson colour, humble and sincere, girt and adorned in the guise which became her very youthful age.

' Thereupon I say in all truth that the spirit of Life, which dwells in the most secret chamber of the heart, began to tremble so forcibly that it was fearfully evident in every vein. And thus trembling it said: " Ecce Deus fortior me, qui veniens dominabitur mihi " (Behold a God stronger than I who cometh to bear rule over me).

' Thereupon the animal spirit which dwells in the deep chamber to which all the spirits of the senses bear their perceptions, began greatly to wonder, and speaking more particularly to the spirits of the sight, said these words: " Now hath your Beatitude appeared ".

' Thereupon the natural (carnal) spirit which dwells in that part to which our nourishment ministers, began to lament and lamenting said these words: " Ah, woe is me for from henceforth I shall be much kept in subjection ".

' From that time forward I declare that Love ruled my soul, which was so readily disposed towards him and began to take over me such great and confident mastery by the power which my imagination gave him that I was constrained to fulfil his behests to the uttermost. Many times he ordered me to try if I could see this most youthful Angel. And many times in my boyhood I went seeking her and I beheld

H

her of mien so noble and worthy to be held in honour that truly of her might be said that phrase of the poet Homer, "No daughter did she appear of mortal man but of God".[1] And although her image which abode continually with me lent boldness to Love in the mastery of me, yet was it of a so noble quality that not once did it suffer Love to rule without the faithful counsel of Reason in those matters wherein it might advantage to hear such counsel. And since it may appear fabulous to speak of surmounting the passions and actions of such early youth I will take leave of them, and passing over many matters which might be drawn from the example in which they lie hid, I will come to those words which are written in more detailed fashion in my memory.'

On the authority of Boccaccio and of Dante's son Pietro it is usual to identify the child 'who was called Beatrice by many who did not know what to call her', with Beatrice Portinari, who afterwards married Simone de' Bardi. There are reasons for doubting this identification, of which not the least is the above allusion to her name, but none for doubting the fact of her actual existence.

The image of the child who awakened in Dante a conscious sense of the beautiful and caused him to react violently against every form of evil, was blended from the first with the notion of a Heavenly force claiming his allegiance. It was an age of symbolism in religion, in art, in poetry and history. Dante was cradled in the mode of thought which finds a hidden truth disguised under every trifling incident in classical or Bible history, under every elaborately prescribed detail of Church ritual. He could not fail to frame an allegory round his early love and make his first attempts in poetizing by discovering some gracious meaning in her every feature.

There are definite moments in the lives of some men when the soul suddenly becomes aware for the first time of love or art or God. Such an awakening or process of 'Conversion' is often attended by a vivid sense that the everyday world is irradiated with unearthly gleams which change all that has

[1] See Aristotle, *Ethics*, Bk. VII, 1. 'The excellence of a hero or god—as Homer makes Priam say of Hector that he was surpassingly good
" nor seemed the child
" Of any mortal man, but of a god." '

gone before and form a starting-point in a New Life, separated as by a gulf from the old. In the case of Dante we learn from the above confession that this crucial moment, akin to regeneration, occurred in his tenth year.

It is important to record that about this time he would be admitted to the rite of Confirmation. It was a solemn season for a boy already mentally far ahead of his years. It would be preceded by his first formal confession to the priest and probably by some instruction in self-examination.

There is good reason to opine that Confession, then a much dreaded ordeal, was secretly disapproved by many Churchmen. Compulsory confession to a priest was a comparatively novel institution when Dante was a boy. It dated only from the Fourth Lateran Council in 1215, and had spread very slowly among the reluctant laity. Even among theologians there was much difference of opinion about it. Gratian marshalled eighty-nine opinions for and against the dogma of confession as necessary for every sin and left it an open question. Peter Lombard, however, declared that without confession to the priest the sinner cannot hope for Paradise, and this sentence carried the day. The enforcement of Confession was the subject of many decrees and the numerous devices for coercing people to submit to it bear witness to the frequency with which it was evaded. It was at first made obligatory once a year only before receiving the Easter Communion. There is much to suggest that the disinclination of the laity to accept this demand on their obedience was largely justified by the low character of the ordinary confessor. Few priests were well prepared for their high office; many had received merely perfunctory instruction in its forms; and some aimed more at extorting fees from their penitents than at amending conduct or deepening religious impressions. So many injunctions were made by the bishops prohibiting the extortion of money from penitents as the price of absolution that it can plainly be seen this was a widespread abuse. It was quite usual to charge a fee, but priests were forbidden to demand payment or refuse absolution if it were refused. They were warned not to gaze wistfully and suggestively at the penitent's purse or exact pledges from the poor to ensure payment. Unfortunately confessors had many indirect methods of bringing penitents to heel. The power to inflict penance put a dangerous weapon into their hands, and we have the witness of St. Bonaventura, who died in this year, that refusal to absolve without payment was very common. Accusations brought by pious bishops against confessors indicate how rarely they were fit to undertake their delicate duties. Grosse-teste, for instance, roundly declared that many among them did not know a single law of the decalogue.

At this stage in his life, before coming into contact with the sins of the flesh which he was afterwards [1] to learn were of the nature of youthful transgressions,[2] Dante describes how he encountered Minos, under whose attributes there seem to lurk the figure of the detested Confessor of that period.

RETRIBUTION FOR SIN

Inf., v, 1-24.
The begin-
ning of pain-
ful experi-
ences.

Thus from the First Zone downward I went
Into the next which compasses less space
But pain much worse and pungent lamentation.

The venal
medieval
Confessor.

There Minos stands—an awful sight—and sneers—
Investigates the crimes in the account,
Judges and orders, according as he binds;[3]

Emphatic
denunciation
of such
practice.

I say that when the sin-stained spirit comes
Into his presence, it confesses all,
And that discriminator of the sins
Perceives what place in hell is (meet) for it,
And winds his tail around so many times
As the grades to which he'll have him put below.

[1] *Inf.*, XI, 70-90. These were sins such as relate to the matter of pleasures and pains. Some of these pleasures Aristotle had taught are necessary, such as those of nutrition, the propagation of the species, and other bodily processes. The animal or natural spirit of man inclines him to yield to the call of the instincts. The errors into which men fall over these pleasures by allowing themselves to be dominated by desires, are to be clearly distinguished from Vices. They are in the nature of youthful transgressions (*akrasia*) but, if they are indulged, the noble part of man becomes entirely enslaved and the death of the soul ensues.

[2] *Ethics*, Bk. III, 12. 'What needs chastening or correction is that which inclines to base things. Now these characteristics are nowhere so strongly marked as in appetite and in childhood. Children live according to their appetites, and the desire for pleasant things is most marked in them.'

[3] *Cf.* St. Matt., xvi, 19. 'Whatsoever ye shall bind on earth. . . .'

Always in front of him are many standing;
They go to judgment, each one in his turn;
They speak, they listen, then they are turned down.

'O thou that comest to the dolorous Inn,'
Said Minos to me, leaving the exercise,
When he perceived me, of his mighty Office,
'Look how thou enter'st, and in whom thou trustest;
'Let not the width deceive thee of the gate'.
And my guide answered him: 'Why thus complain?
'Impede thou not his going—fate ordained.
'Thus it is willed where will and power are one.
'Demand no further'.

Virgil's description of Minos and Rhadamanthus are combined in this figure. He is both judge and lawgiver.

Minos makes part of the apparatus set up by the Church for the government of the world. He stands for the Confessor or Pardoner as he came to be called. In the exercise of so great an office (*l'atto di cotante ufficio*) he imposes on the sin-stained (*animi mal nati*) the task of coming to him and confessing all their misdeeds. There can be no hiding the eyes to the fact that the poet of set purpose lent a grotesque touch to this otherwise reverend figure by providing him with a tail, for in classical usage to append a tail[1] was to throw an air of buffoonery over the proceedings. He was to be regarded as an expert in sin. There were always many waiting to confess; first they spoke; then they listened to what the judge decreed, and then they were turned away down below. The Confessor knew instinctively what zone of hell each one was fitted for. Would not the proceedings appear somewhat in this light to the child approaching it with dread for the first time? In these early days there was no screened confessional and the waiting crowd could watch the constant coming and going and the gestures of the priest and penitent.

The contrast between the awe and terror with which the office was surrounded (*Stavvi Minos orribilmente*), and the grin or sneer which sat on the countenance of the base fellow exalted to be judge, was apparent even to the boy observer, though here as elsewhere the riper thoughts of the philosopher intrude. There were degrees of guilt all very clearly tabulated

[1] *Vide* Facciolati Art: Cauda.

with the penalty which must be paid to procure absolution for each transgression. The prerogative to bind was clearly more in evidence than that to loose. The poet seems to suggest that some juggling or rapid gesture, possibly by aid of the long stole always assumed for this sacred office, took place on the part of the Confessor, and that the penitent was thereby brought without actual words to understand the degree of guilt he had incurred, and hence the proper amount to be paid in order to secure an easy absolution. The lines from which it has been deduced that Minos jerked his tail round his body in coils corresponding to various zones of hell are strangely grotesque if literally accepted. Other hints about Minos bear out his identification with the ignorant Confessor.[1] He was fulfilling his proper office when he warned the child penitent that in entering the ' dolorous inn ' of this life he would find that ' wide is the gate and broad is the way that leadeth to destruction'. His veiled caution against trusting Reason as his escort was in keeping with the attitude of all the guardians of the zones who prophetically foresaw the attacks which the poet under this guidance would make on their domain.

The first stirrings of desire with which, as he reveals, Dante was moved in his tenth year, would meet with abundant illustration in the extracts from Roman poets which formed the basis of his daily tasks. Likening his own noble Beatrice to Athenae it was natural he should set himself to reject with scorn examples of lust which masqueraded under the name of

---

[1] Further allusions to Minos in the *Divina Commedia* are as follows: *Inf.*, XIII, 96. Minos despatches him to the seventh grade.

Inf., XX, 124. 'And he ceased not to rush headlong down the valley to Minos who lays claims on all.'

Inf., XXVII, 124. ' He bore me to Minos. And he directed eight times the tail against my hard back.' (Here the tail stands for the scourge, the infliction of corporal punishment being a common reward of the penitent's candour or perhaps his parsimony.)

Inf., XXIX, 118 ff. ' Minos, of whom it is not conceded that he can ever err, doomed me to the last pit of the ten for alchemy which I practised in the world.' (The supposed infallibility of the Confessor gave occasion for much popular irony.)

Purg., I, 77. ' For this is a live man, and Minos binds me not ' (*non me lega*) in allusion to the much-abused injunction, ' Whatsoever thou shalt bind on earth shall be bound in Heaven'.

Love, while dwelling with avidity on the pains which the poets describe as the lot of all lovers. It was then at this point that the echoes of sorrow began to make themselves heard and the sound of much weeping. It was now that he stepped forward into an atmosphere which vibrated.

While thus precociously in his own person he began to be tormented with restless waves of longing, an event happened in Italy which quickened to the highest pitch his already stirring imagination.

Francesca, the beautiful daughter of Guido Vecchio da Polenta, was betrothed to Gianciotto, elder son of Malatesta, Vicar of Charles of Anjou. The marriage was to cement a political alliance of great importance in Guido's eyes; he had but just established his sway over Ravenna and relied on the aid of Malatesta, himself a tyrant of great reputation in the Guelf faction, to consolidate the victory. The only drawback to the marriage lay in the person of the bridegroom who was lame, deformed, and brutal in character. With a cowardly cunning which suggests that an unmarried daughter did not wholly lack the power of asserting herself, it was arranged among them that Paolo, the handsome younger brother, should not only woo the bride but take the place of Gianciotto as proxy in the wedding ceremony. Paolo was already married, but the love inspired by the bride he had to win for his brother became the ruling devotion of his life. A fatal passion was kindled between the two and the tale of it, doomed as the lovers were by fate from the outset, ran like wildfire through the country. In the version most preferred of the story, which in the year 1275 was on the lips of all, Francesca was not disillusioned about the person of her bridegroom until the actual wedding night, when, awaiting her love, she suddenly found herself in the arms of a strange and savage master, from whose rights there was no appeal.

Such an instance of tragic fate was well fitted to fire the imagination of a boy already steeped in poetic visions. While speculation about Francesca and the abhorred husband resounded on every side, a wondrous image of the lovers, immortally united in desire, began to form in his brain.

103

Inf., v, 25 to
end.

ANGUISH OF DESIRE

Now notes of pain begin to stimulate
Perception; here, where I had come, there smote
Much weeping on my ears.

The first
stirrings of
unsatisfied
desire.

I came into a region void of light
Which, like the ocean in a tempest, moaned,
When by opposing winds 'tis combated.
The infernal cyclone, knowing no repose,
Sweeps on the spirits with its ravishment;

Lovers' pains
as described
by the poets.

Whirling them round and smiting, it perturbs.
When they are brought in presence of their ruin
Then are there shrieks, bewailing and lament;
Then they blaspheme the Power (of Love).

I learned that to the torment thus prepared
Were damned the carnal sinners, who subject
Reason to their desires.
And like the starlings in the wintry weather
Borne by their wings in wide and crowded flocks,
Thus by that blast (were borne) the evil spirits;
Hither and thither they are swept, below, above;
No hope of any rest sustains them ever,
Nor even of less torment.
And like as cranes pass on, chanting their lays,
Forming them in the air into long files,
Thus saw I shadows coming, uttering wails
Carried by that distracting blast aforesaid.

Whereon I said: ' Master, who are this flock
' Whom the black air thus castigates? '

Lovers of old
time brought
to Dante's
notice early
in life by
Virgil.

' The first of those whose story thou wouldst know,'
He then replied, ' of many tongues was Empress,
' And so unbridled in the vice of Lust
' That to efface the blame she had incurred
' She made her laws give licence to desire.
' This is Semiramis of whom one reads
' That she succeeded Ninus, was his spouse
' And held the land the Sultan governs now.
' That other is she who killed herself for love
' And broke faith to the ashes of Sichaeus.
' Next Cleopatra comes luxurious.

" See Helena on whose account there rolled
' So long a time of guilt
" And see the great Achilles, he who fought
' In the end with love. See Paris and Tristan '—
And the shades innumerable he displayed
And, pointing with his finger, named to me
Whom love had separated from our life.
Then after I had heard my teacher name
The ladies of old times and cavaliers
Pity o'ertook me; I was near distraught.

CONTEMPORARY STORY OF FRANCESCA

" Greatly I long, Poet,' I began,
" To speak with those two souls who go together
' And seem to be so light upon the wind.'
And he to me: ' When they come nearer to us
' Thou shalt observe, then do thou implore them
' By that Love which bears them on; and they will come.'

Suddenly as the wind sways them towards us
I lifted up my voice: ' O afflicted souls
' Come speak with us if it be not forbidden.'
As doves called by desire come through the air
To their sweet nest, with wings outstretched and steady,
Borne by their own free will, they issued forth
From out the band where Dido is, and came
Through the malignant air to us;
So powerful was my passionate appeal.

' O gracious creature and benign
' To come through the dark air to visit us
' Who tinged the world with blood;
' Were but the King [1] of the Universe our friend
' We would entreat him for thy (future) peace,
' Since thou hast pity on our fatal ill.
' Of what thou wouldest hear, and wouldest speak,
' We too will hear and we will speak with you
' The while the wind gives pause as it doth now;
' The city [2] where I was born lies on the shore
' Where Po with all its tributary streams
' Descends to flow in peace.

Virgil as Poet is here his Guide.

He has heard of the deceit practised on Francesca and forms a vivid image of the lovers.

Dido's band consisted of women severed by law and duty from their true lovers.

[1] Love.

[2] Ravenna.

105

' LOVE, penetrating swift to noble heart,
' Ensnared this man, so comely in his person—
' Snatched from me and in mode which still offends.
' LOVE, which exempts from loving none beloved,
' Ensnared me with a passionate delight
' In him who still, thou seest, forsakes me not.
' LOVE drew us on together to one death;
' Cain (fratricide) waits there who quenched our life.'
Such were the words conveyed to us from them.

When I had heard these deeply-injured souls
I bowed my face and held it there so long
The Poet said: ' On what art pondering? '
When I made answer I began: ' Alas,
' How many tender thoughts, what fond desire
' Led on these (lovers) to the dolorous pass! '
Thereon I turned to them once more and spoke.

And I began: ' Francesca, thy distresses
' Render me sad and, even to tears, devout.
' But tell me, in the time of the sweet sighings
' By what sign, and in what mode, did LOVE concede
' Thou mightest know thy dimly-felt desires? '

And she to me: ' There is no greater pain
' Than to call back to mind in misery
' The happy times; and that thy Teacher knows.
' Yet if thy passion be so strong to know
' The first root of our LOVE, then I will do
' As one who weeps and tells.
' We were one day reading for our delight
' Of Lancelot, how LOVE enraptured him.
' We were alone and without any fear.
' Many a time that reading would impel
' Our eyes to meet, our faces to change colour.
' But it was one point only conquered us.
' When we read how the kiss of that great Lover
' Rested upon the smile of deep desire,
' He, who shall never more be parted from me,
' Kissed me, all tremulous, upon the mouth.
' Gallehaut was the book and he who wrote it.
' That day we did not farther read in it.'

While the one spirit spoke after this fashion,
The other wept so bitterly I swooned
In my great pity, as I had been dead,
And I fell down as a dead body falls.

New light is shed on these immortal lines if they be regarded as a vision, not of dead shades who expiate a sin, but of living lovers, banished from each other by a cruel fate yet united for all eternity by the strength of their passion. They come before us in the poignant moment when all deception is over and they have attained full realization of the ceaseless torment of unsatisfied desire which is to be their portion. Like all the characters depicted in the *Inferno* they have the gift of second sight and can foresee the final consummation of the tragedy when, some fourteen years later, the smouldering jealousy of Gianciotto suddenly broke loose and in a whirlwind of rage he slew them both. Francesca can plainly see the waiting figure of Cain, the assassin brother. In a double sense he it was who ' extinguishes our life '. With convincing force she urges first the excuse of Paolo, then her own. As a proudly nurtured maiden she is filled with righteous anger at the indignity practised against her on her wedding night. She is still unappeased at the manner of it. It is as *wronged* souls (*anime offense*) to whom great injury has been done, that they are presented.

Dante's own demeanour is most significant. It was as the Poet of Love that he was to be known to all the world. It is as the renowned *Dicitore* that we behold him drawing Francesca to distil the essence of LOVE drop by drop from her heart, and note with what consummate skill he turned to account in later years the vivid image roused in his mind by the story as it first came to his ears when he was ten years old, and was himself already under the sway of a passion destined never to know fruition.

CHAPTER VI

AN EPISODE IN THE DIVIDED CITY

[*Inferno VI*, 1-111. *Third Circle*]

Dante encounters Cerberus, figuring tyrannical powers of ecclesiastical discipline. A picture of Florence with its citizens undergoing penance in the stormy autumn of 1275, when Pope Gregory X passed through the streets, raised the interdict on the city for an hour and renewed it on departure. Ciacco explains to the little boy the causes which had divided the city into contending parties, and covertly warns Dante that he is on the wrong side.

Period covered: Autumn 1275.

Corresponding hour: 10.40 p.m.

BITTER hatred was the cradle in which Florentine children were nursed. Boys were taught from infancy that their first duty was to take vengeance on all who caused injury to their kinsmen. The vendetta curse lay heavy on the generation. In the picture Dante presents of himself in the *New Life* it is noteworthy how far removed we find him from such precocious instincts of hatred. Honour, beauty, and love were the forces already attuning his mind in its most plastic stage to perfection of genius. Indirectly the influence of his Ghibelline mother may have reacted favourably in this direction. Not that the Ghibellines were less barbarous in spirit than the Guelfs. But the mixed lineage must surely have proved a bar to acrimony in the family circle. The attitude of neutrality which prevailed when Alighiero found a useful shield in his wife's family could hardly be broken when their positions were reversed, and may have counted for much by inducing impartial judgments in years to come. Notable events were passing in the world while Dante was filling his imagination with dreams of his child love. Florence stands on the highroad from the kingdom of Naples, through Rome and Viterbo, to France and England. Through her narrow streets streamed all personages who were then making history. Her moneychangers had every facility for keeping their fingers on the pulse of the civilized world.

One dominant factor in Dante's political creed—scorn for the Angevin race—had its seeds in the circumstances of his boyhood, and must not be overlooked in tracing the story of his life. Charles I, who began to dominate Italy at the time of Dante's birth, and whose grandson Robert held her in tight grip some years before Dante's death, was one of the most powerful sovereigns of Europe. Lord of Provence and Anjou, Naples and Sicily, besides many cities of Lombardy and Piedmont, with the islands of Corfu and Epiros, he was Imperial Vicar of Tuscany during the interregnum of the Empire and practically arbiter of the Papal States. Out of his overmastering ambition sprang many of the evils which then and hereafter afflicted Italy. As the Pope's representative he demanded unquestioning obedience from all the Guelf cities. But though overawed by his authority the citizens were very far from approving his deeds. He gave ample cause of offence to both parties of the State and found opportunity in the discord he studiously fomented between them. Ghibellines resented bitterly the cruelties perpetrated on Manfred's defeated army, and the barbarous massacres which took place after Conradin's execution when the inhabitants of entire cities were tortured and put to death. The Guelfs were keenly alive to the crimes committed by Charles in the name of the Church and the extent to which he exploited the Papacy for his own ends. It would be a mistake to suppose that his unscrupulous violence passed uncondemned by the men of his generation. They were even more critical of their public men than their present-day descendants.

Three years before Dante's first encounter with Beatrice, Charles's elder brother, Louis IX of France, died of the plague before Tunis on his last Crusade. Charles had consented to accompany him thither in the hope of advancing his own interests in the East. With his usual skill in striking a bargain he concluded, on the death of Louis, a peace with the Saracens of which the main condition was the transfer of 200,000 gold pistoles from the infidels to his own coffers. To this the more influential crusaders, Philip, now King of France, Edward Prince of Wales, and his cousin Henry of Almayne, son of the Earl of Cornwall, assented in view of the pestilence but with unconcealed disgust. Edward detached himself altogether and went with his army to Acre, sending back his cousin Henry to reduce Gascony, then an English Province, to order. In the course of his journey Henry passed through Viterbo, where eighteen cardinals had been frantically intriguing for over two years without being able to elect a successor to Clement IV. There Henry attended High Mass and at the sacred moment of the elevation of the Host, while actually clinging to the altar for protection, he was brutally murdered by Guy de Montfort in revenge for the execution of his father Simon after the battle of Evesham. Guy, aided by his brother Simon and by a great company of armed men, dragged the dead body of his victim from the church and escaped untouched to take refuge in the Maremma. It was such a deed of vengeance as was all too common, but the time and place of its perpetration raised it from murder to sacrilege and roused universal horror. Henry was a blameless victim who had not even been present at Simon's defeat and execution. In Florence, where the news penetrated within a few hours after the crime had been committed, citizens of all shades of opinion united in condemning their former Podestà, and his master Charles of Anjou. They suspected the Prince of conniving at the crime and blamed him severely, whether or no, for allowing it to pass unpunished.[1] A formal sentence of excommunication was inflicted on the murderer, but he was subsequently pardoned and reinstated in office after performing penance naked in the streets of Florence.

Shortly after this event Tebaldo Visconti, then absent among the Crusaders, was elected Pope under the name of Gregory X (1271-1276). A fateful election for Church and Empire, it was to have also far-reaching consequences for Florence. From the first Gregory reversed the policy of his predecessors and showed himself definitely hostile towards Charles of Anjou, who in addition to his other offices had been permitted to exercise certain Imperial rights. Gregory gave his support to the German princes in electing Rudolph of Hapsburg to be King of the Romans, and thus put an end to the Vicariate of Charles. He summoned a General Council of the Church at Lyons for 1274, and on his way thither, the

[1] Villani, Bk. VII, 39.

year before it was to take place, he paid a visit to Florence
with a view to curbing the tyranny which Charles exercised
in Tuscany and appeasing old animosities. The Florentines
turned out with imposing pageantry to welcome the Pope.
The presence of kings and prelates was no novelty in the city
and highly welcome as a stimulus to trade. A few months
before, the crowds had turned out to witness the funeral
cortège of Louis IX, escorted by Philip III, who was on his
way to be crowned at Rheims. The English Prince, now
Edward I, had lingered there also, while both monarchs had
spent a great deal of money in the city and marked the
occasion by conferring knighthood on young nobles. But
their reception could not compare with that accorded to Pope
Gregory when, with a long train of cardinals and prelates he
rode through the tortuous streets and took up his abode on the
Arno in the Palace of the wealthy Mozzi family whose banking
firm enjoyed the privilege of supplying him with ready money.
Baldwin, the dispossessed Latin Emperor of the East, accompanied him. And Charles of Anjou, uninvited and unwel-
come, put in an appearance to make what mischief he could.

By command of the Pope July 2, 1273, was fixed as a solemn
day of reconciliation between Ghibellines and Guelfs. On
great platforms erected on the banks of the Arno near the
Rubaconte Bridge, chosen representatives of the leading
Ghibelline and Guelf families, with the cynical figure of
Charles standing by, met in the presence of the Pope and
Emperor to swear peace and give each other the kiss on the
mouth which sealed the oath. A great day for the Ghibellines,
and a moving spectacle for the whole city to witness, of
Christian ideals triumphing over the forces of hatred. A
genuine thrill of joy ran through the citizens, for the discord
after all centred in a few powerful families only, and all sensible men deplored its continuance. Every boy in Florence
was assuredly an absorbed spectator of the scene. Dante was
then eight and Gregory X was the first Pope he had seen.

It was one of those delicate situations in which a few malcontents may suffice to upset a newly-balanced equilibrium
established by a rational majority. Peace, however diplo-
matically arranged, meant a certain amount of restitution
and the return to their ancestral homes of some who were
hated and feared. Charles, sending his agents from one to

another of the Guelf nobles chiefly affected, had no difficulty in stirring the unappeasable rage of the Die-hards. They were only too ready to stake their all and defy the Church rather than surrender any part of their booty to its lawful owners. The Ghibelline peacemakers received an intimation that unless they left the city promptly King Charles's Marshal would have them hewn in pieces. It was a threat most certain of execution, and during the night they fled once more from Florence, their fierce stepmother.

In the first flush of pride at the success of his conciliatory policy, Pope Gregory had to learn of its ignominious failure. His anger was hot against all concerned. He left the Mozzi Palace without a moment's delay for the Mugello, where he spent the remainder of the summer, and he pronounced an interdict on the city of Florence.

To understand the feeling roused against Charles among the citizens of Florence it must be realized that of all calamities, fire, pestilence or enemy attack, the curse of the Church was immeasurably the worst for the city. From the moment when the sentence of excommunication was pronounced, no public worship could take place. The churches were closed. The bells were silent. No sacraments save that of baptism, confirmation, and penance were celebrated. Marriages could not take place. Burials were performed without rites. The frequent festivals which animated medieval life ceased. Ordinary social intercourse, which largely centred round ecclesiastical ceremonies, lost all zest. Severe penances were enforced. An air of desolation hung over the streets. And inevitably trade languished.

To add to the general indignation against the Angevin conqueror, the citizens were forced to submit to his presence among them with an overmastering force of French cavalry very expensive to maintain and ill-disposed to respect the laws and customs of the Commune. The only way to rid themselves of this infliction was to turn their attention against rival cities. Accordingly in these years when the interdict spread gloom over the Commune we find the Florentines despatching expeditions under King Charles, with varying success, against Pisa and Bologna. Charles's worst crime was yet to come.

From the moment of his accession, Pope Gregory had bent his mind to make the General Council summoned for 1274 notable for all time in the history of the Church. His great aim was to heal the division between the Eastern and Western Churches and bring all Christians under one head. In technical theological parlance nothing divided them but one word,[1] although in Church government they were widely sundered. The Greek Emperor, Michael Palæologus, who had taken Constantinople from the Latin Emperor Baldwin and felt his position to be highly insecure, was prepared to make wide concessions to Rome as the price of protection from Charles of Anjou. Largely through the efforts of Thomas Aquinas, most saintly and learned of Churchmen, the Greek Patriarch was brought to promise assent to an agreement in which Michael was to recant his former errors and submit on behalf of the entire Greek Church to the supremacy of the Pope. Summoned by the Pope, Thomas left his professorial chair at Naples to attend the Council at Lyons and put the finishing touches to the approaching union of the Churches. He had not travelled far before he fell ill and shortly after he died at Fossa Nuova, March 1274. The rumour that he had been assassinated by order of Charles of Anjou, whose physician was in attendance on him, instantly gained ground and soon crystallized into certainty. Dante never doubted its truth, and later in all good faith embodied it in his denunciation of Charles of Anjou.[2]

The verdict of critical historians on the case is 'Death from natural causes'. But assassinations were then so frequent and hard of detection that public opinion was wont to look no farther for the instigator than the individual who had most to gain by the removal of the victim. Thomas was a real stumbling block in the path of Charles. He was shortly to be made a Cardinal. In the dispute between the Greek and Latin Emperors over the possession of Constantinople his adherence was given to Michael Palæologus, on whose maintenance in power rested the only hope for the union of the Churches. But Charles was already planning to depose

[1] In the Nicene Creed the Western Church reads, 'Which proceedeth from the Father *and* the Son'; the Eastern Church reads, 'from the Father *through* the Son'.

[2] *Purg.*, xx, 67. 'Charles came into Italy and for amends made a victim of Conradin, and for amends despatched Thomas to Heaven.' *Cf.* Villani, Bk. ix, c. 218.

Michael in the interest of his son-in-law Philip, the recent successor of the Latin Emperor. Moreover, so Villani states, the citizens of Aquino, the birth-place of Thomas, had rebelled against Charles and Thomas was believed to be supporting them. These were motives more than sufficient. And to the already lengthy category of Charles's crimes was added without hesitation in Florence and elsewhere that of compassing the death of Thomas and attempting to wreck the union of the Churches.

The Council of Lyons sat from May till June and was successful, notwithstanding the death of its most distinguished delegate, in settling many important matters. Some bold strokes were levelled at abuses in the Church. Gregory was greatly concerned to make the scandalous scenes which had preceded his own election impossible for the future, and he laid down minute regulations for curtailing the Papal election by the shrewd method of progressively curtailing the diet of the Cardinals in conclave. He hit the Florentine bankers very hard by pronouncing usury, which at that time comprised any kind of loan on interest, a deadly sin. He put an end to the long interregnum of the Empire by recognizing Rudolph of Hapsburg as King of the Romans, and obtained the pledge of the imperial electors to respect ecclesiastical liberties and the Papal domains. He formulated a new scheme for the recovery of the Holy Land from the infidels. But the great triumph of the Lyons Council was that it achieved the union so ardently desired between the Eastern and Western branches of the Church and brought the Emperor Michael Palæologus to acknowledge the Roman Pontiff and make confession of orthodoxy. In receiving these pledges Gregory guaranteed the possessions of Michael from attacks by Charles of Anjou, just as he had engaged Rudolph of Hapsburg to abstain from attacking Charles. It was a courageous and equitable bid for a world peace. Rudolph, King of the Romans, Philip the Hardy, King of France, Edward, King of England, James, King of Aragon, and Charles, King of Sicily, were one and all to sink their differences and, accompanied by the Pope in person, were to combine their forces for the recovery of the Holy Sepulchre. Five hundred bishops, seventy mitred abbots, and a thousand other ecclesiastics and monks met at Lyons to ratify these decisions.

Throughout the year 1275 preparations for the Crusade went on apace and the Pope exerted himself unceasingly, too, in the cause of international peace. Only in the peninsula of Italy his efforts were fruitless, for Charles of Anjou was persistently bent on embittering the nobles against each other and his agents were at work nullifying every scheme of reconciliation which was mooted. Over Florence the still unrevoked interdict brooded heavily. The autumn of 1275 was wet and stormy.[1] The Arno was in flood and an unusually severe spell of weather brought hail and snow to deepen the miseries of the city of flowers. The prospect that Gregory, on his way back to Rome, would pass through the city excited some hopes, for the pontiff's presence was traditionally incompatible with the continuance of such a sentence. The citizens were roused accordingly to make a great display of penitence. Gregory was obdurate in demanding solid fruits of penitence, such as the return of some of the dispossessed Ghibellines, and, failing this, he refused to enter the gates. But the flood was so high that his cortège was compelled to pass through some of the streets and to cross the very bridge which had been the scene of the abortive reconciliation between Guelfs and Ghibellines nearly eighteen months before. In the august presence of the Vicar of Christ excommunication could not prevail. But, alas, although the Pope was graciously pleased to raise the interdict during the time occupied in passing through the city this was the extent of his mercy. The inhabitants poured into the streets to display their abject submission, implore his pardon, and receive his blessing. No sooner had he disappeared through the farther gate than the interdict was renewed. We venture to suggest that this scene, most forcibly impressed on the minds of all beholders, with its grim accompaniments of terror, bitter ecclesiastical rule, and reluctantly performed penance, resulting in sullen despair, may not improbably have formed the substratum of fact out of which grew Dante's description of the Third Circle of the *Inferno*.

VISION OF FLORENCE UNDER INTERDICT   *Inf.*, VI, 1-33.

With mind restored—it had been numbed with sorrow
In presence of the grief of the two kinsfolk

[1] Villani, Bk. VII, c. 50.

Which quite bewildered me—I (now) perceive
New torments round me and new souls tormented
Wheresoever I move, where'er I turn,
And in whatever mode I bend my gaze.

In the Third Circle of the Rain I stand.
Eternal and accursed, heavy and cold;
In measure and in quality unchanging.
Hail in great lumps, turbid water and snow
Come pouring down through the tenebrous air,
The ground, as it receives it, stinks.

Cerberus, monster fierce and terrible,
Barks out of three throats, as a dog might do,
Over the folk that are immersed in it.
He has vermilion eyes, beard foul and black,
His belly large, talons upon his hands.
He claws the spirits, flays and tears piecemeal.
The rain drives them to cough like howling dogs.
They shelter them on one side with the other;
Often they turn them round, the impious wretches.

DISCIPLINARY POWER

When Cerberus, the mighty Worm, perceived us
He opened wide his mouths and showed his tusks.
No limb of his but quivered. Then my Guide
Spread out his palms, took earth and with full fists
He flung it down the ravenous throats.
And like a dog that barking craves for meat
And quiets down soon as he gnaws his food—
Solely to gorge it doth he aim and fight—
Thus did those loathsome countenances do
Of demon Cerberus—who admonishes
The souls so loudly they would fain be deaf.

When the dream to which the marriage of Francesca had
given birth had faded, Dante found himself (1275) in a region
where rain, cursed, cold, and heavy, was falling incessantly.
No change in the sky was ever discernible. Enormous hail-
storms swept over the country; the river rushed down in a
turbid stream; through the gloomy air came flakes of snow,
melting as they fell, making a filthy mixture on ground which

116

was already putrid from overflowing cesspools. Face downwards prostrate on the ground lay a host of wretched penitents vainly attempting to shield themselves from the weather. So closely were they packed and so preoccupied that Dante passing along the street trod on more than one without his presence being noticed. They were coughing in chorus, like dogs barking, as the rain soaked through their bodies. Constantly changing their posture, first on one side and then on another, they found no refuge from the wet. A more miserable crew it would be impossible to imagine.

A picture of hell torments? So it seems. A symbolic description of the physical and mental discomforts of the ' cold humours ' endured by the gluttonous and drunkards? Probably. But also a *chose vue*, a picture indelibly impressed on the mind of the little boy who walked the street, with ashes on his head. It is evident that a definite purpose underlies the figure of the Virgilian Hound, so queerly transported to a place of high authority in the administration of Divine Justice. There are indications that under the image of Cerberus, the watch-dog of the infernal regions, the poet satirized those disciplinary powers of the medieval Church, which, committed to unworthy hands, were the occasion of so much tyranny and woe.

Cerberus was the Worm,[1] the Serpent, or Dragon of Revelation [2] which seduced the whole world, the accuser of the brethren night and day before God, having great wrath because his time is short.

Like all the other Guardians of the zones Cerberus showed hostility at the first sight of Dante, who was strenuously to oppose his power in later years. Like Gerione and Lucifer, Cerberus had three heads, typifying probably the three-fold aspect of ecclesiastical administration, Episcopal, Monastic, Inquisitorial, all of which had power to inflict penances on those under their jurisdiction and to claim the assistance of the civil authorities in carrying out their sentences. Not only such reformers as might be suspected of heresy, but bishops

[1] *Vermo* meant any kind of loathsome reptile. Mr. W. W. Vernon quotes Milton:

' O Eve in evil hour thou didst give ear
To that false worm.'

Paradise Lost, IX, 1067, 1068.

[2] *Rev.,* xii, 10 ff.

and monks of strict orthodoxy are found inveighing·against the impudent greed characteristic of the guardians of the people's morals. 'They not only flay their sheep', said Bishop Grosseteste, 'but strip the flesh from their bones and grind the bones.' They devised degrading penances and heavily fined all who resisted. It was in such a sense that Cerberus was painted in act to flay the shades and rend them piecemeal. He barked fiercely and currishly over the sheep he had been set to tend. His eyes were bloodthirsty. His beard was black in contrast with that of Cato, emblem of God's righteous judgments, and like that of Lucifer it was fouled, instead of being anointed with the holy unction of Divine Grace which rested on Aaron's beard. The belly, seat of greed, was enormous. The hands, used for extortion, were armed with claws or hooks,[1] as were those of all the demons in the *Inferno*. These hooks were the ironical mark of avaricious bishops, borrowed from the crook on the pastoral staff. Every holy quality which should be found in religious officials, chosen to advance God's kingdom on earth, was reversed. The demon harangued (intronisaret)[2] the spirits, so that they would fain have been deaf.

Cerberus *graffia gli spirti*. The word 'graffiare'[3] was the technical term for the performance of the 'graffier's' or clerk's duty. To note down the names of transgressors against

---

[1] The hook on the bishop's staff was a common subject of satire in the fourteenth century. Cf. *Vision of Piers Plowman*:

> Do best is above bothe
> And berith a Bishop's Crois
> And is hokid on that on end
> To halie men fro helle,
> And a pike is in the poynt
> To put adon the wyked.

[2] *Vide* Ducange. Art.: *Intronisare* is the technical term for addressing penitents prior to their receiving absolution. 'Archiepiscopus poenitentes de more apud ecclesiasm intronisaret.'

[3] *Vide* Ducange. Art.: Graffiare. The double sense of the word (*a*) to hook or grip, and (*b*) to write down, made it useful in satire. Cf. *Canterbury Tales*—'The Frere's Tale':

> For ere the Bishop caught hem in his hook
> They weren in the Archedeknes' book.

The process of having the name noted strikes terror into the illiterate even to this day.

the innumerable regulations which had been made to keep the laity in submission was the first step in the long chain of proceedings which ended very often in the wretch who had incurred the displeasure of an ecclesiastic being stripped of all he possessed.

Dante beheld the unhappy 'profane persons' who had shirked fulfilling their obligations, and had been classed as contumacious, in the act of fulfilling their very disagreeable penance. As a devout Catholic, not one of the 'profane', Dante procured immunity by means of a money payment, graphically depicted as offering a 'sop' to Cerberus. Emphasis is laid on the fact that with all his pretence of keeping people in order Cerberus had but one end in view, that of filling his rapacious gullets.

The prostrate crowd was well aware that the moment Gregory had passed beyond the gates 'the great sentence', which they must hear lying on their faces, would again be pronounced in their ears; the churches would be closed and gloom irrevocable would settle on the doomed city. Hence the abject attitude of the penitents in the streets, receiving from the outstretched hands of the Pope only the blessing of an hour. And thus it came about that by order of the Bishop the citizens lay prone on the evil-smelling ground, tortured by the rain and horrible slush, which made a *sozza mistura* with the hail and snow and seemed an emblem of the wrath of Heaven.

FIRST PERCEPTIONS OF POLITICAL DIVISIONS

Inf., VI, 34-III.

Among the shades o'ercome by the heavy rain
We passed above setting our feet upon
Their nullity which seemeth like a person.
They were lying one and all upon the ground,
Save one, who swiftly rose and sat him down
When he perceived us pass in front of him.
' O thou that art conducted through this hell ',
He said to me: ' recall me if thou canst;
' Before I was undone, thou wert in being.'
And I to him: ' The anguish that thou hast
' Perchance withdraws thee from my memory,
' So that it doth not seem I saw thee ever.
' But tell me who thou art, that to a place

Figure of a reluctant penitent.

' Art sent so doleful, with penance ordained
' None more disgusting, though some heavier.'

And he to me: ' Thy City which is full
' Of envy so the sack already bursts
' Held me as hers during the life serene.
' Ciacco you citizens nicknamed me (Hog)
' For the damnable sin of gluttony,
' As thou mayest see, I languish in the rain.
' A wretched spirit am I, and not alone
' For all these undergo the self-same penance
' For self-same sins.' He spake no farther word.

I answered him: ' Ciacco, thy grievous plight
' Weighs on me so it rouses me to tears;
' But tell me if thou canst to what will come
' The citizens of the divided City?
' Is there any one just? Tell me the cause
' Why such great discord hath assaulted it? '

And he to me: ' After long-drawn dispute
' They'll come to bloodshed and the Forest ᵃ Party
' Shall with much injury pursue the Other,ᵇ ¹
' And later this,ᶜ within three suns, must fall,
' And the other ᵈ must prevail by force of him
' That lately came to shore. Long time he'll hold
' His head on high, holding the Other down
' Under great weights however it may weep
' And be ashamed thereat.
' Two men are just, but not there listened to.
' Pride, Envy, Avarice are the three sparks
' Which have set hearts on fire.' Here ended he
The lamentable strain. And I to him:
' Again I would thou'dst teach me and bestow
' The benefit of further speech on me.

He had broken the fast enjoined by the Bishop.

Forecast of Dante's political career (1) as a triumphant Guelf; (2) as an oppressed Ghibelline.
ᵃ *Guelf.*
ᵇ *Ghibelline.*
ᶜ *Ghibelline.*
ᵈ *Guelf.*

¹   Dopo lunga tenzone
Verranno al sangue, e la parte selvaggia
Caccera l'altra con molta offensione.
Poi appresso convien che *questa* caggia.

According to grammatical usage ' questa ' refers back to the pronoun nearest to it—to l'altra. The reader perceives that the word *altra* thrice repeated is responsible for the designed ambiguity of the prophecy.

' Farinata and Tegghiaio, so worthy once,
' Jacopo Rusticucci, and Arrigo
' With Mosca and the rest who set their minds
' On doing good, tell me where they are now;
' Contrive that I may know them; great desire
' Constrains me to find out if Heaven soothes
' Their lot or if the Inferno poisons them.'

He enquires into the fate of the exiles.

And he: ' These are among the blackest of the souls;
' Horrid offence down weighs them to the depth.
' If thou descend so far thou mayest see them.
' But when thou art within the gentle world
' Prithee recall me to the mind of others.
' I say no more; farther I answer not.'

And learns he will one day share it.

Then his straight eyes he turned asquint on me,
Gazed for a moment and bowed down his head.
And my Guide said to me: ' He wakes no more
' Until the sounding of the angelic trump;
' When there shall come the enemy Podestà.
' Each one shall then re-visit his sad house (tomba)
' Resume his flesh and figure (as a man)
' And hear what echoes to eternity.'

Those under penance must await the renewed sentence of excommunication.

Thus we passed through the filthy mixture formed
Of shadows and of rain with lingering steps,
Touching somewhat upon the life to come.
Whereon I said: ' Master, will these afflictions
' Grow worse, diminish, or stay as acute
' After the mighty sentence? '
And he to me: ' Back to thy Science turn
' Which has it that the more perfect the thing
' The more its sense of good and so of pain.
' Although these folk accursed can never get
' To true perfection, yet they look to be
' After, rather than now (more near to it).'

Yet with some hope of its mitigation.

The dialogue with Ciacco assumes a new aspect if examined in accordance with the theory that all the incidents in the *Inferno* are grounded on actual happenings. Much that is apparently grotesque disappears, and an air of spontaneity is thrown over the whole conversation if we take it that Ciacco was no shade but a live man, reluctantly undergoing penance, whom Dante remembered in the act of saying and doing pretty much what is related of him. As a lively reminiscence it owes its place in the poem, we may surmise, to the light it throws on the disciplinary methods of the Church and on the mischievous spirit of discord in the city.

Let it then be assumed that on the occasion of the Pope's visit to Florence in that wet winter of 1275 Dante was one of the spectators, that he witnessed the penance inflicted on the recalcitrant, and that he was accosted by one of the prostrate figures, who, momentarily screened from the observation of the ecclesiastic on guard, stirred himself to a less uneasy posture and began to talk.

Round this person the remainder of the canto centres. Ciacco means a hog, and the nickname was bestowed on him presumably in virtue of his intemperate habits. His entreaty to be brought to the mind of others when Dante should come to take a part in the gentle world [1] (of letters), suggests unsuccessful authorship of some kind, and he betrays a literary flavour in his speech. Dante reluctantly admitted that he did not remember Ciacco at first, but the remark ' I want you once again to instruct me ' seems to hint at a time of previous instruction and might imply that Ciacco was once his tutor. Ciacco declared he was *unmade*—ruined—before Dante was born, and the expression implies that he was a victim of some previous revolution. The questions Dante put to him were of an artless description, very natural queries for a boy of ten, but a little out of the picture when referred to the year 1301, and set in the mouth of the leading statesman in Florence, addressing a drunkard.

The striking object-lesson which ecclesiastical discipline administered in retribution for the abortive scene of reconciliation was, it may well be believed, Dante's first introduction to politics. To know who was right and why the other side was wrong, to understand why all this misery had invaded the town, these were the natural preoccupations of an inquiring mind. None, least of all the boys of the city, could help taking sides in the contests which entered every home and were fought out in every square. But the boy Dante was not

---

[1] ' Dolce mondo ' and ' vita serena ' both have reference to the life of the intellect in contrast to that of the body.

of the stuff which takes side because of the colour of a ribbo·
or even because his own kin were involved in the strife. We
seem to behold in these interrogations some early attempts at
reasoning on the events which were taking place in the
città partita.

We find him greatly exercised for the first time about the
rival claims of Guelfs and Ghibellines, much concerned to
know why the city was thus divided, and what was likely to
come of it. Ciacco was ready enough to explain that he and
the rest were condemned to this disgusting penance ' for the
damnable sin of gluttony', in other words for breaking the
fast enjoined by the Bishop and being found out. Drunken-
ness and gluttony were gentle vices too common to be visited
with ecclesiastical reprobation under normal circumstances.
They became ' damnable ' only when they took the form of
eating prohibited viands on days of fasting and abstinence.
Ciacco's contempt for the whole proceeding was shown plainly
enough at the end when he turned a squinting eye of grim
mockery intently on his interlocutor. Dante was intentionally
enigmatic in retailing Ciacco's prophecy. He worded it in
such a way that it held tolerably good either for the year 1301
(the date of the ostensible narrative) or for the earlier date of
1275, which is more immediately intended. No one, however,
could have doubted what was meant by the *Parte Selvaggia* or
Woodland Party in 1275, when the Captain of the Guelf
Militia under Charles of Anjou was the celebrated Count
Guido *Selvatico*; the party he led was plainly the Forest Party.
Moreover ' selvaggia ' had a very familiar esoteric sense, and
it cannot be doubted that it was used with this intention by
Ciacco. Though obscure to Dante at the time it came to indicate for him also that Guelfism which stood for the material
as opposed to the spiritual. It was the essence of that dark
WOOD in which his own steps were to go astray. It could not
be used in this sense by any but a Ghibelline, and we are thus
brought to a comprehension of the inner mind of Ciacco himself who, speaking to the son of a Guelf noble, one whose
kindred were deeply engaged on the Guelf side in the city
politics, chose this ambiguous way of displaying his partisan-
ship. After long contention, Ciacco foresaw open warfare
would break out and the ' Forest Party,' that is the prevailing
popular party in Florence, would be completely triumphant.

Spoken of a city where blood was daily shed like water in the streets the expression 'they will come to bloodshed' ('veranno al sangue') suggests a pitched battle of some importance. To what battle was Ciacco alluding? All the prophecies have veiled references to facts in Dante's life, and we surmise that Ciacco was hinting at the battle of Campaldino when Dante himself would make one of the triumphant Forest Party which was to scatter the Other with great slaughter. 'Then', he continued in his melancholy story (of Ghibelline woes), 'it must needs be that this Other [the last named or Ghibelline party already pursued with great injury] will be altogether abased within the course of three years and that the other [the Forest or Guelf Party] will prevail with the force of him who has but lately come to shore.'

Instead of first one party triumphing and then the other, triumph was to lie exclusively with the Guelfs. This is what happened, for the administration with which Dante was to be personally connected, although on the eve of his disgrace it was beginning to divide into Blacks and Whites, was distinctly a Guelf one.

The wheel of fortune was to bring it about that when the Forest Party became really dominant, Dante himself would be among those whom it kept down under heavy burdens. It was within the space of three years, 1301 to 1304, that the Whites, by this time allied to the Ghibellines, would be reduced to impotency. Many citizens, wealthy, powerful, and respected in 1275, were during those fateful years brought to a homeless state and Dante was to be among them.

But who was the conqueror who was to keep under the Ghibellines and had but lately come to shore? The birth of Charles's grandson Robert, in this very year 1275, was assuredly an event not likely to pass unnoticed in the city which owed him allegiance.

At the time when Dante wrote the *Divina Commedia*, King Robert the Wise of Naples, Champion of the Guelfs, Papal Vicar of Tuscany, exercised so widespread a tyranny in Italy that none who dared openly to satirize him could have found sanctuary. Hence the necessity for the guarded references to the tyrant, which will be found scattered throughout the *Inferno*.[1]

[1] Robert is alluded to as 'Polyphemus' in the Eclogues exchanged between Dante and Giovanni di Virgilio about the year 1316.

'Piaggiare' means literally to come to shore, and Ciacco, speaking in the year of Robert's birth, is prophesying that this newborn infant, just landing on the shores of this world, is he who in years to come shall bring disgrace and disaster upon the Imperial cause.

The denunciation of the pride, envy, and avarice of the Florentines is more than once renewed in the *Inferno*. At the mention of the two who were just, but to whom no attention was paid (and surely Ciacco meant to imply that he himself was one of them), a very natural desire arose in the mind of his hearer to know what was going to happen to the many exiles whose reputation stood high in the city. Every successive revolution added to the number of citizens unjustly robbed of their houses and estates. Florence was a stern stepmother and had no scruples in reducing those who served her to ruin. Not only the Ghibelline Farinata who in 1260 saved the city from destruction at the risk of his own life; but the Guelf Tegghiaio and Rusticucci, alike renowned for their disinterested patriotism, had suffered the loss of all they possessed. The family of the Farinata, with their descendants, had been banished for ever from Florence. Tegghiaio and Rusticucci, who in all equity ought to have received back their property when the Guelfs triumphed, had remained beggared and their demolished houses were still lying in ruins, a monument to past barbarity, when an inventory was made in 1295.[1] What more natural for a boy who was often passing the ruins than to wonder at the fate incurred by men whose names were still household words, who had done their best for their city. Damnation was much in the air. Were these worthy citizens really in Hell that they and their heirs had received such harsh treatment? To this there could be only one answer and it was one impossible to give to this Guelf youth, viz., that the men who now held power in the city were betraying its interests instead of guarding its honour. Innocent, indeed, was he who should expect to find virtue rewarded in the Inferno of this world. It was in bitter irony that the old Ghibelline informed his young interlocutor that the patriots he named were among the blackest of the black in this Inferno, and that he would encounter them himself if ever he got down low enough. Clearly Ciacco foresaw with the prophetic eye pos-

---

[1] Del Lungo. *Una vendetta in Firenze.*

sessed by all in the *Inferno* that Dante would himself one day find himself among the outcasts, once reckoned as 'worthy', who had been betrayed to ignominy by their own city. Thereupon Ciacco turned with a contemptuous gesture to fulfil his part in the unpleasant penance enjoined on him.

The reader's interpretation of the succeeding passage will be guided by the meaning he attaches to the 'Angelic Trump' and the 'Enemy Podestà'. Clearly as they may seem to refer to the Last Judgment, it may be suggested that the first expression alludes to the trumpet which was to announce Gregory's anxiously awaited *fiat* concerning the interdict, the word 'Angel' being frequently used of Popes and Bishops in conformity with its use in the Apocalypse. By the 'enemy Podestà' Dante assuredly did not mean Christ. In a city which had lately petitioned against the exclusive appointment of Frenchmen by Charles of Anjou to hold the principal offices of justice in Florence the words need no explanation. The civil powers of the Podestà reinforced the spiritual thunders of the Church. The penitents were to remain in their uneasy posture until the Pope had renewed his solemn interdict against the city, for it was compulsory to fall upon the face when the sentence of excommunication was read. After that each might go home, not to his 'tomb' but to his house, the same word in Low Latin being in use for both, and resume his flesh and figure—his human posture. The sentences of the Pope took effect not only in this world but in the world to come; it was claimed for them in effect that they reverberated into eternity.

Doubtless the matter which interested the whole city was that on which Dante was speculating as he left the scene, whether after the 'gran Sentenza' of the Pope it would be found that they were worse off, or better, or much as before. And the enigmatic reply merely accentuates the fact that though the Florentines who were under a curse were very far from perfect, and by no means very sensitive either to good or evil, yet they could hardly be worse off than in the present moment, and might perhaps expect some alleviation of their lot.

CHAPTER VII

SATAN AND THE POPES

[Inferno VI, 112-115; VII, 1-96. Fourth Circle]

Dante encounters Pluto, figuring the venal Papal Conclave conspicuous in the election of Nicholas III. He records his own recollection of the disquieting popular rumour that the devil had carried off John XXI and the other short-lived Popes. Symbolic description of the gambling scenes witnessed in Florence during the frequent Conclaves. Veiled eulogy of Imperial principles, in opposition to a superstitious belief in blind chance.

Period covered: 1277.

Corresponding hour: 11.20 p.m.

Pope Gregory did not live to raise the interdict from the city of Florence. Nor had he time to complete the bargain he had made to crown Rudolph of Hapsburg King of the Romans and Emperor of the West in return for the surrender of Romagna. In the midst of the preparations for the Imperial Coronation Gregory died of a mysterious fever, leaving many wise reforms incomplete to be swept away by his successors. The interests of Charles of Anjou had been so seriously threatened by the proposed recognition of Rudolph that he was exposed to the groundless suspicion of having contrived the Pope's death. It happened most opportunely for the King of Naples. He was able to influence the College of Cardinals to appoint a Frenchman, Innocent V, pledged to an anti-Imperial policy. And the postponement of the Imperial Coronation *sine die* was recognized as a signal victory for the Guelfs.

Innocent V was consecrated in February and died four months later. During his short reign he raised the interdict on Florence. Adrian V, elected in June, died twenty-nine days later before he could be consecrated. His successor, John XXI, consecrated in September, died the following May, 1277, after a reign of four months. Thus were four Popes in succession hurried to their grave within seventeen months, 'two by Divine Judgment,' says a Ghibelline chronicler, 'and two from poison'.

In an age when the active intervention of the devil in the affairs of mankind was universally taken for granted, it was inevitable that these appalling events should be ascribed to Satanic agency. The death of John XXI was of a nature to turn popular suspicion to certainty. He was a man of deep learning, addicted to the study of science and astronomy, hence vulgarly reputed to be a magician. He was killed while asleep by the falling of a ceiling in a room he had newly added on to the Papal Palace at Viterbo. Villani relates[1] with complete conviction a mysterious occurrence which had turned to certainty the general suspicion that the devil had carried him off. The night before John XXI died a Florentine merchant, by name Berti Borzetti, possessed of well attested occult powers, was on board ship, journeying to Acre. Suddenly he called out, 'Alas, alas . . . I see a gigantic man in black with a great club in his hand and he is about to break down a pillar above which is a ceiling'. And after a time he cried out again and said: 'He has broken it down and he is dead.' Being asked 'Who?' he replied 'The Pope'. His companions wrote down the words and the night, and when they were come to Acre a short time after there came to them the news of the death of the said Pope, which came to pass that same night. There was no room for doubt that the gigantic black figure beheld in the act of carrying off by a violent death his intimate the Pope was the devil in person. Villani was only a year old at the time, but he tells us that in later years he heard the story with his own ears from the very merchants who had witnessed the scene on board ship, and he gives his testimony that they were 'men of great authority and worthy of credence', and that 'the fame of this thing resounded through the city'. There is the witness of the text to the impression made upon one Florentine boy, in whose mind these memories were to be turned hereafter to rich account.

Nowhere, not even in the place appointed for the sitting of the Conclave, were the illicit dealings of the Cardinals during their period of deliberation better known than in Florence. Every detail of the transactions through which the contending factions laboured to secure a majority in favour of a candidate

[1] Bk. VII, 50.

pledged to their interests was laid bare in the city, for it was the Florentine bankers who furnished the gold on which the issue turned.

The scenes which accompanied a long drawn out Papal election afforded the moralist a vivid illustration of the fourth Deadly Sin—Love of money displayed in hoarding and in reckless squandering. The greed of the electing Cardinals was reflected in hundreds of minor officials, dependent for a place and bread upon the turn of the event. The advent of a new Pope disturbed the balance for a horde of ' clerics ' who lived in one way or another on Church funds; it brought some to opulence, ruined others and stirred the entire ant-hill to prodigious activity. There was much wagering on the event, and the chances of the leading Cardinals were feverishly canvassed from day to day, as parties within the Conclave formed and were dissolved only to form again. Notwithstanding the exaggerated secrecy thrown around the proceedings by minute regulations, every child in Florence could guess what was going on. It may be judged whether such scenes, five times repeated within a couple of years, inclined men to reverence a Head of the Church whose main qualification for office was the power to outwit and out-bribe all the rest.

When at length, six months after the sensational demise of John XXI, John Gustavus Orsino was elected Pope under the name of Nicholas III, the expectation of reform still cherished by many Churchmen faded into despair. Of this Pope who had served under eight of his predecessors, and had himself taken part in seven Conclaves, nothing was to be expected but that he would perpetuate the worst abuses of the Curia. It was of him that Dante hereafter declared: ' It was of shepherds like ye that the Evangelist was ware when SHE that sitteth upon the waters was seen by him committing fornication with Kings.'[1]

While such events were being enacted under the awe-struck vision of the devout, and the ribald scoffs of the populace, Dante, far beyond his years in knowledge and penetration, was pursuing his studies either at some Florentine high school, possibly attached to a monastery, or under a private tutor. The seventh Canto of the *Inferno* gives vivid support to the supposition that he was fully cognizant of the disreputable

[1] *Inf.*, xix, 106. *Cf.* Rev., xviii, 3.

manœuvres which were bringing shame on the Papal Conclave in his twelfth and thirteenth years.

In the midst of the dismay occasioned by the mysterious death of John XXI, while men clamoured for vengeance on the incriminated Cardinals, there arose the exculpatory cry, not untinged with a kind of unholy triumph (for this is implied in the word *Chioccia*) that it was Satan himself who bore off to swift judgment Popes who had surrendered themselves to his service. But at the height of Dante's doubtful consternation the calm voice of reason stilled his fears.

Inf., VI, 112-115.
The corrupt election of the Popes was recognized as the source of all the evils in the Church.
Inf., VII, 1-15.

IMAGE OF THE VENAL PAPAL CONCLAVE

On we went winding round about that way
Saying a good deal more than I repeat.
We reached the point where degradation starts.
Here we found Pluto, the Arch Enemy.

[Pape Satan, Pape Satan aleppe]
' Satan, Satan snatcheth away the Popes ',
Pluto began, with clucking emphasis.

And that wise Sage, he who knew everything,
To cheer me, said: ' Let not fear mislead thee;
' Whatever power he hath, the going down
' Shall not take this Rock from thee.'
Then to that swollen lip he turned and said:
' Be silent, Wolf accursed; devour thyself
' Within thine own mad rage; not without cause
' The journey to the Deep. 'Tis willed on High
' Where Michael took revenge on the proud whoredom.'

As sails inflated by the wind collapse
Entangled, when it snaps the mast, so fell
To earth that cruel monster.

It was near the beginning of Dante's pilgrimage that he was startled by a cry which proceeded from a strange figure in his path, ' Pluto, the Great Enemy,' beginning an oration of which only three words are recorded: ' *Pape Satan, Pape Satan, aleppe* '. It would seem that Dante understood what Pluto was trying to say, for the words caused him the most lively discomfiture. Virgil, while administering comfort, did not attempt to explain the cryptic utterance, and it has always been reckoned one of the most obscure in the *Divina Commedia*. We venture to suggest that the most puzzling word of the three admits of a simple philological interpretation, and that the entire passage was based on the tragic train of circumstances narrated above which occurred while Dante was twelve years old.

Taking the word ' Satan ' as the subject of the sentence, in its natural sense as the devil, and ' Pape ' also in its usual meaning as the plural of Papa (Pope), the only puzzling word in the phrase is *Aleppe*. Its meaning has been vainly sought in Greek and Hebrew, yet it is the third person singular, present tense, of the verb *Aleppare*. Leppare or Aleppare [1] is a base form of the Latin Levare (Fr. *enlever*) to carry off or snatch away suddenly.

Leppare was a word in common use by the medieval. Such words lent themselves readily, but usually with some slight change of meaning, to an affix, as Portare, Apportare; menare, amenare (*voce antica*); levare, allevare. Accepting then the word *Aleppare* in its signification ' To carry off suddenly ', the enigmatic sentence resolves itself into the declaration, ' Satan, Satan (himself) is carrying off the Popes, the Popes '.

To identify the incidents which elicited Pluto's declaration must involve some attempt to apprehend a deeper meaning underlying the grotesque figure of Pluto himself. By classical tradition Pluto was guardian of the infernal regions. He held the KEYS in his hands. He was inexorable, invisible. In these particulars he corresponded to that Papal Conclave on which the government of the world depended, in whose power it lay to deliver the KEYS to whomsoever it would by a decision impersonal, subject to no appeal. Dante had at once perceived on first becoming aware of this portentous figure that here was ' il grande nemico '. Devout Churchmen, more especially Pope Gregory X, had long been persuaded that this august assembly in its corrupt condition had become the great obstacle to reform. The avarice of the Cardinals, the shameless traffic in votes which accompanied every election were an open scandal throughout Christendom.

It was Virgil's part to refute the implication that Satan held power over life and death.

[1] *Vocabolaria dell' Accad: della Crusca.*

Not without Divine cause had the passing of the Popes to the unknown depth (*cupo*) of eternity taken place. It was willed in Heaven, where Michael had once been set to take vengeance on the proud whoredom of the rebellious angels. The words were not merely a rebuke, they were a threat. What had befallen such men as Innocent V, elected by foreign bribery, might yet befall the rest. In the eyes of the moralist it was the crime of ' committing fornication with the Kings ' which had brought upon the Conclave and its nominees the fate they superstitiously ascribed to the operation of Satan. Wondering and awe-struck Dante beheld prophetically the moment when the Conclave, as a rotten mast, which upheld the inflated sails of Anti-Christ, would be swept away, and the whole structure become involved in its downfall.

In the succeeding passage it would seem we are to behold the disgraceful scenes of bribery and corruption which the election of a new Pope opened up before the observer. Dante had taken a step forward and downward in the dismal region which ' the evil of the universe ', *i.e.* the ill-governed Church, swallowed up in its sack.

Inf., VII, 16-60.

An exhibition of avarice.

GAMBLING ON THE ELECTION OF A NEW POPE

Thus we descended into the Fourth Lake
Learning yet more about the doleful Slope
Which is appropriated utterly
By the Evil One of the universe.
Ah, Justice of God, who could agglomerate
So many torments new and penalties
As those I saw; why doth our sin thus waste us?

Symbolic picture of the gambling which attended every fresh Papal election.

As there above Charybdis breaks the surge
Against the wave that it encounters, thus
Here must the people meet in opposition.
Here I saw many folk more than elsewhere
On one side and the other, with great shouts
Turning the scales by vigour of their chests.
They came in contact, then precisely there
Each one, recoiling, backward turned him round,
Yelling: ' Why hoardest? ' ' Why squanderest thou? '
Thus they revolved about the sordid track
From either hand to the point opposite,

Re-echoing their shameful measure still.
Then each one turned, when he had (over) reached,
Along his half track to play other trick.

And I who felt my heart as it were stricken
Said: ' Now my Master, pray unfold to me
' What folk are these, and whether they were all,
' These tonsured on our left, ecclesiastics? '
And he to me: ' So squint-eyed one and all
' Were they in mind during their early life,
' They made no spending with due moderation.
' Their voices clear enough are baying this
' When to the two points of the track they come
' Where guilt discordant severs each from each.
' These were ecclesiastics on whose head
' No covering rests of hair; moreover Popes
' And Cardinals in whom finds Avarice
' Use for its worst excesses.'

And I: ' Master, midst such as these I ought
' Surely to recognize some who were stained
' By these iniquities.' And he to me:
' Vain thoughts are these thou gatherest.
' The undiscerning life which made them foul
' Makes them obscure from any recognition.
' For all eternity they will collide
' In double shock; these with closed fists will rise,
' The others with shorn hair from out the grave.
' Ill-giving and ill-keeping has bereft them
' Of the fair world, and set them to this buffet.
' To say what like it is needs no fair words.'

Spendthrifts
and misers
alike con-
tend des-
perately to
ensure the
return of the
Cardinal to
whose inter-
ests they were
pledged.

Many Popes
owed their
election to
bribery
practised
when
Cardinals.

The gossip
of the day
was con-
cerned ex-
clusively with
the inner
secret of the
conclave.

In setting Pluto to image the Conclave Dante was not un-
mindful of the links which connected him with Plutus, god of
riches. In both senses his figure harmonizes with the ostensible as well as the allegorical meaning of the poem.

Invoking the Justice of God, not because he beheld it manifest, but because he was horrified at its apparent absence,
Dante became lost in wonder at the piling up of so many new
pains and penances as had been devised.

It is implied by the metaphor that the actors in the drama

lay between Scylla and Charybdis; they must either take bribes or give them. Here were to be seen men not above playing false with each other and the Church, turning the weights of the scale by the force of their own chests, a familiar metaphor for cheating.

The scene was extremely lively and an astonishing number of persons, principally ecclesiastics, was involved. Half were clamouring for bribes, ' Why dost thou withhold? ' The rest were more guarded, refusing to be beguiled. ' Why dost thou squander? ' So they went through the dreary round, constantly encountering, then drawing back; in the end returning to the same place. Then they changed tactics and tried the other joust. Is not this a vivid picture of the proceedings at many a hotly-disputed election, not only at a thirteenth-century conclave? Modes of bribery differ little from one century to another.

Ecclesiastics were shaved on the crown of their heads as a token that they renounced all worldly possessions, hair being the symbol for material preoccupations, for was not Esau a hairy man? Thus in their outward semblance avaricious priests, Cardinals, and Popes perforce exhibited the fact that they had renounced by solemn oath all participation in the riches for which they were contending. Emphasis is laid on the participation of the Cardinals in the disgraceful ' Circus ' presented by the Conclave, and hence by the Popes themselves.

The eager questioner went on to ask for further information, longing to know the names of bribers and bribed, many of whom were Florentine bankers. But his mentor, refusing to gratify his curiosity, rebuked him for his interest in vain rumours. No reasonable men cherished any hope of a reformed Conclave after the utter failure of the plan devised by Gregory X.

Such as the conclave was, such it would always be. To all eternity bribers and bribed would go on butting at one another with their horns. Even when they rose from the dead they would have their fists full of bribes, and their hair shorn in visible token of perjury. Evil-giving (bribery) and evil-keeping (avarice) had stolen from them that sweet world (of the intellect) the loss of which Ciacco too lamented, while he foresaw that it was to be the refuge of the boy Dante.

FIRST NOTICE OF DISINTERESTED IMPERIAL RULE
(Virgil continues)

' Now mayst thou see, my son, the transient farce
' Of the goods delivered unto fortune
' For which the human race for ever wrangles;
' Not all the gold that is beneath the Moon,
' Or ever was, could bring tranquillity
' To any one of these fore-wearied souls.'

' Master ', said I, ' now tell me more again;
' This Fortune, that thou touchest on with me,
' This that within its clutches holds so tight
' The good things of the world, what may this be? '

And he to me: ' O foolish human beings
' How great the ignorance that injures you!
' *My* judgment on it now do thou receive.
' He, whose omniscience transcendeth all,
' Not only made the Heavens but appointed
' Those that should guide them, so that every part
' Shines out to every part, distributing
' Light equally. In like mode He ordained
' A Mistress and Conductor general
' For worldly splendours, who should in due course
' Change from nation to nation, race from race,
' Beyond defence of human argument,
' Vain (temporal) possessions, so that hence
' One people rules, another languishes,
' Obeying Her decree which is concealed
' Like snake in grass.
' Your knowledge hath no counter-stand to Her.
' She foresees, judges and maintains her rule
' As do the other Deities their own;
' No truces hath she in her permutations;
' Necessity compels her to be swift;
' Since oft comes one pursuing revolution.
' This is SHE, so greatly execrated
' Even by those who ought to give her praise,
' Blaming her wrongfully with evil words.
' Yet is She happy and she hears it not.
' Joyously with the other Primal Creatures
' She wheels her sphere and tastes her blessedness.'

Inf., VII, 61-96.

The Imperial Idea presented in opposition to the system of blind chance to which the Papal elections had sunk.

Virgil scorns the theory that the world is ruled by fortune.

Veiled reference to the Holy Roman Empire.

The ideal Imperial policy.

This appears to have been the time when the first notions of imperial rights, the first conception of what imperial rule at its best might mean to the world, were presented to Dante's mind. Possibly some relative, secretly inclined to the Ghibelline doctrine, was responsible for the brief epitome of the theory of universal monarchy which is put into the mouth of Virgil. It has been usually taken for a distinctly pagan eulogy of Fortune. Yet Virgil uttered a grave rebuke of the stupidity of those who believed that the Universe was governed by blind chance.

Nothing could be further from the philosophy revealed in Dante's work than the notion of Fortune like a heathen god ruling the affairs of men. The design of the whole passage is to refute this pagan theory and present a veiled exposition of Imperial Authority as God's ordinance, marking a strong contrast with the hazardous system of the Papacy. In the *Monarchy* precisely the same thought occurs in prose: ' Just as the whole heaven in all its parts, motions and movers, is regulated by a single motion (to wit of the *primum mobile*) and a single motor, God . . . it follows . . . that the human race is then best disposed when it is ruled in its motors and motions by a single prince as single motor and by a single law as single motion'. All that is declared about the 'general Mistress and Guide of mundane splendours' is to be applied not to Fortune but to the Empire. The theory that God could have committed temporal possessions to blind chance provoked at the outset from Virgil an exclamation of disgust at such ignorance. God Who appointed rulers over the Heavens did *not* leave the world without a general Mistress and Guide. It is part of the Imperial authority to set up a balance of power among the nations. This imperial Mistress of human affairs lies beyond the power of the best human wits to circumvent. Her judgments lie hidden from mortal eye even as a snake (symbol of wisdom) lies hid in the grass. The Master complained, however, that the knowledge of Dante and his Guelf friends (*vostro saver*) took no account of this element in public affairs. The permutations of national rule, one nation rising to power and another declining, go on without ceasing; they take place of necessity because so often there comes one (an ambitious tyrant) who deliberately aims at causing a turn of events (*vicenda conseque*) and subverting the state. It is this principle of imperial rule which is so constantly abused, even by those who live under its administration and ought to honour it as their surest protection from tyranny. They blame it wrongfully and with evil words. Men judge of Empire as it appears thwarted by the perversity of human wills. Yet in its essence it is as pure as the other primal creatures who are set to move the spheres. As ' Idea ', eternal in God's sight, the principle of imperial authority rejoices in its sphere, and can no more come short of its Maker's intent than can the other Divine Beings.

Under some such cryptic form was the notion of a force apart from and independent of the Church, yet working in accord with it, set to govern the world by Divine authority, presented to the mind of Dante. He was prepared for it by the disgraceful scenes of bribery which he witnessed during the five successive sittings of the Papal Conclave. The new outbreak of disorders and warfare consequent on the surrender of the Romagna to the Church were drawing men irresistibly at this date to the perception that existing modes of world government were out of harmony with Divine Wisdom.

CHAPTER VIII

MONASTIC REFUGE FROM CIVIL STRIFE

[Inferno VII, 97-130; VIII, 1-64. Fifth Circle]

Symbolic Picture of civil war, in which men are beheld destroying themselves and each other in a swamp of Hatred. Unsatisfactory détour made by Dante, with eyes fixed on the filth. Appearance of the Tower beheld signalling afar to another Tower. Encounter with Phlegyas, figuring Monastic Authority. Dante carried safely through this dangerous part of his journey in the boat of Monastic Rule. Attempt of the Man of Wrath (Charles of Anjou) to drag him into the strife, frustrated by Reason. Ultimate retribution of Charles foreseen.

Period covered: 1278-1283.

Corresponding hours: 11.40 p.m.—1.20 a.m.

DANTE LOST his mother about the year 1278. There is one reference to her and only one in the *Divina Commedia*, and, as will be shown below, it is a very significant one. 'Blessed is she that bore thee'.

Very soon after the death of Bella, Alighiero married again. Dante's stepmother was Lapa, daughter of Chiarissimo Cialuffi, and she bore three children in quick succession, Francesco, Tana (Gaetana), and another girl. The union lasted four or five years only. Before 1283 Alighiero was dead. The sale of certain property by Dante in that year is attested by documents in which he is mentioned as 'heir of his late father Alighiero of the quarter of San Martino del Vescovo'.

While one bereavement succeeded another, bringing inevitably depression and uncertainty into the life of the adolescent, a new period of strife, more intense than before, was devastating Italy.

Pope Nicholas III (1277-1280) began his reign by making a formal settlement with the Emperor Rudolph of Germany. On the strength of a long series of deeds of gift, the Church claimed extensive territories in Italy which fell within the Imperial domains, including the rich province of Romagna,

138

the ' orchard of the Empire '. All were now surrendered by Rudolph without reserve as the price of the Pope's sanction to his coronation with permission to resume the Imperial rights in Tuscany, which Charles of Anjou had been allowed to usurp since the death of Manfred. Rudolph was deplorably duped over this bargain. Nicholas died before he could fulfil his promise of carrying out the formal coronation at Rome for which Rudolph had stipulated, and his successor, Martin IV (1281-1285), who was completely under the influence of Charles of Anjou, kept tight hold of the ceded provinces but deferred the coronation *sine die*.

The ratification of this agreement between Nicholas and Rudolph involved great administrative changes both in Tuscany and in Romagna. The French Vicar, who, with a host of officials backed by lawless bodies of French troops, had hitherto collected exactions for Charles of Anjou in the Tuscan cities, was replaced by a new administration under which a Vicar appointed by Rudolph attempted to collect the long pretermitted contribution to the Imperial exchequer. The withdrawal from Florence and neighbouring cities of the ' enemy Podestà ' and the French soldiery could not but awake rejoicing, and the Imperial hand seems to have rested lightly enough on the municipalities in comparison. Within a short while Florence and the other cities had compounded with the Emperor for their Imperial dues by payment of a lump sum down and became to all intents and purposes free cities. Nicholas took pains to secure a rapprochement between the rival parties in the state, by sending his nephew, Cardinal Latino, to visit Florence and negotiate something like a truce between the most bellicose Guelf and Ghibelline families. Open warfare was avoided, and the acute misgivings of the Guelfs lest all the exiles should hurry back and turn out the present occupiers of the land and dwellings were not realized.

Far otherwise was it in Romagna. The surrender to the Church of the great tract of country stretching north-east of Florence, beyond the Apennines to the seacoast, including the great university city of Bologna, provoked a fierce civil war which rapidly spread to other parts of Italy. The settled order of rule by great landowners exercising long-established feudal rights was suddenly overthrown; a long period of anarchy followed, and the new system of rule by Papal envoy succeeded only in making religion odious. The surrender was hailed as a great Guelf triumph and it made the position of the old Ghibelline nobles in the district to the last degree insecure. The story of Italy for the next twenty years is largely made up of civil war in Romagna in which, and to this Litta's records bear striking witness,[1] every noble family took an active part. Many great clans like the Conti Guidi were divided in politics with the result that near relations fought against each other. Every city was engulfed in this senseless strife. Their history in this century under the Papal sceptre is one of incessant revolt, a never-ending struggle of men unjustly dispossessed to regain their patrimony.

Before long the Two Sicilies likewise were in a blaze, and Charles of Anjou came near to being overwhelmed by his enemies and ejected from Italy. The two principal allies against him were the Greek Emperor Palæologus, who was excommunicated by Martin IV in order to please Charles, and secondly Peter III of Aragon, whose wife Constance, daughter of Manfred and niece of Conradin, was regarded by the Sicilians as their lawful sovereign. John of Procida, a Spanish agent despatched to Sicily to sow disaffection towards Charles and rouse hopes of support should a revolt ensue, found it only too easy to excite an insurrection, but the savage nature of it surpassed all expectations. Moved to fury by an insult offered to a married woman by one of the French soldiers, the Sicilians suddenly rose and on 31st March 1282 massacred every man, woman, and child of French nationality in the island. This savage butchery, known as the Sicilian Vespers, created a profound sensation even at a time when massacres were too frequent to secure more than a line or two of notice in the chronicles of the period.

Peter of Aragon at once accepted the invitation of the islanders to take possession of Sicily in the name of Queen Constance. He and Palæologus had for some time been preparing a great fleet in anticipation of a rising, and they headed a formidable expedition to depose Charles. Instantly all Italy took sides, the Ghibellines espousing with ardour the claims of Constance to her father's patrimony, the Guelfs obeying the call of Martin IV to a new Crusade on behalf of Charles.

Such were the events in progress during the impressionable

[1] *Pompeo Litta*—continued by *L. Passerini*. Famiglie Celebri Italiane.

years of Dante's passage from boyhood to adolescence. None could live in Florence and not share in the hourly excitement roused by these stirring events as the news, collected from agents at Rome and elsewhere, was brought hot-foot by couriers to the Communal authorities. There are open allusions in Dante's writings to the vices of Charles and his son,[1] to the gross self-indulgence of Martin IV [2] 'who held the Church in his arms' at this time, to the illegal cession of Imperial territories to the Church, to the Sicilian Vespers, as the result of bad government. We venture to maintain that these events were woven into the cryptic fabric of the *Inferno* and are discernible under the strange incidents recorded by Dante on his way through the sorrowful valley.

(Virgil is speaking)

TIME REFERENCE

' Now let us descend to deeper wretchedness.
' Every star sinks already which arose
' When I set out. To linger is forbidden.'

Inf., VII, 97 to end.
Key date.
Hour: Past Midnight.
Year 1280.

CIVIL WAR

We crossed the Circle to the opposite bank
Over a spring that bubbling gushes down
Into a gully that was formed by it.
Black was the water—darker far than perse—
And we accompanying its gloomy waves
Entered below upon a ghastly path.
This dismal streamlet, when it has flowed down
To the foot of the malignant dusky shores
Creates a swamp which has the name of Styx.

The Styx, an image of Hatred.

And I, who stood intent to gaze, perceived
People be-mired and naked in that bog,
With aspect injured and injurious.
They struck each other, not with hand alone
But also with the head, the chest, the feet,
Rending each other piece-meal with their teeth.

Picture of internecine conflict.

---

[1] *Purg.*, XX, 67-124; *Para.*, VI, 106-108; XX, 63; *De Vulg. El.*, I, 12.
[2] *Purg.*, XXIV, 20-22.

Said the good Master: ' Son, thou seest now
' The souls of men whom anger dominated.
' Moreover I would have thee surely know

' The water holds folk underneath, who sigh,
' Making this water bubble at the top
' As thine eye tells, whichever way it turns.
' Stuck in the mud they say: " Sullen were we

' " In the sweet air made joyous by the Sun,
' " Nursing within us smoke accidious.
' " Now we lie sullenly in the black ooze".
' This canticle they gurgle in their throats;
' With unobstructed words they cannot say it '.

Thus a great arc of that foul fen we compass,
Between the dry bank and the marshy ground,
With eyes turned on the men who gulp down filth.

To the bottom of a Tower we came at length.

It was nightfall, about 7 p.m., when Dante began his journey. The setting of the stars indicates that it was now past midnight. He had already been five hours on the way, but so far they had traversed only four circles. When the twenty-four hours of the day are synchronized with the seventy-two years of man's approximate life-time, each hour corresponds to three years. When the stars were setting about midnight some fifteen years had elapsed since the journey began, and the date was about 1280. The salient events of the first fifteen years of life are reflected in the scenes which passed under review during these five hours: conception, birth, infancy, early education ; early impressions of sin and punishment; first thoughts about love; crude religious fears; first introduction to political discord. A definite stage in the journey had been accomplished which marked the end of Dante's childhood. From this point he was to descend to far more poignant sorrow than he had yet tasted.

With his home broken up by the death of both parents Dante had to make choice of a future career. There could have been no more unpropitious time for a youth of studious habits and sensitive disposition to be launched upon the world. It may be assumed that he had already assimilated such learning as his grammar school teachers or private tutor had to impart and had made himself master, so far as his scholarship extended, of all the books within his reach. From hints already afforded in the New Life it may be deduced that he had already begun to exercise a talent for writing verses, an art then much in vogue among young men, and that his early love-lyrics had brought him fame among his compeers. None of these poetical assays have survived, with the exception of an enigmatic correspondence between Forese dei Donati and himself. Six sonnets have been discovered in which the friends directed somewhat scathing personalities against each other and also against the father of Dante and the wife of Forese. One very interesting trait in Dante's character emerges. He absolutely refused to take part in the family vendetta which had arisen out of the murder of Geri del Bello, his great uncle, by a member of the Sacchetti family, one of whom Geri himself had slain. Forese taunted Dante with cowardice for setting up a standard of morality for himself in this respect directly contrary to that observed among his friends. Referring to the murder of Geri, Forese says:

> ' Why if thou hadst hewn one (of them)
> ' In bits for it, 'twere early still for peace.
> ' But then thy head's so heaped with things like these
> ' That they would weigh two sumpter horses down.
> ' Thou hast taught us a fair fashion, sooth to say,—
> ' That whoso lays a stick well to thy back,
> ' Thy comrade and thy brother he shall be.'

The sonnets seem to show that Dante's gift had brought him precociously among a group of convivial wits, many much older than himself, in whose company he drifted, after his mother's death, into a way of living devoid of any purpose save the pleasure of the moment. It is a matter of common observation that temptations to dissolute habits are increased a hundredfold in war-time when public morality in all directions is relaxed. If the authenticity of the Forese sonnets be admitted, it is to these years that they must be referred, for they allude to Alighiero (who died in 1283) as still alive. When Dante encountered Forese in Purgatory he made definite confession of a time of dissipation in his company of which both were by that time bitterly ashamed. ' If thou bring back to mind what thou hast been with me and what I have been with thee, the present memory will still be grievous.'[1] This season, when restraint was lacking and little progress was made in the higher life, may have succeeded his mother's death.

It may be judged whether the above quoted vision of the Styx does not vividly reflect Dante's position in these years, when, uncertain of the future, he found himself confronted by a black tide of civil warfare which blocked his onward path.

The scene depicted in the Styx carries its interpretation on the surface. It is a picture familiar in all ages of the insane conditions attaching to civil war. Here in a black swamp of hatred men's energies were displayed solely in the task of destruction. They were to be seen naked, stripped as refugees of all their possessions, mad with revenge and blood-lust, recklessly intent on tearing each other tooth and nail, injuring themselves even more than their adversaries. Virgil comments strongly on a perverse feature of Italian misrule. There was a sullen undercurrent of discontent and rebellion which was largely responsible for troubling the waters. Hidden out of sight were the men to whom he had alluded in his recent vindication of Imperial rule, men who had railed on the laws under which they had lived in safety, and had secretly plotted to overthrow Imperial rule. The inhabitants of the Romagna who had never ceased complaining of foreign rule were now singing to another tune. They had to confess they had been discontented in 'the sweet air which the Sun gently illumines'. Now they were engulfed in the hideous swamp which flowed from a fount of avarice.[2]

Dante's own movements are highly significant. The condition of the ground on which he trod is constantly mentioned throughout the journey, assuredly not without some purpose. He tells us that if at this stage he did not actually dip his feet in the swamp, neither did he choose for his path the dry bank which rose above it. He walked between the two, his whole attention absorbed by the belligerents. Thus it came to pass that he made a wide détour, impeded in his onward course by bitter strife near at hand, conscious all the time of gloom and

---

[1] *Purg.*, xxiii, 115-117.

[2] *Inf.*, vii, 100-108. The course of the Styx is traced direct from the scene of corruption which marked the election of the Pope.

disillusion. The impression is subtly conveyed that he was profoundly dissatisfied with the path he trod and that he had no better prospect before him.

At this moment he found himself confronted by the Tower.

Nothing could present a more powerful contrast to the morass than this Tower. It stood out among the treacherous shallows of the Styx as an emblem of permanence and security. We are reminded that Dante more than once spoke of Reason or Knowledge as a Tower, ' la diritta Torre della Ragione ',[1] and apprehend that he had now arrived at the new starting-point in his career. The time wasted in circling the Styx is indeterminate, but it is not improbable that the death of Alighiero may have broken up this devious course. Certain it is that the death of his father synchronized with that new vision of Beatrice which occurred when Dante was nearly nineteen,[1] and marked a new starting-point in his life, a period of intense absorption in study. The Tower contained no door. Hence it serves only one purpose in the allegory—that of flashing a signal, perchance of such a nature as those of which Dante sang in the Banquet,[2] lightning flashes of intuition which strike down from above to burst asunder men's inborn vices.

At the close of a passage which describes their effect in raising men above their lower nature, Dante exhorted his readers to lift their eyes on high to behold these flamelets, instead of keeping them fixed on the mud (fango) created by their own stupidity.[3] Thus in the text do we behold Dante lifting his eyes from the mud to catch sight of the beacon flaming over his head.

The parallel with the New Life revelation is remarkable. Dante turned to ' the sea of all knowledge ' to interpret the

---

[1] New Life, c. III.

[2] Banquet, III, Ode 2:

> Her beauty scatters little flames of fire
> Impregnated with life by a noble spirit—
> He Who of all good thoughts is the Creator—
> Like thunder do they burst the inborn vice
> Which makes men vile.

[3] Ibid., III, 5. ' O ineffable Wisdom, that has ordered thus. How poorly our minds can comprehend Thee. And ye for whose use and pleasure I write, in what blindness ye live, never raising your eyes towards these things, but keeping them on the mud of your stupidity.'

flashes of intuition with which his mind was illumined. From the Tower flashed signals revealing the existence of a stronghold which lay shrouded from view in the mist arising out of the waters of strife. How could the gulf be bridged? In other words how was Dante in the position he was now in, fatherless, without settled home, and in a city given over to partisan warfare, so to frame his life that he could devote himself to the intellectual life which called to him. His obvious refuge was a monastery.

THE MONASTIC REFUGE

Inf., VIII, 1-30. The Tower of Knowledge closely allied to the Tower of Law.

Continuing, I say that long before
We reached the bottom of the lofty Tower
Our eyes rose up above it to its summit
By reason of two flamelets that we saw
Thereon displayed, and far away another
Making a signal (faint) such as the eye
Could scarcely apprehend it.

Flashes of Intuition raising the eyes from earthly things.

Call to monastic restraint.

Then to the Sea of all Intelligence
Turning I said:—
' What saith this fire? And what replies that other?
' And they that kindle it, who may they be? '

And he to me: ' Over the squalid waves
' Thou mayest e'en now discern what is expected
' If the marsh fog conceal it not from thee '.

Phlegyas symbol of monastic authority.

Cool reception of the postulant seeking only temporary protection.

Never did cord hurl from itself a dart
That ran its course more swiftly through the air
Than I perceived a tiny boat advancing
Over the water towards us; in the which
An oarsman, under one sole governance,
Who called: ' Now guilty soul, thou hast arrived '.

' Phlegyas, Phlegyas ', my Lord replied,
' Thou callest for a Vow. This time no more
' Thou'lt have of us than while we cross the wash.'

As one who hearkens to some great deception
Practised upon him, then chafes under it,
Such Phlegyas became in wrath restrained.

146

Into the skiff my Guide descended; then
After him made me enter; and it seemed
Only when I was in it laden down.
Soon as the Guide and I were in the boat
The ancient prow moved on, cutting more deep
Into the water than its wont with others.

Dante took
his vocation
seriously.

No undocumented facts in the life of Dante are more
worthy of credence than his connection with the Franciscan
Friars and with the university of Bologna. Even without the
weight of tradition it might reasonably be assumed that in the
disturbed state of the country he took refuge in a monastery
for a time after his father's death and that he kept the terms
at the university proper for men of his birth and understanding.

The *Inferno* narrative contributes remarkable testimony to
the same effect. For at this point, when the future looked
black and Dante's onward path was blocked by bloodthirsty
men eager to involve him in their disputes, a strange figure
addressed by Virgil as Phlegyas appeared, as the signal
flashed from the Tower, to ferry the pilgrims securely in his
tiny boat over the troubled waters. The ultimate decision to
resort to this help was made very suddenly, and at once, like
an arrow shot from a cord, Phlegyas was at hand. He is
represented as playing a part not unlike that which Virgil assigned him in the *Aeneid*, where he discharged an honourable
office, proclaiming to the shades: ' Discite justitiam moniti,
et non temnere Divos '. In more than one particular Phlegyas
played a part similar to that undertaken by ' Monastic Rule '.
To the individual novice the Rule was harsh and the new-
comer was received as a brand snatched from the wrath of
God. The boat was very small (*piccioletta*), adapted to receive one passenger only, a possible indication of the peculiarly
individual nature of the obligation assumed. Virgil could not
weigh it down perhaps because Reason is unaffected by the
curbs on appetite implied in the discipline. Dante weighed
down ' the time-honoured bark ' more than many others;
and this may be a confession that he brought with him a heavy
consciousness of ' innate vices ' he was anxious to discard.

It is impossible to resist the suspicion that Dante used the
word ' voto ' in a double sense in the remark made by Virgil,
' Flegias, Flegias, tu gridi *a voto* '. The stern guardian implied

that Dante had come to stay: ' Now thou art at thy destination (*sei giunta*), thou sin-stained spirit '. And Virgil is commonly supposed to reply: ' Thou shoutest in vain '. But ' voto ' also means a vow, and in this sense the retort was: ' Thou callest for a vow? Thou shalt have no more of us this time but solely in crossing the swamp '. Phlegyas was sharply disappointed when he learned that this particular novice had not come to stay. Dante was quite obviously a promising recruit, and the monks may have made it a grievance when he firmly refused to take irrevocable vows and become a member of the order ' at this time ', whatever he might do hereafter. The Franciscans were accused a little later on of keeping boy students by force to make them monks, and the restrained (*accolta*) indignation with which Dante was treated as a temporary inmate is entirely in keeping. He was thrust forth, perhaps with some show of rejection when the moment came for leaving the shelter of the Boat. It stood him, however, in good stead. Phlegyas is the most respectable of all the ministers of Dis whom he encountered on the journey. Without his boat Dante could not have crossed the Styx. By no other means would it have been possible for a young man at that epoch to have resisted pressure put upon him by relatives or party chiefs to join in disastrous civil strife. It was not long before a determined effort was made to drag him from seclusion into the swamp of hatred.

THE BIZARRE FLORENTINE

Inf., VIII, 31-64.

Charles of Anjou, man of Wrath.

While we were running through the dread morass
ONE, full of mud, rose up before me, saying:
' Thou that hast come before thine hour, who art? '
And I to him: ' I stay not, if I come.
' But who art thou, that hast become so foul? '
' Thou seest ', he answered, ' I am one who weep.'
And I to him: ' With weeping and with woe
' Do thou remain, spirit accursed.
' Yet I can recognize thee, all befouled.'

Effort to enlist Dante in his service.

Then to the boat he stretched out both his hands;
Whereat the wary Master thrust him back
Saying: ' Away, there with the other dogs '.

148

Thereupon round my neck he flung his arms;
He kissed my face and said: ' Disdainful soul,
' Blessed is she that bore thee in her womb.
' This in the world was a proud personage;
' Goodness there's none his memory to adorn.
' Therefore his shadow here is furious.
' How many count themselves to be great Kings
' Above there now, who here like hogs in mire
' Shall wallow, leaving frightful reproach behind.'

And I: ' Master, I should be much content
' To see him plunged into this broth himself
' Before we disembark from off the lake '.
And he to me: ' Even before the shore
' Comes to thy view thou shalt be satisfied.
' 'Tis meet such wish of thine should be fulfilled.'
Soon after this I saw the miry throng
Make such an onslaught on him, even now
I praise and render thanks to God for it.
All shouted: ' (Turn) to Philip; (give us) Money.'
The spirit of the fantastic Florentine
Turned with his teeth upon himself.
We left him here. No more I tell of him.
But on my ears there struck a sound of woes,
Whereat I clear mine eye to gaze ahead.

Hint that Dante owed his right principles to his mother's influence.

His career epitomized by Reason.

Many desired his downfall.

Image of his crushing defeat. His unpaid troops deserted. His only hope of help was from Philip of France.

While Dante was under the charge of Phlegyas a remarkable incident proved decisively that it was no imaginary danger to which he had been exposed in the Styx. Among all the incitements to take arms by which men were beset none was more imperative than that made by the agents of Charles of Anjou, who were actively engaged all over Italy in the work of securing recruits for the Sicilian war. In particular great pressure was put upon all Tuscan cities to send levies of men and money. The Prince of Salerno, Charles's eldest son, visited Florence in 1282 and raised a troop of volunteers to go out under Guido da Battifollo. They went off amidst great excitement bearing the Florentine flag but, alas, they were speedily cut to pieces by the Spaniards and very few survived to return home.

The following year Charles of Anjou came himself to Florence. There is much to suggest that it was the personality of this King which is concealed under the image of the ' persona orgogliosa '. We suggest that Dante here recalls an actual encounter with Charles who, avid for recruits in the state of emergency succeeding the Sicilian Vespers, attempted metaphorically to drag Dante by force from his self-chosen refuge in order to immerse him in the waters of strife.

Too much attention need not be paid to the guess of early commentators who have tried to identify the Man of Wrath, on the strength of the outcry ' A Filippo Argenti ', with a cavalier named Filippo whose horses were shod with silver. In connection with this foolish blusterer (even if he existed and was used as a stalking-horse) the assault on Dante seems strangely meaningless and the warmth of Virgil's embrace quite unaccountable. Bullies such as this were all too common; his exploits were assuredly not of sufficient importance to secure him a place among those ' well-known to fame ', with whom the *Divina Commedia* is exclusively concerned.[1]

It has been seen that the hour of midnight, not long past, synchronizes in the Time Scheme with the year 1280, and that the incident is thus fixed approximately for the time when the King of Naples was putting great pressure on his so-called subjects in Florence to join in his fatal wars. Many striking indications can be discerned which link this ' bizarre Florentine ' with the figure of Charles of Anjou, by conquest and frequent residence in the city a questionable kind of Florentine indeed.

Virgil plainly gave his disciple to understand that this was a very great man from the world's point of view. His arrogant spirit was filled with fury at the hatred excited against him; his memory was adorned with no deeds of generosity. Clearly he held himself to be a great king, for it is said of him that many other great kings are in reality like him.

The scene is extraordinarily vivid. Intense and most unusual antagonism was displayed by Dante towards the figure which invaded his solitude. His measured pronouncement that the ruin of this Man roused him even in after years to thank God, could be nothing but empty hyperbole if the offender were merely a common swashbuckler, and thus an

---

[1] Cf. *Para.*, xvii, 133-138. This is a key passage for the identification of the shades. It definitely declares that souls known to fame and these only have been selected for notice.

air of insincerity would rest upon the lines which assuredly were not written without a full consciousness of their gravity. The invective which he permitted himself against the ' accursed spirit ' is hardly equalled in bitterness throughout the darkest scenes of the *Inferno*. And its severity was underlined by the whole-hearted approval of Virgil, which absolved the speaker from any taint of personal malice and set the rebuke on a lofty plane as of Divine Judgment. The closely following reference to Bella ' Blessed is she that bare thee ', distinctly implies that she had no small part in planting in her son's mind the sentiments which led him at the critical moment to a right decision.

The cryptic dialogue is not very easy to follow, but if the above interpretation be admitted it resolves itself into a highly condensed offer of patronage by Charles and a refusal on Dante's part translated from conventional courtly language into an expression of brutal truth; then a final attempt at coercion (both hands outstretched to drag Dante from his point of vantage) checkmated by the monastic authorities.

Nothing could be more natural than that Charles should wish to attach Dante to his service. He had many Florentines in his court at Naples. Some were employed in the King's library, in the work of translating Aristotle into Latin by the help of Arabic scribes. One was head of the Royal Mint. Another was Judge of the High Court. Many were among his troops. In his youth Charles had been a lover of the troubadours. It was at his court that Sordello found protection. Amid all his worldly ambitions he continued a patron of the arts and his interest in the universities of his kingdom never flagged, though his patronage was all too frequently displayed in demands for subsidies with which to prosecute his wars. He had an eye for talent wherever he found it, and when he visited Florence in 1283 he may well have summoned Dante to his presence and suggested to him a place in his retinue. In his address: ' Who art thou who arrivest before thine hour? ' we trace no offensive meaning but rather the condescending greeting of the monarch whose taste for literature was not entirely blunted by war, addressed to the latest successor of the troubadours, the boy poet with whose genius Florence was ringing.

Dante's reply, ' If I arrive I do not mean to stay where I

am ', proclaimed the consciousness that his goal in life was not the production of ' dolci rime d'amor ' with which to adorn a dissipated court. And in the words: ' But thou, who art thou who hast made thyself so foul? ' the interview passes into a searching mental interrogatory in which Dante tested the man who would be his master. The answer: ' Thou seest that I am one who weep ' is, as it were, a confession that this broken conqueror, heavily in debt, bankrupt in credit, his kingdom slipping away from him, weighed down by horrible crimes, had nothing to offer a new adherent but to become a partaker in his wretchedness. The spirit of *hubris* or righteous exaltation at just punishment with which Dante denounced the speaker strikes an entirely justifiable note directed against a notorious political offender, but was altogether out of the picture if a mere provincial bully were in question.

Lastly it may be noted that Virgil's rebuff ' Away, there with the other dogs ' is even more scathing than it sounds. For it recalls the words in the Apocalypse wherein the Apostle, after describing the New Heaven and the New Earth, added the warning, ' *Without are the dogs and poisoners* '. It is a forcible if covert allusion to the last and basest of the crimes of which Dante later accused Charles, the assassination of Thomas Aquinas by poison.

If it were Charles whom Dante desired to behold falling a victim to his own lust for bloodshed the desire was shared by a good many of his subjects and it was shortly to be gratified. Charles left Florence to learn that his son had rashly engaged the enemy without orders, that the Prince had been taken captive, and that the entire Angevin fleet, got together at prodigious cost, had been destroyed. Naples was in a flame of revolt. All the French in the city, including some of the highest officials, were ' assaulted, wounded, robbed, banished, or massacred '. All hope of regaining Sicily was at an end, and it seemed likely that the Neapolitan Kingdom also would be forfeited. Charles struggled fiercely to the end. Dante beheld him swamped in the conflicts he had brewed, and outraged by his infuriated subjects. Around him the cry for French subsidies echoed unceasingly, all shouting on ' Philip ' as their only hope, while unpaid troops clamoured angrily for ' Money ' (*argenti*). In his ignominious end Charles dragged his nephew down with him. Philip III threw himself too im petuously into the Sicilian war. He ruined his exchequer by the demands he made on it to aid Charles, and with the sands of his life fast running out he set out in person to make a counter attack on Aragon. He survived his ambitious kinsman, the Man of Wrath, but a few months.

Contrasted with the accounts circulated under ecclesiastical authority of the edifying end made by Charles in the odour of sanctity, the picture of his unrepentant fury presented by Dante unfolds a stern moral rebuke. It fully justified the secrecy with which the identity of Charles was shrouded. It was permitted to declaim against the vices of a dead King. To dispute the power of the Church to procure for him an easy passage through Purgatory was heresy.

CHAPTER IX

AT BOLOGNA—THE STRONGHOLD OF THE JURISTS

[Inferno VIII, 67 to end. Before the City of Dis]

Approach to barred gates, figuring rigid ecclesiastical control over every branch of knowledge. Determined resistance of the jurists collectively to the advance of Reason. Dante found all intellectual progress obstructed and remained for a time in deep discouragement and doubt. The symbols employed suggest an atmosphere of opposition to free thought, rather than personal aggression towards himself.

Period covered about 1283 to about 1286.

Corresponding hour: from about 1 a.m. to 2 a.m.

AFTER THE hour of midnight the record of Dante's adventures in the Lower World run parallel for a few years with the story of the *New Life*. He was about eighteen when the call of Beatrice rescued him from absorption in base things and introduced him to a higher intellectual life. In the *Inferno* it was just past one a.m. In the world it was the year 1283-4. Both in the *Inferno* and in the *New Life* Dante enigmatically presented himself as involved at this epoch in a desperate struggle for the life of the intellect against powerful forces which he did not specifically define. But whether we behold him stranded alone in darkness on an unknown shore, faced by iron walls and barred gates, Reason discomfited, the onward path obstructed by formidable adversaries: or whether we watch him stretched on his bed in anguish, denied the salutation of Beatrice and filled with apprehensions of her total loss, the story is one of terror and despair. It is plain that the mental crisis which occurred during these student years was of a twofold nature. The *Inferno* (Cantos VIII and IX) depicts symbolically the objective adverse forces which hampered the advance of his mind towards freedom. The *New Life* presents the same conflict subjectively, as it took place in his own mind, and analyses the successive phases through which he passed on his way from the Old Thought (or Belief) to the New Spirit of Love. These apparently simultaneous experiences demand separate consideration. Each throws light on the other. And neither can be understood without reference to the actual circumstances of Dante's life, and the influences to which he was exposed during these years of stress. The same period is briefly summarized in the opening canto of the *Inferno*, where it is called ' the valley which pricked my heart with fear '; ' the night I passed with so much piety '; ' the Pass that no live person ever abandoned '.[1] And Virgil uses the same expression in reassuring Dante: ' Fear not; our Pass none can take from us.' [2]

In one of the rare passages in which Dante openly gave information about his life he stated that for about two years and a half he studied in schools belonging to the religious orders, and attended disputations of philosophers.[3] The words can only mean that he surrendered his entire time to an extensive course of reading, and hardly save at one of the universities could he have had access to the manuscripts demanded for such a course.

In the thirteenth century higher education included as a matter of course a period of university study, and Boccaccio relates the tradition that during these years Dante studied at the universities of Bologna, Pisa, and Paris. Good reasons can be given for placing the visit to the Paris university some years later. The disturbed condition of Pisa, in the year 1284 and for some long time after, owing to her crushing defeat by the city of Genoa in the battle of Meloria, makes it highly improbable that it would be chosen as a place of study by a young Florentine. There remains the university of Bologna which then ranked as equal to that of the universities of Paris and Oxford. Benvenuta da Imola, who lectured on the *Divina Commedia* within sixty years of Dante's death, commenting on the allusion to the leaning Tower of the Garisenda in

---

[1] *Inf.*, I, 14, 20, 26. [2] *Ibid.*, VIII, 104.
[3] *Banquet*, Bk. II, c. 13. I began to go where she (Philosophy) was in very truth revealed, to wit, to the schools of the religious orders, and to the disputations of philosophers, so that in a short time, I suppose some thirty months, I began to perceive so much of her sweetness that the love of her expelled and destroyed every other thought.

Inferno XXXI, 136, remarked: 'The author had noticed this when he studied at Bologna as a young man,' and confirmation of this surmise has been afforded by the discovery of a sonnet on the same subject, now universally recognized as the work of Dante, inscribed in the Register of the Memoriali under the year 1287 by one Enrichetto delle Quercie. That some of Dante's poems were early in circulation at Bologna is proved by other extracts, copied into the Registers, as, for instance, a good part of the Ode '*Donne che avete intelletto d'amore*' appears inscribed in the Register, in the second week of 1292, of Pietroda Allegranza, a notary and doctor of laws. Such carefully, perhaps secretly, preserved specimens of his verse testify to early celebrity. It may be taken then as an ascertained fact that Dante studied at Bologna.

A certain period of study at the Bologna University was an essential qualification, not merely for obtaining ecclesiastical, legal, and professorial posts, but also that of Podestà, an office eagerly sought after by men of good family as opening up unlimited opportunities for increasing their influence and extending their domains. Dante is found expressing great scorn for self-interested students. The lines in which he contrasts the joys of true philosophy with studies tainted by expectations of gain or plunder give a lively picture of the aims of students at the medieval university:

> O mad solicitude that fills mankind,
> How false the arguments are those with which
> Thou art enticed to beat thy wings below.
> One after laws, one after aphorisms
> Went questing, and one after priesthood strove,
> And one to dominate, by force or quibble,
> And one to plunder, one to civil business,
> One, tangled in the pleasures of the flesh,
> Wore himself out, and one to ease surrendered,
> The while from all these things released, above
> With Beatrice I was welcomed gloriously
> In Heaven.
>
> *Paradiso*, XI, 1-12.

The Constitution of the Bologna University differed from that of any other. The governing power resided in the students, who were of all ages between seventeen and forty.

They were divided into two groups, the Citra or Cismontana, who came from Rome and Tuscany, and the Ultramontana, numbering about this time as many as fourteen nations. Among the heterogeneous assemblage which formed the university, great divergence existed as regards the course of study selected and the lectures attended. Men who were preparing for the bachelor's degree with a view to becoming members of the legal or medical profession were, it is true, subject to a prescribed course of study. But the rank and file who were merely ' up ' for a year or two, and had no intention of taking a degree, could apparently choose their own subjects.

The scholar was nominally compelled to attend at least three lectures a week. He took the oath of obedience to the Rector on entering, and on payment of certain fees was admitted to the corporation of students which made up the University. His privileges comprised protection of his purse from extortionate landlords, tradesmen, and producers of books or copyists. It also included protection in some degree of his person. The university stood by its members. They could not be murdered without vengeance being exacted. They could not be tortured unless the Rector himself gave consent and was present at the function. The university conferred on them in fact a modified citizenship in the foreign city where they sojourned. On the other hand the oath of obedience to the Rector was a legal and religious ceremony. To break it was a mortal sin, and exposed a man to the rigours of the law which might give him over to the Inquisition to be prosecuted as a heretic. Giovanni Livi [1] shows documentary evidence for the existence of *hospitia* near the Garisenda Tower, at this time much frequented by Florentine students, and concludes that Dante was in residence in this locality. There were no university buildings at this time, and the scholars assembled in the houses of their lecturers or in a room hired for the purpose. Large assemblies of the students and all ' congregations ' were held in churches or public places—at Bologna, usually in the Convent of S. Dominic, the burial place of the saint. Vast numbers of the students made themselves ' clerici ' for the purposes of obtaining the immunities of an ecclesiastic. They could pass over into the ranks of those protected by ecclesiastic privilege from all civil actions merely

[1] Giovanni Livi, *Dante in Bologna.*

by receiving the tonsure from a Bishop, adopting clerical dress, and remaining nominally celibate. It was not even necessary to assume minor orders. Notorious abuses resulted from this practice.

The main studies at Bologna related to Civil and Canon law, and gradually these centred more and more round the Decretum of Gratian which strongly reinforced the cause of Papalism against Imperialism. Five books of Decretals were added to Gratian's Decretum in 1234.[1] Together the Decretals made up a code which the Church sought to impose upon the world. They were never universally recognized, and the later ones conflicted strangely with the rights of nations.

Resistance to this distorted Code was the basis of Imperialist principles throughout Europe during Dante's lifetime, and his attitude cannot be rightly understood without appreciation of this fact.

Next in importance to the school of law at Bologna was that of medicine. The medical university embraced students in medicine, surgery, philosophy, astrology, logic, rhetoric, and grammar, though only students of medicine ranked as scholars and were entitled to a vote in the congregations. Astrology included the science of mathematics; a taint as of illicit knowledge lay on it and brought it under suspicion.[2]

The arts course comprised certain treatises of Aristotle. Logic formed the main subject of instruction.

In every course all was cut and dried, dead and finished with. It was the boast of medieval teachers at this period that all truth had been ascertained and philosophy completed. All that was necessary for the student was to make himself master of the conclusions at which other men had arrived. 'In each science there was a book which summed up the actual state of that science, and the study of that science was confounded with the study of this book.'[3]

There was no Theological Faculty at Bologna. Theological degrees had to be taken at Paris. Strictly theological speculation was practically banished, and with it all the religious thought and life to which speculation gives rise.[4]

---

[1] Boniface VIII issued a sixth book in 1298, and Clement V prepared another, which was published after his death.
[2] Bacon, *Opus Minus*.   [3] *Ibid.*
[4] See Rashdall, *Universities of Europe in the Middle Ages.*

There is good cause for surmising that Dante's mind reacted forcibly against the restraints imposed by this system, and that he was foremost among the few who battled for the life of the intellect under professors dead to reality and progress. Below the surface of apparent conformity with authority lay a seething intellectual ferment, which from time to time manifested itself unguardedly in some recognizable form, and brought deadly suspicion to rest on all concerned.

The great Watch Tower of Reason, as Dante has it in his *Monarchy*,[1] was Imperial Law, and of this in former days the University of Bologna had been the great stronghold. Here, if anywhere, the basic principles should have been demonstrated which enabled rulers to govern mankind aright. But the student, eager to apprehend right principles of government, found his reading limited to digests of the Decretals framed to cover and condone Papal usurpation. He learned how to gloss over open wrongs by legal subtleties, and was called on to subject his reason at every turn to doubtful authorities. Not justice but skill to overreach the poorer claimant was the end in view. The profits of legal chicanery were enormous, and the power of the lawyers grew apace. They had secured the richest offices in the state. Canonists filled many important episcopal sees and their influence in the Curia was overwhelming. There was ground for the complaint that the Church had become a hierarchy of lawyers.

The ' presumptuous jurists ' or Decretalists formed a class of men whom Dante exposed in the *Monarchy* as people fighting against the truth. These men were ' totally ignorant ', he said, in every kind of theology and philosophy; and laid all their weight upon their Decretals, which they declare to be the foundation of the faith. A marked feature in the jurists was their contentiousness which had risen to such a pitch that ' whereas in other cases ignorance is the cause of contentiousness, with them contentiousness is the cause of ignorance '. By this it may plainly be perceived that the very act of investigation into the truth had become an offence against the law.

It could not escape the acute wits, who were deterred from research by the threats of ignorant professors, that the ecclesiastical lawyers were playing precisely the same part that

---

[1] *Mon.*, Bk. II, c. 12.

lawyers had played once before when they incurred the rebuke of the Master: 'Woe unto you, lawyers! for ye have taken away the key of knowledge: ye entered not in yourselves, and them that were entering in ye hindered.' [1] The nature of the obstruction was evident. Students were required to surrender their Reason without reserve to Authority. Their rôle lay in slavish, lifeless subjection to the dictates of professors and the dogmas of the text book. If reason revolted against discrepancies in the comment, so much the worse for reason. Its use must be abandoned. The reasoning faculties must be forever imprisoned. Such was the iron wall which an innumerable host of hostile authorities, 'learned in the Law', reared against investigation. It was under such conditions that Dante first began to ponder over the ancient scripts on which Authority based itself, and dared (the fruits of this daring are to be plainly seen in the *Banquet* and the *Monarchy*) to examine dispassionately the credentials under which ecclesiastics aspired to supersede Reason in the government of the world.

Inf., VIII, 67.

BOLOGNA CENTRE OF THE PAPAL ADMINISTRATION

The City of Dis a Vision of the University.

Said the good Master: 'Now my Son draw near
'The City that hath Dis for name—therewith
'Its weighty citizens, its great array.'
And I : 'Master, already I can see
'Its *mosques* distinctly, in the valley there,

Knowledge of Aristotle derived from Mahommedans damned to everlasting flames.

'Bright red as though they had come out of fire.'
Then he said to me: 'The fire eternal
'That kindles them within makes them look red,
'As in this Nether Hell thou canst perceive.'
At length within the deep moats we arrived
Which fortify that City of Despair.
Its walls appeared to me as though of iron.

Dante leaves the monastery to become a student.

Not without making a wide circuit first
We reached a point at which the helmsman loud
Shouted: 'Here is the entrance; get you forth.'

Discordant jurists refusing access to any live mind.

Above the gates I saw innumerable
Beings rained down from Heaven who angrily
Cried: 'Who is this, that without Death goes through

[1] St. Luke, xi, 52.

' The Kingdom of the people (that are) dead? '
And my wise Master made a sign, as though
Desirous separately to talk with them.

Then they suppressed somewhat their great disdain,
And said: ' Come thou alone; let him be gone
' Who hath so valiantly entered this Realm.
' Let him, an if he knows, bring proof; for thou
' That led him to so dark a land shalt stay.'

They spurn
Reason and
invite Dante
to enslave it.

Imagine, Reader, if I were dismayed
At sound of the accursed words, for I
Believed not I should ever win back hence.

' O my beloved Leader, thou who more
' Than seven times hast brought me back to safety
' And rescued from deep peril facing me,
' Leave me not thus,' I said, ' undone. And if
' All farther progress be denied to us
' Swiftly let us retrace our steps together.'

Instinctive
recoil from
the conflict
with dogma.

That Lord who thither had conducted me
Said to me: ' Fear thou not; for none can take
' Our Pass from us, bestowed by One so mighty.
' But here await me: strengthen thou and feed
' Thy wearied spirit with good hope; in truth
' I will not leave thee in the Lower World.'

Abstract
Reason seeks
a foothold

Thus goes the gentle Father—leaves me here,
And I remain in doubt, for ' Yes ' and ' No '
Contend for mastery within my head.
I could not give assent to what they held.
But he not long stood there with them, when each
Betook himself to proof. They shut the gates,
These our opponents, on my Signor's breast,
Who stayed outside, and turned with lagging steps
Towards me. On the ground he kept his eyes
And of all boldness he had shorn his brows.

and is baffled.

With sighs he said: ' Who hath denied to me
' The doleful houses? ' And to me he said:
' Though I was wrath, yet be not thou dismayed.

Allusion to
the Pharisees
and lawyers
who strove
to bar the
gate of
Salvation.

' For I shall overcome the disputation
' Whoever may combine within for hindrance.
' Their overcogitation is not new.
' Once they employed it at less secret Gate
' Which still is found without a fastening.
' Over it thou didst see th' inscription dead.
' And even now descends this side the steep
' One, passing unescorted down the Circles,
' By whom the City shall be opened for us.'

There is a curious reference to Bologna in the Latin pastoral
with which Dante replied to a letter couched in similar form
from his disciple Giovanni del Virgilio about 1315. He wrote
in cryptic language, evidently with the design of concealing
his meaning from the authorities should the letter be opened.
Indeed, it would seem that he was surrounded by spies, for he
alludes to the manner in which he baffled politely one
Meliboeus who looked over his shoulder while he read the
letter. Giovanni had begged him to visit Bologna, and Dante
declined with some heat. He avoided mentioning any place
or person by name, disguising all under classical images.
Bologna, as the headquarters where the weapons of the Papal
Curia were forged, he transformed to Etna, ' where among
parched rocks in the caves of the Cyclops, the thunderbolts
of the gods are fashioned '. The place held by Etna in the
cosmogony of the ancients answered pretty closely to that held
by Bologna in the modern world. Here briefs, citations, bulls,
and sentences were forged. All the legal instruments by means
of which the Papal Curia made itself feared and obeyed issued
from Bologna as from an inexhaustible armoury. Rome was
merely the nominal centre of Christendom. Bologna was the
veritable City appertaining to Dis.

The enigmatic reference to Bologna in a private letter
affords a glimpse into the mode of secret writing forced upon
men of independent minds during this dark period of repression. The manner of it corresponds with the cryptic
record of his own life and times we have endeavoured to unfold in the *Inferno*. It remains to examine the disputed entrance of Dante and Virgil to the City of Dis, noting the many
curious details which suggest the identity of this infernal City
with Bologna University, stronghold of ecclesiastical lawyers.

Among Dante's first impressions of the University was a vision of 'Meschite', mosques or Mahommedan places of worship; the very professors who banished independent thought as heresy were themselves compelled to worship, as it were, at the shrine of Mahommedan scholars such as Averroes and Avicenna, translators of Aristotle, whom they believed to be burning in hell-fire.

The renowned university ' with its grave citizens and great company ', beheld from afar with reverence, resolved itself on a nearer view into an impassable barrier bristling with innumerable beings all insisting, as it were with one voice, that Dante should surrender his Reason to bondage. From the very beginning he found himself in a position of one waiting outside the barred gates of knowledge, while a despicable crew obstructed his forward path.

The objections raised were not to his presence but to his attitude. He was *alive*—eager to use eyes, ears, memory, above all Reason. And there was no room in the scheme of things at Bologna for any who were not *dead*.[1] He was sternly bidden to turn back in his path of folly; to weave if he had the skill a web of meaningless proofs (*provi se sa*), and above all to surrender Reason which had brought him to so gloomy a region. We find Dante laying aside for the moment all personal predilections, in order to apply abstract reason to the task before him, and are reminded of St. Augustine's attitude in a similar mental impasse: ' All this time I restrained my heart from assenting to anything, fearing to fall headlong, but by hanging in suspense I was worse off.'[2] Thus Reason pondered, unbiassed by will and desire, while a sub-current of assent and dissent, of 'yes' and 'no ',[3] left Dante in suspense. Reason was completely baffled.

[1] *Banquet*, IV, 7. ' In man living consists in the exercise of the reason. Hence if man's existence consists in his having life, to relinquish the exercise of reason is to relinquish his existence and so to become *dead*. . . . Some may say " how is he dead and yet walks? " I answer that the man is dead but the beast survives.'

[2] *Confessions*, vi, 14.

[3] The form of reasoning known as the *Sic et Non* was Abélard's famous exposition of knowledge. He applied it to a long list of apparent discrepancies and, without admitting that the Scriptures can err, claimed that we have perfect freedom of judgment and retain our right to dissent from doctrines even when supported by the Fathers of the Church.

Virgil retreated murmuring ' Who has denied me entrance to the houses of torment? ' (*le case dolenti*). We suggest that his dilemma amounted then to this, that Reason was rigidly excluded from any place in the Church's system of punishment. To examine the system under which men were subjected to penalties in this world and the next was pre-eminently within the province of Reason, and in Tartarus, as Virgil conceived it, punishment was meted out in accordance with men's deeds. All the denizens of his hell were criminals. It was far otherwise with the prisons to which saintly divines and righteous statesmen were relegated on suspicion of holding opinions obnoxious to authority. To these ' *case dolenti* ' Reason had no access.

The images employed by Dante in depicting this block to his onward progress are such as are familiar in every record of mental doubt and anguish. His feet were set in the midst of a swamp. Darkness brooded over the scene. Thick fog enveloped him. Iron walls and barred gates made advance impossible. Long drawn out expectation of he knew not what culminated in a suspense tinged with fear.

Some effort must be made to probe into the causes of the dread which possessed Dante in this stage of his journey. The story of the *New Life* bears repeated witness to the same dread, and allusions are made to it in the *Banquet* on divers occasions.[1] The part played by the Inquisition Courts in obstructing the mental development of Dante and his contemporaries must now be explored.

[1] *Banquet*, IV, 8. I who am speaking in this treatise in the presence of so many adversaries. . . . See also *Mon.*, Bk. III, I.

CHAPTER X

THE PENAL CODE OF THE CHURCH

[*Inferno IX*, 1-8; 31-68]

Procedure and power of the Inquisition Courts. Evil reputation of Inquisitors exposed in *Il Fiore*. Certain noted victims, 1272-1290. Satire of ecclesiastical courts veiled under image of the Furies. Sentence of excommunication pictured as the Gorgon's Head.

(Note on Erichtho, *Inferno IX*, 16-33)

IT is of the utmost importance for the right understanding of Dante's life and works to study the methods adopted by the rulers of the Church to retain their hold on the very large body of Christians who, moved by various reasons, were secretly renouncing allegiance to the Papacy.

From the moment of their first introduction in the twelfth century the Inquisition Courts had brought a new element of doubt and danger into the free cities of Italy. They were expressly designed to intensify the penal code of the Church, at all times fairly severe. The Bishops had always held power to try in their own courts all accused of disobedience in the performance of their religious duties, to exact fines, impose penances; in the last resort, to excommunicate, a sentence which meant ruin in this world and the next. But in a certain sense the Bishop as a temporal ruler with a local jurisdiction came to stand between his flock and the Curia. He was jealous of interference with his prerogative, and would often exercise his power for protection no less vigorously than for punishment. It might happen that he had Ghibelline leanings and was disposed to take a lenient view in matters of strict orthodoxy. In like manner a judicious Father Abbot might act as a father to his monks and protect them from molestation. When the Courts of the Bishop and the Abbot were superseded in matters of doctrine by that of Inquisitors appointed direct from Rome and very imperfectly supervised, citizens found themselves exposed without appeal to a secret, deadly, and irresponsible tribunal of unparalleled ferocity.

Those who read into the *New Life* merely a story of chivalrous devotion to a hopeless love and deduce from it a Florence gay and flourishing wherein, as in some idyllic May week at Cambridge, fair ladies diversified by their presence the sports and serious occupations of studious youths, have overlooked the fact that at the period to which it relates, the years immediately preceding 1290, the city was overshadowed by the horror of an intensive campaign of the Inquisition Courts.

Since the methods of the Inquisitors early became standardized, and varied little from one country to another, it is possible from researches made into the original registers of French Inquisitors to form a fairly clear notion of the system of terrorism employed. The first business of the Inquisitor in a city under suspicion, yet outwardly conforming to every requirement of the Holy See, was to obtain a sufficiently large list of 'suspects'. To this end a host of spies and informers was kept busy by the familiars or assistants of the Inquisitor in the endeavour to beguile the unwary into fatal confidences. Every individual was enjoined on peril of excommunication to give information to his Confessor and notice to the Inquisitor of any who departed from 'the common life, conversation and customs of the faithful'.[1] Husbands were required to denounce their wives, and wives their husbands; children to betray their parents. Convicted thieves, perjurers, and harlots, whose evidence was admitted in no other court, might traduce citizens against whom no other witnesses were forthcoming. But these were less to be feared than the treachery of close friends who knew the secrets of a man's heart.

The mode of trial in the Inquisitor's Court constituted an outrage on justice and humanity from beginning to end. Once accused, the victim was treated as guilty, and the proceedings were designed with diabolical ingenuity to extort confession and compel him to implicate others in his guilt.[2]

---

[1] Bull of Nicholas III, '*Noverit universitas vestras*', 1280. To love solitude, or to abstain from flesh meat, cheese, or strong drink was sufficient to provoke 'light' suspicion.

[2] The list compiled by the Inquisitors often assumed enormous proportions, and since none were ever safe whose name had once been inscribed, on however frivolous a pretext, it was not uncommon for insurrections to take place in which these fatal registers were seized and burnt.

He was entitled to hear what charge had been brought against him; it was his only privilege; but the names of witnesses were withheld on the pretext that reprisals might be attempted. If on interrogation in court the victim refused to admit that the accusation brought against him were true, or to betray the name of associates, he was relegated to another chamber, where, confronted with instruments of torture, he was again interrogated. If still obdurate, he (or she) was stripped of all clothing and subjected to such extremities of anguish as could be inflicted without external effusion of blood, actual mutilation or immediate death. The process might be gone through again and again with long or short intervals of harsh imprisonment intervening for, though torture might not legally be repeated, this availed little, the Inquisition Courts having decreed that it might be *continued*. Sometimes the accused was suffered after the first interrogation to remain in prison for long periods, extending in some recorded cases to ten or even twenty years, uncondemned, awaiting his trial. Numerous devices were invented to break his spirit, confuse him in his replies, and entrap him into a confession of guilt. Acquittal was very rare. Steadfastness in maintaining innocence under atrocious forms of torture was regarded as diabolical obstinacy to be punished with utmost rigour. Confessions of guilt provoked a continuance of torture to extort the names of fellow heretics. These confessions had to be repeated and signed by the victim, after a day or two, in order that the judge, by a base quibble, might certify that they had not been proffered under the influence of torture.

The penalties were designed not merely to punish but to stamp with perpetual ignominy. *Excommunication* in itself closed all professions, public offices, or lucrative employments against the accused. The excommunicate could not be admitted as a witness, nor succeed to property, nor collect his debts, nor sue in any court, nor be heard in his own defence against any accusation. In the case of a manumitted slave the emancipation was cancelled. The lightest penalty consisted in *Money Fines*, which were continually inflicted in spite of many edicts prohibiting them. The penance of ' *Pious Works* ', consisted in fines exacted for the erection of churches or monasteries. The sentence of ' *Flagellation* ' was extremely common. It was carried out in public with degrading accom-

paniments, usually on Sundays or holidays before the cele-
bration of High Mass, when the nearly naked penitents were
savagely scourged at different points on the route, and again
during the service in Church. The penalty of ' *Pilgrimages* '
might be either major or minor. The former were practically
sentences of banishment extending over periods of from two
to five years. The line of route to distant shrines, such as St.
James of Compostella, SS. Peter and Paul at Rome, St.
Thomas of Canterbury, was strictly prescribed; distinctive
apparel made the heretic pilgrim the object of scorn and fear,
and he was kept under observation wherever he went. The
sentence of wearing ' *Crosses* ' was far worse than it sounds.
The victim was compelled to sew two crosses of yellow felt,
two and a half palms long by two broad, on all his outer gar-
ments, and must never appear without them. The result was
to bring insult upon him wherever he showed his face and, in
fact, to put him under the ban of society, none daring to trade
or consort with him. All the above were reckoned minor
penalties.

The more serious sentences were *Total Confiscation* of all
property, a dangerously lucrative sentence for judges who
shared the proceeds in the proportion of one-third. *Perpetual
Imprisonment* had three degrees of severity. Under the lightest
form some degree of communication with the outside world
might be hoped for, if gaolers could be bribed, while food and
other comforts might possibly be received from friends.
Rigorous imprisonment involved complete isolation, chains,
and scanty diet, while the strictest of all plunged the victim
into an underground cell where, in darkness and most brutally
chained, with the ' bread and water of affliction ', he might possibly linger on for many years. The worst sentence of all,
though not always, alas, the least merciful, was delivery to the
hands of the civil authorities, who were allowed no choice in
the disposition of the culprit. It was their duty, under pain of
excommunication, to burn alive all heretics delivered up to
them.

Lastly, the Inquisition took pains to stretch forth its long
arm to involve in the persecution of its victims all their relations and dependants. As, for instance, all the sons (in the
case of male heretics, all grandsons also), even though yet unborn, were debarred from holding any office in the Church or

State. Children of manumitted slaves were reduced once more to a state of slavery by the conviction of father or mother. The very dwelling-place, with its precincts, of a heretic condemned to death was treated as infect. It might never be inhabited, nor could it even be pulled down and assigned to another owner without special permit from the Pope; in the wealthiest quarters of many cities were often desolate areas bearing witness to the terrors of the Inquisition. The judges did not disdain to wreak vengeance on the bodies of heretics condemned as such after death, when the corpse would be torn from the tomb, burnt with every circumstance of ignominy and its ashes scattered.

The conviction that Inquisitors were appointed in no sense to hold the scales of justice, but expressly to strike terror by condemnation, is established by the circumstance that their future advancement depended on the number of suspects they could procure and bring to ruin, while a third of the spoils brought in by fines and confiscations was delivered into their hands.

It was under the shadow of this awful menace that Dante and his comrades struggled for intellectual freedom. Against the dark background of the Inquisition, his Odes and Sonnets were composed. With innumerable adversaries on the watch to entangle him in argument and penetrate to the secrets of his inner life, he steadfastly sought a way by which he might press forward towards the truth. There were times, and to this the *New Life* no less than the *Inferno* bears abundant witness, when doubt overwhelmed him and his footing was well nigh gone.

THE BAN OF THE CHURCH

Inf., IX, 1-15.

That shade lent to my face by cowardice
When I beheld my Leader turn him back,
Sudden effaced his own new shade (of wrath).
He stopped attentive like a man who listens;
Because his eye could not carry him far
Through the black air of the dense ignorance.

' Yet must it be that we shall win the fight,
' Unless '—began he—' such appeared to us.
' Ah, what delay ere comes Another here.'

Reason flinches before the dread of excommunication.

169

I well perceived how he had covered up
His opening with the Other that came after
For these were words differing from the first.
But none the less his speech stirred terror in me,
Because perchance I turned his broken words
To a worse sentence than it really held.

We behold Dante oppressed by the labours of sustaining single-handed a mental contest in which every step forward threatened to stamp him as a heretic. He cast round to see if there were not one to stand by his side in his struggle to open the obstructed gate of knowledge, and his search for a kindred mind is typified in Virgil's attitude. He stood like a man who listens, very attentive, unable to see very far because of the darkness of ignorance. Had Dante been at this time more learned, had his reason been more exercised in sounding the minds of other writers, he might have perceived much to encourage him in this thick fog of doubt. But he was merely at the beginning of his lifetime of research. There was no one in his line of vision among his contemporaries who could reinforce his resistance to legal casuistry. He seemed to himself to stand absolutely alone. Meantime the dread of incurring excommunication pursued him, a ' worse sentence ' perchance than Reason held it to be, a phrase which seems to veil the perception that at this period he attached more weight to the Church's anathema than Reason justified.

Uncertain which way to turn, expecting he knew not what, Dante turned as often before to the pages of his Master for enlightenment. So obscure is his appeal to Virgil, so extraordinary the response, that it would almost appear to be inserted in the narrative in order to divert attention from the dangerous condition of mental perplexity suggested, and fasten it more securely on the ostensible Hell theme.

At critical moments, as for instance in the Prelude, Virgil seems to exchange the impersonal voice of Reason or Conscience for the authentic voice of the antique poet, transmitted through the medium of his own verse. The first grade in Dante's *Inferno* was Limbo, wherein he set in the gracious surroundings of the Elysian fields (quite contrary to orthodox doctrine) the souls of heathen poets and philosophers. We find him then in his hour of doubt questioning whether heathen philosophers had to go through a similar struggle with received opinion on their way towards truth, and Virgil, instancing his own experience, brought him encouragement, even though he was unable in his own person to force the barriers of ecclesiastical authority.[1]

Throughout the whole course of the Middle Ages no open allusion is made by any lay writer to the Inquisition Courts. Even in the pages of Chaucer, even in daring Ghibelline chronicles, and in the secret *Cronaca delle Tribolazioni* there is dead silence about this horrible tribunal which was able to petrify the whole world of letters. In the year 1881 a remarkable manuscript was discovered tacked on to an ancient copy of the *Roman de la Rose* in the library at Montpellier. It is in part a *rifacimento* of part of Jean de Meung's continuation of the *Roman de la Rose* and has been named ' The Flower ', but it contains a good deal of new matter dealing with the condition of the Church in Italy towards the close of the thirteenth century. Some Italian scholars of high repute detect in it the handiwork of Dante himself; in this the present writer is unable to concur. But certain passages reflect remarkably the bitter under-current of protest against ecclesiastical legal malpractices which we believe to be alluded to in the ninth canto of the *Inferno*, and depict with brutal directness the figures of evil Inquisitors. Owing to the extreme vigilance of ecclesiastical authority, ceaselessly exercised during many centuries, almost every scrap of evidence has been destroyed which could betray contemporary opinion about the measures of repression employed to subjugate the intellect of mankind. Many of the sonnets of *Il Fiore* are such as could never have seen the light; they must have been handed about in furtive secrecy with great precautions among the initiate only. The anonymous poet produces his strongest effects by setting the Inquisitor himself, under the name of False Pretences, to boast of his methods:

' I am one of the servants of Antichrist, one of those thieves *Il Fiore,* who, saith the Scripture, have a holy outside show and are one Sonnet 123. and all hypocrites. A pious lamb he seems when he is viewed; outside he puts on a gentle bearing; within he is a Wolf that devours the flock of Jesus Christ. Thus we hold sea and land

[1] See Note on Erichtho at end of chapter.

in our clutches; everywhere we publish our ordinances. He who observes it not we declare to err from the faith. Such great treachery have we done that all the world is at war with us. But we despatch them all to perdition.'

Sonnet 124.   ' I find out in City or in Castle, wherever a Patarin finds refuge. Do ye believe he is consoled thereby or rather not but is rebellious towards me? Whether he be a priest, or little clerk who keeps a mistress, or jolly prelate, through me must he be chastised. Each one stands in doubt about me so deadly dangerous am I. . . . From every one I have ill will. But whatsoever anguish thou feelst, thou wilt not speak. Thus powerfully do I deliver my judgment.'

Sonnet 125.   ' Such as would escape from my fury, behold now.' He enumerates many kinds of rich food and drink continuing: ' These are the things to gain my love. . . . When you shall have used such bait no need for you to proffer loud denials; say I am joking and joke with all the guests.'

Sonnet 126.   ' They who have not bethought them of such sort of armour as I have told you of, or of precious wines or of fine bags of florins, on them will my sentences be desperately heavy. Let them not put their trust still in the Scriptures. For let them make trial with my Masters of Divinity; I will prove that they are Patarins and will make them *feel the great flames*. Or at least I will so do that they are walled up, or will administer such hard penances that better were it they had not been born. At Prato, at Arezzo and at Florence many have I destroyed and banished. Wretched is that man who falls under my decrees.'

Sonnet 92.   ' All do I overthrow by my fraud.
               ' If there come any great scholar
               ' Who would uncover my crime,
               ' I confound him with all the force I possess.
               ' Master Sighier did not go long content;
               ' I made him die in great anguish (*a ghiado*)
               ' At the Court of Rome, at Orvieto.
               ' I made them cast out Master Guillaume from France
               ' The good Guillaume of Sant'Amor
               ' Banishing him with great uproar from the realm.'

This remarkable poem, rescued as by a miracle from destruction, presents the authentic spirit of the century which witnessed the developments of Inquisition methods; it illustrates the reign of terror inaugurated more especially in France and Italy, with its inevitable effect of rendering orthodox religion odious and undermining the spiritual forces of the Church. The practices enjoined upon Inquisitors were such as decent men in all ages have abhorred. It is perhaps misleading to assume of any past age that a lower conception of justice prevailed than that of civilized nations to-day. The ideals of the noble-minded Italian, trained to reverence Roman law, were not inferior to those of modern judges. But Inquisitors whose gains depended on the extent of their confiscations, and their office on the number of condemnations, would seem to have been selected, not by reason of their zeal for pure doctrine, but for their cunning and ferocity in tracking down their victims. These men were scorned and detested. In particular there is every reason to believe that their persecution of learned divines, students zealous in research, and young Franciscan monks who aspired to imitate the poverty and holiness of Francis, roused the most violent resentment, exaggerated by personal apprehensions, among the disciples and comrades of the victims.

Every student of the *Roman de la Rose* must have been struck by the remarkable anger and contempt it displays against a certain section of the Mendicant Orders, clearly distinguished from the worthy Friars ' serving their Lord in praise and prayer'. The accusations made against these Friars are, indeed, extraordinary. They can be understood only under the supposition that they are directed against those Dominicans and Franciscans, with their underlings, to whom the Holy Office had been committed. A brief résumé of the charges made against these officials will suffice to show that they could hardly have been levelled against any ordinary body of monks:

1. They inspire the prelates or bishops with great fear:

> ' No prelate dare my work defeat,
> ' Saving our Lord the Pope alone,
> ' From whom this privilege was won.' (11932 ff.)

2. They have power to appease people by granting remission from every kind of sin and flouting every law:

> ' Though royal or imperial
> ' No one dare 'gainst me judgment give,
> ' Exempted from their rule I live.' (11791 ff.)

3. They have a vast and powerful organization. Friar Louveteau, the chief [Inquisitor] can procure Bulls from the Pope himself, ' cite you before the Court And ruin you in two short days '.

4. They have enormous wealth:

> ' Their hoard might buy St. Peter's Chair.'

5. Their jurisdiction extends over the whole world:

> ' *Curate to all the world am I*
> ' But from the Pope a Bull I've got,
> ' For he, good man, suspects me not.'

6. They disclose the secrets of the Confessional—a monstrous crime yet enjoined on Inquisitors. (12250 ff.)

7. If exposed in their iniquities or refused a bribe they set on foot a secret campaign of deadly calumny:

>   ' We'll bring
> ' Against him such a grievous string
> ' Of crimes that if not burned alive
> ' He will but wretchedly survive
> ' Beneath a penance of a kind
> ' That heavier tax than doles he'll find.' (12438 ff.)

8. They are the servants of Antichrist. (12369.)

9. They have unlimited powers over all, and threaten if resisted:

>   ' Round his neck I'll fit
> ' A cord and drag him to the stake
> ' E'en though his howls the city shake,
> ' Or to deep cell will have him cast
> ' To languish till his life be past.'

All these powers were notoriously exercised by the Inquisi-- tors who wrung privileges and authority from successive Popes until they were able secretly to dominate all Christen-- dom. But the Friars, apart from this malign element which permeated both Orders, possessed no such powers. Some no, doubt were licentious and preyed upon the poor, but the crimes attributed by Jean de Meung to their confrères were entirely outside their range.

Paris was for a long time the storm centre. Its theological faculty had attracted great minds to demonstrate the unity of ¯ truth, and attempt to harmonize Aristotelian philosophy with the dogmas of the Church. It was a dangerous line of re-- search. The demonstrations of Thomas Aquinas awakened on the one hand dark suspicions of his orthodoxy among wary authorities, and on the other hand provoked acute students of Aristotle to detect flaws in the supposed harmony. Attention was closely concentrated on the distinction between demon- strable truths and dogmatic assertions. The authorities took fright. Edicts were made in 1272 and again in 1275 to pro-- hibit discussions on questions impinging on faith. The only result was to drive the forward party to meet in secret. A further edict prohibited any master or bachelor of any faculty from reading any books save grammar or logic in. private places.

Before his death in 1274 Thomas had prohibited the students from speaking *in corners* of the point at issue. A dread of free discussion possessed the authorities, and provoked savage measures of repression which had the inevitable result of stimulating ' the art of dissimulation '. Some light is thrown on prevailing conditions in the Church by the edict of the Papal Legate in Paris, excommunicating, among others, ' ecclesiastics who during Divine Office throw dice on the Altars and blaspheme the name of God, the Virgin and the Saints, not without marked heretical depravity '. So nervous had the authorities become that the orthodoxy of Thomas Aquinas was openly impugned. The Bishop of Paris making inquiry at the Pope's request into the state of the University condemned over two hundred propositions, and struck no less at the doctrines of Thomas than of his opponents. Censure of Thomas found expression at Oxford, and the Archbishop of Canterbury condemned thirty propositions closely connected with his teaching. It was now that the policy of repression began to intensify. In 1277 the Generals of the Dominicans and Franciscans met in Paris to ratify accord between the two Orders. The Franciscan General, Jerome d'Ascoli, afterwards Pope Nicholas IV, under the advice of certain minor Friars, ' condemned and reprobated the doctrine of Friar Roger Bacon, Englishman, master of Sacred Theology, containing certain suspicious novelties', on which account the said Roger Bacon (he was then about sixty-three) was condemned to perpetual prison.

In the same year Simon du Val, Inquisitor of France, cited Siger de Brabant, together with a certain Canon of Liége, ' probably and vehemently suspected of having committed the crime of heresy ' in the Kingdom of France ' to make reply touching their faith. Siger, as is revealed in *Il Fiore*, was judged and condemned at the Court of Rome so that he must have appealed to the Pope. Dante's allusion to him in the *Paradiso* proves that his death was slow and agonizing, and Mandonnet conjectures that he was sentenced to prison in perpetuity, a cell underground, darkness, chains, the bread and water of affliction. The death he so earnestly craved visited him in 1284, or shortly before, as is proved by an allusion to it in a letter of Archbishop Peckham of that date.

The impression made upon the Universities by these sensational prosecutions may be imagined. A bond of common enthusiasm and belief-linked students ' of sane intellects ' in France, Italy, England, and Germany. The same illimitable power, backed by tribunals which played the punitive part allotted by Virgil to the Furies in Tartarus, now threatened them all. Hitherto the Inquisition had sought to terrorize the multitude by arraigning peasants and burghers, with selected victims from the rank and file of priests and monks who displayed suspicious symptoms of religious fervour. The attack on Siger, coupled with the imprisonment of Bacon, was a demonstration of hostility towards all abstract speculation and research. It was followed up by a wave of intense activity on the part of Inquisitors which culminated when Jerome d'Ascoli, the Franciscan General who had persecuted Bacon, was made Pope under the title of Nicholas IV in 1288. Under his auspices a veritable reign of terror succeeded among the Franciscans, including the seculars or the Tertiary Order, who were now brought under Papal jurisdiction. Heads of communities were charged to bring to the notice of the Inquisition all monks, and specially the younger members of the Orders, who were tainted with the doctrines known as Spiritual. Not learning only but devotion to the ancient ideals of Francis became suspect. The minor offence of ' allowing oneself to be suspected ' was created. The spy system was organized to a terrible pitch of efficiency, and the Sonnets of the period bear witness to the existence of ' false lovers ' in whose presence caution was enjoined.[1]

It may readily be supposed that a good deal of friction was set stirring between the Inquisition Courts, with their powers of confiscating all the goods of heretics, and the civil authorities. Great discord in addition ensued between the Bishops and the Inquisitors. Their relations with each other were not settled till the Council of Vienne in 1309, and meantime though nominally the Bishop and Inquisitor worked together, the concurrence of the Bishop in the sentences pronounced was a mere formality, and the Chief Inquisitor held practically unlimited power. Philip of France was roused in 1301 to make a strong protest against his subjects being delivered over to the judgment or imagination of one sole person, possibly ignorant and influenced by passion; the protest was occasioned by the complaints made against the Inquisitor at Toulouse for his extortions. Unprecedented outrages had caused horrible suffering to many imprisoned under pretext of heresy in order to make them confess crimes they had not committed.

In his record of personal experience, Dante depicted above in a perfectly comprehensible manner the darkness which brooded over his student days, his perception of hidden dangers threatening destruction, the complete check on any forward movement produced by the powerful organization confronting him. In the sudden vision of the Furies swooping down to an attack—not on himself but on some other daring spirit—we believe him to have ventured on a symbolic presentment of the ecclesiastical courts, ready to confound all who fell under suspicion of disloyalty to Rome.

[1] Guido Cavalcanti warns Dante not to trust Lapo Gianni.

ALLEGORIC VISION OF ECCLESIASTICAL COURTS

Inf., IX, 31-63.

(Virgil continues:)
' This swamp emitting the great stench begirds
' The wretched city round, where without wrath
' We may not enter now.' And more he said,
But in my memory I hold it not.

The Law.

Rival Courts
of Justice.

Because my eye had wholly drawn me towards
The lofty Tower with flaming summit where
At one spot sudden there were (Codes of) Rights
(Like to) three hellish furies, stained with blood,
Their charters despicable and their deeds.
Circled they were with snakes most venomous;
They wore, instead of hair, vipers with horns
Wherewith their cruel courts of law abounded.

¹ The Curia.

And he, who knew full well the hand-maidens
Belonging to the Queen of Endless Tears ¹
Said to me: ' Mark the fierce Erinnyes.
' This is Megæra on the left-hand side.
' She is Alecto on the right, that weeps;
' Tisiphone is in the midst.' At that,
The mighty one, he held his peace.
Each her own breast was rending with her claws;
They smote each other for the victory;
And shrieked so loud that in my fear I pressed
Close to the Poet. Then gazing below
' Let come Medusa ', one and all they said;
' This shall turn him into stone; for ill
' Did we avenge on Theseus his assault '.

' Do thou turn backward, and thine eyes keep closed,
' For if the Gorgon shows and thou perceive her
' There would be no returning up again.'
Thus said the Master, turned me round himself,
And did not hold my hands, for he as yet
Had not completely circled me with his.

O ye that have sane intellects, admire
The doctrine that is hidden neath the veil
Of the strained verses.

The swiftness of the attack, the tumult of noise which echoes through the rhythm of the verse, the tangle of venomous reptiles, the vivid colouring thrown into high relief by the flaming summit of the Tower as contrasted with the dun shadows round the poets, the bloodthirsty rage of the attacking three, finally their violent invocation of a resistless fatal power, all serve to make up a scene which renews its horror at every fresh perusal.

The most conspicuous feature of Bologna, the City of Dis, was the lofty Tower with its glowing summit which symbolized one sacred immutable Law. The Tower of Law was the necessary corollary to the Tower of Knowledge, and Dante had already beheld signals flashing from one to the other beckoning to him across the waters of strife that he might come to a fuller knowledge of God's eternal purpose for man. Fire is the symbol of the law since Moses set it before the children of Israel 'flaming in God's Right Hand '.[1] Later in life, when he had come to a higher understanding of Imperial Law, Dante boldly declared:

' Now let the presumptuous jurists see how far they stand below the *WATCH TOWER* of Reason (Law) when the human mind surveys these principles [of Imperial rule] and let them hold their peace.' [2] He rebuked the lawyers or *Legis-periti* in the same treatise for issuing out of their boundaries and over-running the encampment of others; ' understanding naught themselves and in no degree understood, they provoke some to anger, some to scorn, and some to laughter.' [3] Was not this very much what Virgil meant when he told his disciple none could enter the citadel of the Papal Curia or contemplate the Canon Law at Bologna, without anger?

The great Watch Tower of Reason, God's Law, which ostensibly was the pivot round which the learning of the University revolved, had been neglected and forgotten. In its place, arising out of it as by some infernal jugglery, there became visible to the student's eyes three fiercely contending *Furies* which set themselves up above it, and contended fiercely for the mastery one with the other. Difficult as it is to see eye to eye with the medieval in his impressions of the institutions

---

[1] Deut., xxxiii, 2. Fire destroys the evil and tests the good.
[2] *Mon.*, Bk. II, 11.   [3] *Ibid.*, Bk. III, 3.

of his own day, it is possible, nevertheless, to grasp the main lines of the allegory. For there were three Handmaids of the Papal Curia, contending jurisdictions [*Diritte*] under which the people were oppressed: (1) the episcopal; (2) the monastic; (3) the Inquisition. These three were at variance. All were blood-stained. All were jealous of their privileges, and more concerned to extend them than to administer justice. All three had their courts,[1] ' temples ' which abounded with the horned serpents [2] Dante introduced in *Inferno*, xxv, as typical of sacrilegious thieves. The membra [3] or charters of the Furies were *femminili*[4] or contemptible and, indeed, the frequent forgeries of the period had weakened their value.

In contrast with the feebleness of their legal titles they were girt with hydras which were ' *verdissimi* ' or intensely vigorous. And these seem to typify the claims they put forth against their victims which were of such a nature that as soon as one was demolished others sprang up in its place.

The activities of these fierce rival jurisdictions corresponded strangely to the function exercised in the heathen cosmogony by the Furies, handmaids of Dis. It was in their province to punish men both in this world and the next. Virgil supplied the comment on their proceedings with extreme caution, and the interpretation is offered as merely conjectural. Alecto standing on the right hand, may be considered from that position to be the most legitimate of the three, and by the fact that she was wailing it may be presumed that she was labouring under a sense of injury because the others had the upper hand. She may therefore stand for the episcopal rights, seriously encroached upon by the new penal measures devised by the Curia.

Possibly Megæra on the left may indicate the ever-increas-

---

[1] The word ' temple ' was used either of the forehead (Lat. *tempora*), or of a building (Lat. *templum*) often legal in character. Latin plurals in ' a ' became either masculine or feminine in early Italian.

[2] The ' Ceraste ' were horned vipers, and it will be noticed how often in the *Inferno* the horn (cornu) is used as a distinctive mark of the demons. The biretta worn by ecclesiastics and professors was horned. Med. Lat. corneta, Fr. Cornette.

[3] Membra was contracted from membrana—a parchment or deed. *Vide* Ducange.

[4] ' Femminis ' is often used allegorically in the classics for weak or despicable. *Vide* Facciolati.

ing power exercised by the 'regular' ecclesiastics. Of the ferocity of the penal courts to which monks were subject within their respective orders there are many testimonies. There were undrained dungeons deep underground, ponderous chains to affix the victims to the ground, long intervals during which even the bread and water of affliction were withheld; penances which just stopped short of death penalty; finally for the condemned the ghastly process of enmuring.

There remains Tisiphone. Enough has been said above of the terrible tribunal which usurped so often the functions of the other ecclesiastical courts. None dared mention the Inquisition Courts. They had become the central figure in the administration of justice by the easy device of bestowing the name of heresy on any crime at will. Reason was silent in this awful presence.

At the moment when the attention of Dante was suddenly called to these contending authorities, they were for once united against an unnamed offender. They were rending their own breasts with their hooked claws, a sign that they were engaged upon something illegal, and were urging themselves on to victory (*a palme*). One and all shrieked: 'Let Medusa come, so will we turn him to stone.'

It was in the usual course of events for the courts to invoke excommunication against offenders who could not be reached in other ways.

The Gorgon's Head appears to be an excellent image of the MEDUSA. rite of excommunication as abused in this epoch. As originally used in the Church it was a ceremony whereby members of the Christian community might eject any who openly discredited their profession of faith. But as a frequent political weapon of the Papacy it had been gradually reduced to a grotesque though still formidable engine, capable of inspiring terror but incapable of acting as a restraint. The curse of the Church lost in dignity as it gained in vituperation.

The practical inconveniences of being excommunicated were numerous. Almost every form of advancement centred in the Church save the profession of arms. Under excommunication no doctor or lawyer could hope for a clientèle, no trader for custom, no author even for personal safety, no landowner for the collection of his rents. The Ghibelline Leaders who defied excommunication were perpetually restless under it, and strove for a remission of their sentence with all the resources they could command. While the ribald jested they feared. They told each other they did not believe in the efficacy of the curse and could point to many notorious fiascos in its working. But they shunned it with remarkable dexterity. As a horrible bogey, appealing to overwhelming currents of superstition in the minds of the vulgar, it made men shudder. Its vaunted power to turn men to stone, and shut the doors of mercy irrevocably in time and eternity, rendered it a veritable Gorgon's Head on which no man could look and live.

Over Dante and his like, men of religious fervour, passionately attached to their Church, but awakening to a consciousness of its misgovernment, it hovered as a fateful penalty invoked in the last resort by every ecclesiastical authority. It had power to sweep away all that they counted dear in life, intellectual progress, individual advancement, every outlet to service in the State, every spiritual privilege. We behold Dante in the midst of his intellectual revolt bowing like the rest before the portent.

'And he did not hold on to my hands, for with his own he had not yet closed me about.' Reason had *not yet* firmly grasped him by the hand, to be his shelter from vain fears. Such it may be inferred was the doctrine which the poet bid his disciples set themselves to discover in his strained verses.

Appendix to Chapter X

Inf., IX, 16-33.

VIRGIL AND ERICHTHO

'Doth there ever descend to this deep place
'Within the dreary shell, any who come
'From the First Grade, where as sole penalty
'Hope is cut short?' Thus I questioned him;
And he replied: 'Rarely it happeneth
'One of us take the road I go upon.
'True is it once before I was down here
'Evoked by that crude Thessalian witch
'Who summoned back the shades into their bodies.
'Not long in being was my flesh forlorn
'When she compelled me pass within that wall
'To bring a spirit from the Traitor's Circle.

'That is the lowest spot, the most obscure,
'The farthest from the Heaven which circles all.
'Well do I know the way. Be reassured.
'This swamp, emitting the great stench, begirds
'The wretched City round, where without wrath
'We may not enter now.'

Dante was fully aware by this time that Virgil, personifying Reason, had come to an end of his resources. These eminently unreasonable adversaries were not to be dominated by argument. Intensely lonely, he hungered for a kindred spirit, and sought blindly yet not without hope for another Guide.

It was while seeking for this 'other' that Dante turned to the pages of Virgil, and interrogated his favourite author as to whether he himself or any other of the ancients relegated by the Church to Limbo had ever gone through a similar experience.

ERICHTHO
THE MUSE.

Virgil's reply, literally understood, was most extraordinary. The usual explanation suggested is that Erichtho, a sorceress of Thessaly, named by Lucan but, so far as is known, by nobody else, had shortly after Virgil's death used her magic arts to compel him to go down to the bottom of hell to bring up the ghost of a traitor whose name is not mentioned. Dante did not leave the reader in doubt as to Virgil's opinion of witches, and it is surely a perversion of the philosophy attributed to him throughout the *Divina Commedia* to attribute to him belief in the power of Erichtho to dispatch him on such an errand. The obvious thing for Erichtho to do was to conjure up the spirit of the traitor for herself if she could. In this as in so many instances throughout the *Inferno* the surface meaning is sacrificed to the higher claims of the allegory. The reader is driven, probably by the express intention of the author, here designedly obscure, to the conviction that this cannot be the true meaning of the passage.

The First Grade in Dante's *Inferno* was Limbo, in which he garnered (contrary to orthodox doctrine) the souls of heathen poets and philosophers.

The query amounted to this: 'Did heathen philosophers go through the struggle against received opinion, or is this the portion only of the Christian?' Virgil had no hesitation in replying that very few of the ancients had been exposed to this kind of trial. Then to console Dante he related how in his own youth he too had wrestled with doubt, so that the citadel before which they stood was for him no untrodden path.

' *Di poco era di me la carne nuda.*'

The words can be rendered either as: ' When the flesh had been naked of me but a short while', that is, *soon after I died*, and this is the conventional interpretation; or, ' When the naked flesh of me had subsisted but a short while', that is: ' While I was still but a very young man,' and this is the sense which accords with the allegorical meaning:

' *Ver è ch'altra fiata quaggiù fui.*'

' True is it that once I was below here' (before the gates of the citadel of doubt).

' *Congiurato da quella Eriton cruda*
' *Che richiamava l'ombre a' corpi sui.*'

' Under the spell of that crude Thessalian witch who was wont to call back the shades to their bodies.' Thessaly was the home of the Muse and the crude Muse is the Muse of a young man as Virgil was when he wrote the *Ciris*. Like Dante himself he could, indeed, compel the shades to resume the very habit in which they lived. And so Virgil is relating that as a very young man, when his Muse was immature, he had actually under her influence penetrated to the gates of this castle of human errors, and plunged so deep into the secrets of human crime that he had depicted an example of the worst form of treachery, such as would one day be exposed to Dante's eyes in the circle of Judas.

Dante had betaken himself to wondering whether his great Master had had to struggle through difficulties similar to those he was experiencing. The amazing vitality of these frequent self-communings, which take the form of dialogues between Dante and Virgil, is due to the dramatic power which never lost sight of Virgil's own personality, even when the question and answer echoed the most intimate strivings of Dante's own soul. Was it possible that even before the Christian era this desolate encounter with the forces of authority had been experienced by those whose wisdom Dante revered? He found small trace of such doubts in the writings of the ancients, ' Rarely do they descend to the spot'. But in the works of Virgil there is one conspicuous allusion to his having in early youth trod the same path which Dante was now following, and tasted the same difficulties. '*True is it that I was once before below here.*' It would appear then that Dante derived encouragement in that great encounter with false opinion by the discovery that Virgil too, when a young man, had pursued investigations of a similar bewildering nature into the errors of mankind. And to enlighten the reader who might be puzzled to find in the works of Virgil the passage referred to, Dante put into his mouth the further detail that this condition of philosophic doubt, on Virgil's part, was connected with the production of a poem depicting an instance of exaggerated treachery. We have now only to enquire: ' Did Virgil in his youth compose a poem containing indications of some such mental crisis as Dante depicts in the eighth and ninth cantos of the *Inferno*, and was this in any way connected with the story of a cruel traitor guilty of betraying a benefactor? '

The point we have now reached is the point where facts seem at first entirely to fail. The *Æneid*, the *Georgics*, the *Eclogues*, even the more authentic minor poems of Virgil, present no such strong indications, as are alluded to in the text, of his acquaintance with philosophic doubt, nor does any one of them contain for a principal character, a denizen of the circle of Judas. But one poem had been overlooked, the poem, now no longer attributed to Virgil, known as the *Ciris*. When once this had been mastered, all difficulties vanished. In Dante's day the authenticity of the *Ciris* as the work of Virgil had never been called in question. Indeed, so late as the seventeenth century it is mentioned by Dryden in his *Life of Virgil* as an authentic work. The *Ciris* recounts the mythus of Scylla, daughter of Nisus, King of Megara. When Megara was besieged by Minos, Scylla was taken with so great a passion for the invader, that she pulled out the hyacinthine lock on the top of her father's head on which she knew his life depended, his ' exterior soul ' in short, and surrendered the city to Minos. In disgust at her treachery Minos fastened her to the poop of his vessel and drowned her in the depths of the sea. Here then is the wretch from the circle of Judas whom the Muse compelled Virgil to clothe anew with flesh and blood. And oddly enough Virgil writes as if the Muse had

compelled him to the subject against his own will and inclina-
tions. In the sense of being inspired by a ' crude ' Muse, the
poem speaks with no uncertain voice. It is a poor performance even when full allowance is made for the deplorably
corrupt condition of the text. In dedicating it to Messala,
Virgil apologized for its deficiencies in the following terms:

' Since I am now first being born to these great arts, since
I now first strengthen my muscles to this end. Accept these
early rudiments of youth.'

The lines were held as evidence that the poem was the first
Virgil ever attempted. Finally we find conclusive evidence
that the poem was composed during a period of intense mental
depression which justified Dante in regarding it as parallel to
his own night of anguish and *pietà*. In recapitulating the
causes of his love, Virgil complains he has been plagued by
empty desire of glory. He has found by experience the vanity
of the rewards yielded by the deceptive mob. His Muse, girt
for very different studies and toils, rises higher to the stars of
the great universe, and has dared to ascend the Mount (of
scientific investigation) which has charms for few. Then he
goes on to allude to his aspirations after philosophic truth, and
his struggles to obtain a survey of the *errors of all mankind*, in
order that he might despise the sordid cares of the world.

These are just such allusions to personal difficulties and
perplexities as can be passed over unheeding by a generation
no longer interested in Virgil's inner history, but were
fraught with intense concern to disciples who pored over his
works intent on gleaning every rare reference to the working
of the Master's mind. That Virgil should confess to turning
reluctantly under controlling influence of the Muse from deep
philosophic researches into the nature of human error, in
order to make his first poetic attempt, was a fact of tremendous
import to one at least of his disciples. Unless we can constrain
ourselves to behold Virgil for a moment with medieval eyes
we miss the entire force of this remarkable incident, the most
perplexing reference to Virgil which occurs throughout the
Divina Commedia.

CHAPTER XI

THE WITNESS OF OLIVI

[Inferno IX, 64-105. Before the City of Dis]

Suggested identification of the Divine Ambassador with the Spiritual leader Petrus Johannis Olivi, Leader of the Spiritual Party in the Church; corresponding incidents in his life and character. Parallel between Dante's imagery and that used by Jean de Meung in the *Roman de la Rose*.

Period covered: 1286-7.

Corresponding hour: about 2.20-40 a.m.

CONFRONTED BY perils from which Reason was powerless to deliver him, Dante remained, so he intimates, steadfastly fixed in his purpose of intellectual progress—in other words he was bent on pressing forward with Virgil. The impersonal character of the adversaries massed against him suggest that they represent the innumerable host of orthodox commentators, tutors, professors, whose combined utterances made up the course of instruction permitted, with the result that they effectually barred the gates of knowledge in the face of inquiring students. There is no indication of the length of time he spent in this gloom and uncertainty. It may possibly have lasted all the time he was at Bologna, for the gates when opened at last gave no entrance to a city but merely to a cemetery. He is not the only one who has found himself beating against impalpable barriers in the quest for knowledge. It is clearly suggested that the beings who denied Dante the use of his own Reason were strongly reinforced by infernal agents, to whose fatal machinations he believed himself to be in danger of falling a victim. In this hour of despair he witnessed the arrival of an ambassador of God who quelled his despicable opponents, proved that there were in reality no bars at all on the gates, and sent Dante on his way rejoicing.

187

THE MESSENGER OF GOD

Inf., IX, 64-105.

Blast of
popular in-
dignation
against the
jurists.

And now across the turbid waves there came
A tumult of a sound fraught with alarm
Whereat the parapets both trembled;
No otherwise affected than by a blast
Set stirring violently by adverse passions
That without any pause attacks the Wood,
Shatters the boughs, beats down and bears them off;
Sweeping the dust in front, it goes superb
And puts to flight wild beasts and pastors both.

He loosed my eyes and said: ' Now turn about

Their
discomfiture.

' Thy nerve of vision, through that ancient scum
' Where the smoke lies most pungent, yonder there.'

As frogs before the serpent adversary
Scatter them through the water, running all
Until each one squats huddled on the ground,
Thus saw I myriads of souls destroyed

Ambassador
of God
recognized
by Reason.

Flee before One who at the (ferry) Pass
With soles unwetted passed over the Styx.
He waved from off his face that unctuous air
Moving it with his left hand constantly;
By that affliction solely seemed he tired.
Full well I knew him for a Messenger
From Heaven, and I turned me to my Master;
And he made sign to me I should stand quiet.
Moreover that I should bow down to him.
Oh, how he seemed to me full of disdain;
He reached the Gate, and with a little rod
He opened it;—it had no fastening.

His rebuke
to those who
obstructed
intellectual
advance.

' O despicable crew, shut out from Heaven,'
Upon the threshold he began;
' Whence is the cause this over-cogitation

Allusion to
punitive code
as super-
seded.

' Allures you thus? Why do you kick against
' That Will whose end can never be frustrate,
' And many times hath added to your grief?
' What profits it to butt against the Fates?
' Your Cerberus if you remember well,
' Still beareth chin and throat all shorn from this.'

Then through the filthy way he turned him back, *His recall.*
And spake no words to us, but had the air
Of one restrained, bitten by other care
Than that of him who stands in front of him.

And we moved our feet on towards the City *Reassurance*
In confidence after his holy words. *of Dante after*
hearing his
message.

We venture to suggest that the ambassador of God who de-livered Dante from the powers of darkness may have been the famous Apostle of the Spiritual movement, Petrus Johannis Olivi, round whom one of the fiercest legal battles of this epoch was waged. When he defeated the jurists on their own ground, and was acquitted of any taint of heresy by the tribunal summoned to condemn him, an immense wave of enthusiasm uplifted the vast company of his disciples. It seemed that the battle against old abuses had been won. On the crest of this wave came the election of Pope Celestine V in 1294. Men held it for certain that the New Age of the Spirit was about to dawn.

It was no part of Dante's scheme to unfold in the *Inferno* the mysteries of the New Age. But he could, and we believe that he did, in recording some of the main incidents of his own life, present a vivid allegorical description of the gloom which enwrapped him when he first became acquainted with the limitations imposed by authority on any intellectual advance. And he could introduce with telling effect into his narrative the impression made on his mind by the leading liberating personality of his age. He shows in a parable, which is strongly reminiscent of the figurative language common to Olivi and his disciples, the popular tumult occasioned by the master's acquittal. He depicts ironically the alarm of the jurists when their stronghold was shaken and seemed likely to be overthrown; the blast of public indignation, generated by adverse passions, which burst against the Wood, symbol of Guelf materialism; the flight of the wild beasts posing as shepherds, the pitiful state of the loquacious Decretalists collapsing like frightened frogs before their wise adversary.

The Deliverer is represented in the act of rebuke, wielding the rod of the teacher, defending himself with the left or less worthy hand from the unctuous vapour (of false accusation) which obscured his face—a weary task which had for years sapped the energies of Olivi. For the right-hand was the higher task of setting down the oracles of God for the enlightenment of the faithful.

Dante accepted him instantly as a Divine messenger. Reason not only approved but induced a reverent attitude as towards one inspired by God. It was the mark of the true Apostle, the perfected, to set stirring in the disciple instant inward recognition of his Divine authority.

The Master made himself known on this occasion solely by the scathing force of the rebuke he administered to those who barred the gates of knowledge, while within (as discovered later) they were busy building the sepulchres of the prophets they had done to death.[1]

Almost every sentence in Olivi's authentic utterances is derived from Holy Scripture, which was the base of all allegorical writings and the justification for the symbolic use of language.

He came calming the tumult, his feet unstained by strife, and before his restraining presence the Furies were momentarily quelled. It was not solely against them but against that which called them into being that he directed his wrath. ' *Your* Cerberus ' he proclaimed as the source of the whole mischief.

In Cerberus, shorn of dignity and for ever degraded by Hercules (who under many aspects of his career presents a figure of Christ Himself) it seems we are to recognize the Law in the evil ecclesiastical sense associated with it by S. Paul. This was the purely punitive law, designed to hold men in subjection. It embodied the corrupt elements of priestcraft as manifested first in the Jewish and later in the Carnal Christian Church. It was the Law which ' worketh wrath ' [2]; the Law which constitutes ' the strength of sin '; [3] the Law

---

[1] See S. Luke, xi, 47-52. ' Woe unto you! for ye build the sepulchres of the prophets, and your fathers killed them. Therefore also said the wisdom of God, I will send them prophets and apostles, and some of them they shall slay and persecute: That the blood of all the prophets— may be required of this generation.—Woe unto you lawyers, for ye have taken away the key of knowledge; ye enter not in yourselves, and them that were entering in ye hinder.'

[2] Romans, iv, 15.   [3] 1 Corinthians, xv, 56.

which is the curse from which Christ has redeemed us; [1] the Law of ' commandments in ordinances ' which Christ has abolished. [2] This conception of Cerberus is less far-fetched than may appear at first sight.

The figure of Cerberus is found in the *Roman de la Rose* in a ôle corresponding very closely to that which it holds in the *Inferno*, with the Furies as its coadjutor. Cerberus is first encountered in the *Inferno* as the agent of Dis (the Papal Curia). His office is to keep in subjection and afflict with disgusting penances the merely sensual offenders, guilty of breaking the fasts ordained by the Church and thus rebelling against authority. Later in the journey of life Dante witnessed before the City of Dis the fate of such as committed graver offences against ecclesiastical law—men who resisted the usurping claims of the Curia or had persisted in the exercise of their own intellect. Against them the Furies raged, petrifying them with the great Curse. But we are made to understand by the Messenger that it was Cerberus who had set the Furies in motion, and that they acted under his orders.

It was to Petrus Johannis Olivi that men of all degrees, at this time, and more particularly the young intellectuals, were looking as their champion against the oppression of the ecclesiastical code.

Olivi was a Franciscan monk of Provence, who by the vigour of his intellect had early gained distinction in his own Order, and became in course of time the most famous exponent of the Gospel of Divine Love. By virtue of his singular magnetic charm he communicated his own zeal to all who came in contact with him. It was his great aim to restore in his Order the ideals of Francis, whose doctrine of Holy Poverty restricted the monks to the simplest necessaries of food, drink, clothing, and shelter. Great offence was given by Olivi's ardour for Holy Poverty to the most influential section of the Order, men who recoiled from austerity of life and claimed that since the real owner of all the Franciscan possessions was Holy Church, the monks were at liberty to enjoy the use of whatever the Pope might allow them. On this account Olivi was bitterly attacked within his own Order. Moreover he exposed with entire frankness the vices which disgraced monks and priests and prelates. They were too

---

[1] Galatians, iii, 13.   [2] Ephesians, ii, 15.

notorious to be controverted. Yet there are many indications that his message was by no means wholly minatory; it brought into men's hearts a new and spiritual conception of Christianity based upon Divine Love which completely altered the lives of all who accepted it in sincerity, and led them cheerfully to endure every kind of persecution under the radiance of its great light.

In these controversies it was never thought advisable by ecclesiastics to bring the real matters at issue into the open. It was impossible to attack Olivi's main doctrines, his plea for a return to Gospel simplicity and purity under the in-dwelling power of the Holy Spirit. It was even inadvisable to press against him his insistence on the life of poverty within the cloisters lest men might suspect the Order of laxness. But it was comparatively easy in the case of a voluminous writer and preacher to pick out propositions open to objection. No form of expression has ever proved more efficacious either for disguising or for imputing opinions than the scholastic. The Parisian doctors, skilled in this extraordinary method of com-plicating plain statements, had already sent Siger to his death at the hands of Inquisitors by the path of the syllogism. They now compassed the destruction of Olivi by the same means. The storm broke on the occasion of the General Meeting of the Franciscan Order at Strasburg in 1282, when Olivi was confronted with twenty-four questions relating chiefly to philosophic definitions. For five years he was interrogated at intervals, his writings were sequestrated, his appeals for an opportunity of vindicating himself were set aside. In his de-fence he plainly declared that the decrees of the Parisian doctors, though worthy of respect, were not infallible, and that the formal doctrinal decisions of the Roman See were alone entitled to unconditional acceptance. This was to cut away a vast entanglement set up by the lawyers for the un-doing of their opponents. It is tolerably clear that the whole future of the Spiritual party was at stake in this long-drawn-out controversy. It was not so much the consubstantiality of the human soul in its threefold-strand, vegetative, sensory, intellectual, that was the vital matter, but the power of the Holy Spirit revealed in Love, superseding mechanical ritual observances.

Olivi's exegetical writings were sought out and destroyed

in years to come by agents of the Inquisition with a pertin-
acity which testified to the fear they had inspired, and left
small trace of his eloquence to posterity. It is very evident
that his influence spread far beyond his own Order and his
own country. Charles II of Naples toyed with the Spiritual
doctrines, and hailed with enthusiasm the election of Celestine
V. His eldest son Charles Martel, beloved of Dante, embraced them ardently. We find Olivi in intimate correspondence with the younger members of the Angevin family. His
doctrines were highly esteemed by several Cardinals, and by
Dominicans hardly less than by Franciscans. Multitudes of
loyal Guelfs who pressed for a reform of existing abuses in the
Church were among his followers. The Ghibellines found in
his fearless attitude towards their oppressors and in his
liberal outlook some hope of ultimate reconciliation. The
old Joachist distinction was revived between the ' Carnal
Church, called universal, Catholic, Militant', and the
Spiritual Church of the New Age, pure and undefiled, the
New Jerusalem of the Apocalypse. Of this latter Olivi was
acclaimed the Prophet, and he led men to anticipate that the
Sixth Age of the Apocalypse was at hand wherein after great
persecutions of the faithful the New Age of the Spirit would
be inaugurated.

Both in Florence and in Bologna Dante was unquestionably
at this time brought into close contact with men who embraced secretly, but with ardour, the promise of the New Age.
So far Olivi as the great Apostle of reform within the Church
had steadily gained in authority and in influence. The attacks now made upon him were cunningly devised to throw
doubts upon his orthodoxy and cast a taint of heresy over all
his doctrines. Everyone knew that his condemnation would
be followed by cruel persecution undertaken against all such
as might be suspected of sharing his views. Accordingly the
years during which, with the dice heavily loaded against him,
Olivi laboured to defend himself, were a time of deep discouragement and suspense to those who were taking part in
the forward movement.

It was in 1287 that a General Council of the Order was
held at Montpellier under the new Franciscan General
Matteo Aquasparta, shortly to be made a Cardinal; at this
Olivi's fate was decided. To the amaze and discomfiture of

his foes all censures promulgated against him were annulled, and in recognition of his complete loyalty to the Church he was promoted to the responsible office of Lector in the school of his own Order in Florence. If we are correct in the surmise that the Messenger of God who brought Dante courage in his dark hour was no other than Olivi himself, this may have been the occasion when, after subduing the Furies and frustrating the Gorgon's head of excommunication, the Prophet put fear into the hearts of the lawyers, and proved that the gates they barred had no real bolts. Olivi's power of caustic rebuke was notorious. The rod of the teacher was apt to become in his hands a rod for the castigation of the obdurate. The words put into his mouth in the text are in keeping with his reputation, and may even be a reminiscence of what he actually said. Dante has told us it was his own custom to frequent the schools of the religious orders and, on this triumphant first appearance of Olivi, vindicated as authentic ambassador of God, the applauding concourse would number all who could in any way obtain admission. Olivi came to Florence. He rebuked his opponents after his usual fashion, openly to their faces, as Christ rebuked the lawyers of His day. Then, it would seem, before he had time to use his right arm and press that message of the Divine Love which was ever his main concern, he was recalled. An even weightier charge, the Lectorship of the great Franciscan School at Montpellier, was conferred upon him, and his début at Florence was followed almost at once by his sudden departure. The impression he gave was that some higher care absorbed his mind and bit into his soul. And who can doubt that to testify to the truth among his compeers and fellow-countrymen was the thing which lay nearest to his heart?

On Dante, as he recounts the incident, the effect was instantaneous. The vindication of Olivi, for the time being at any rate, cleared the air of suspicion and brought a wave of hope and courage to those who loathed the iniquities of the governing clique in the Carnal Church.

In attempting to identify this great contemporary of Dante it has been necessary to supply a very brief summary of almost forgotten speculations on the part of men whose works were systematically destroyed, whose very existence has been commonly overlooked by students of Dante. The utmost that can safely be done is to form a working hypothesis, and outline the facts which appear to support it. Of all the men able to afford encouragement to Dante during his student years none has a stronger claim to consideration in this respect than Petrus Johannis Olivi. It must be left to another occasion to demonstrate how deeply Dante was imbued with the doctrine of the Spirituals.

CORRESPONDING IMAGERY IN THE *ROMAN DE LA ROSE*

At the close of the *Roman de la Rose,* in the anti-Papal satire of Jean de Meung, he introduced on the scene the figure of Genius in order to present a striking contrast between the vices of Papal administration and the virtues preached and practised by the Spirituals. Whereas in the *Inferno* Dis is the central malign power, in the *Roman* it is Atropos. Both hold a secondary meaning as of Death, but under this figure can be discerned in both the sinister and detested image of the Carnal Church inspired with deadly hatred against intellectual freedom in any direction.

The Cerberus of Jean de Meung is the rapacious hound of Atropos; he calls incessantly for fresh victims, never sated, while she casts in his triple throat without pause an endless succession of hearts and souls of men and women. Cerberus stands it would seem, as in the *Inferno,* for the dreaded ecclesiastical punitive code under which power was committed to a priesthood, often unworthy, of inflicting many degrees of penitential discipline, or of exacting fines in lieu of it. Atropos has much ado to fill the jaws of the ' ribald Cerberus ', who lusts after the destruction of those he devours, and pesters the base wretch for more and more victims. It was the popular notion that new penalties had constantly to be imposed in order to satisfy the extortionate officials clamouring for the fees which depended on their exactions. A significant description is furnished of the three Furies, Alecto, Megara, and Tisiphone who, themselves impious and disloyal, were the avengers of impious misdeeds, struggling to keep Cerberus satisfied and fill his maws. We are to behold them ' sitting in full Consistory ' while their three Provosts rack the victims with tortures to extort confession of all the misdeeds they have committed from the hour of birth. To this end ' they chain, beat, scourge, strangle, buffet, tear the flesh, press it with weights, scorch, drown, burn, grill, and boil '. 'Before them all the people tremble.' Under the hell covering the shadow of the Inquisition Courts shows up with terrible realism. As for the crimes which call down such chastisement the author declares that Nature whispered them in his ear at Mass. He reckons they are twenty-six in number, and declares he has revealed them in the romance of the Rose. Thereupon he proceeds to give apparently as an illustration of these direly-punished crimes, an allegorical picture of Joachist doctrines, their beauty and their peace, akin to the vision of the Earthly Paradise in the *Purgatorio*. The gist of it, loosely disguised under classical imagery, lies in the daring distinction which is drawn between the walled in *Garden*, figuring the Roman Catholic Church, and the free and open *Park* of Spiritual Truth. The former is a fable. The Lover looked into this Garden in his dream, and was allured by the vision of dance and song, flowers and pleasure he beheld therein. The great feature of the Garden is the Fountain, ' fed so they say, by two perpetual springs '. But one of these is to be suspected as due to an alien source. It has a marble brim of stone (*marbre de pierre*). Above the Fountain, guarding it, is a Pine-tree with boughs spreading wide and far.

The Fountain is clearly the doctrine of the Church deriving from the double source of Holy Scripture and the impure source of Tradition. The *Pine* takes its name from the Pina di San Pietro, a well-known image of the Papal Curia, employed by Dante with great effect in his description of the Giants or World Powers in the Pozzo. It derived from the huge bronze fir-cone which in Dante's time stood in the outer court of the old basilica of S. Peter, and is now in the Vatican garden. 'They boast', says our Author, ' there was never such a Pine since the days of Pepin '—an allusion to the immense powers conferred on the Pope by the famous Donation of the Frankish King. But all that the Lover saw in the garden, continues the author, was nothing but idle tales and nonsense—(*trufles de fanfeluës*). ' For the Lord's sake, Sir, take heed how you believe such things.' There is nothing stable there. All is corruptible. Atropos, nurse of Cerberus, is ever spying upon it, and uses her powers against everyone.

As for the *Park* it is full of unspeakable joys. There springs an eternal fount at which all the beasts may drink, once they have severed themselves from the ' black flock '. Those who drink of this water shall never thirst again nor shall they taste of death. They follow the Lamb with joy which lasts eternally. Far different is the fountain from that which owns the *marbre de pierre*. The true Fount [of doctrine] is sweet and clear and living. It flows from three conduits which are in effect but One—always three and always one. For the base of the Joachist doctrine was the Holy Trinity. No *Pine-tree* guards it. But as it descends from on high a lowly *Olive-tree* is found, under which its waters flow. All the roots of this Olive are moistened by this sweet water; it grows and is enriched with leaves and flowers till it becomes taller and more wide spreading than that Pine he tells of which never put forth more boughs, nor offered such abundant shade as this. The Olive as it stands protects the fountain, and under it the beasts find pasture, while the flowers and tender grass are bedewed by its spray. There hangs from the Olive-tree a little roll in tiny script which saith to those who read therein, those who repose under its shadow:

' Here runs the Fount of Life
' Beneath this Olive, full of leaf
' Which puts forth the fruit of Salvation.'

What Pine hath ever equalled this in value?

Within this fount there shines a marvellous Carbuncle. ' The foolish hardly credit it and many reckon it a fable.' Then follows an Apocalyptic vision describing the inner mystic Light which illumines the New Jerusalem ' having the Glory of God; and her light like unto a stone most precious, even like a jasper-stone clear as crystal '. For Olivi taught his disciples that the promise of the New Jerusalem would be fulfilled in the dawning of the Age of the Spirit, albeit preceded by terrible persecutions of the faithful.

The author proceeded with even clearer deliberate intention to enter his testimony against the vices of the Papal Court, and to acclaim the pure doctrines of Olivi and the Spirituals:

Por Diex, Signor, donc que vous semble?
Judge between *the Park* and *the Garden*.

Pronounce in reasonable terms—which, deem ye, shows the greater beauty? Look at the two founts; which has the most healing leaves, is most virtuous, most pure, and judge the nature of the two. Judge which of the precious stones hold the most virtue. And then *judge between the Pine and the Olive* which guards the living fount. The one impregnates the living with death. The other gives the dead new life. The Author summed up with the injunction: ' *Honour ye Nature.* Serve it by hard work. However things happen submit to *Reason*. Restore the goods you may possess of other men. Approach not near to deeds of blood. Be loyal and pitiful. Keep hands and mouth clean.' The words of Genius end on a high note of pure Evangelic doctrine.

The above brief summary of one of the concluding passages in the *Roman de la Rose* does not profess to exhaust by any means the significant testimony afforded by Jean de Meung to the rising tide of Joachist doctrine, together with the popular revulsion against Papal infringements of liberty. It affords remarkable testimony to the recognized position of Olivi as Prophet of the New Age.

CHAPTER XII

A DIALOGUE WITH THE DEAD

[Inferno IX, 106-133; X. Sixth Circle]

Reflection on the past. Vision of patriots, philosophers, and reformers condemned to everlasting flames by Papal authority. Dante depicts himself in the act to gain light on the future by invoking the dead. Farinata subtly warns Dante he will one day stand in the same position towards Florence as Farinata himself at Mont Aperti. Cavalcante warns him of the impending death of Guido.

Period covered: 1287.
Corresponding hour: 2 a.m.

In the stinging rebuke which Christ addressed to the lawyers who sought to entangle Him, He reproached them for building the sepulchres of the prophets whom their fathers had killed. The conclusion is irresistible that this rebuke was in Dante's mind when, depicting himself in act to push forward and observe what the despicable crew were hiding in their stronghold, he discovered a region filled from end to end with red-hot sepulchres. Flames in the *Inferno* typify the sentence of eternal damnation very freely pronounced against offenders by the Papal agents. It was a symbol actually in use by the Inquisition Courts which labelled the backs of heretics with hideous tongues as of fire. Hence the tombs of those who had incurred the displeasure of the Holy See are here depicted alive with flames.

INSIDE THE WALLS OF DIS

Inf., ix, 106-133.

There without any strife we came within.
And I, who had the wish to scrutinize
The state of those locked up in such a fortress,
Soon as I was within, cast my eyes round
And saw on either hand a spacious plain
All filled with anguish and with evil torment.

As sepulchres make all the place uneven
At Arles, there where the Rhone stagnates, so too
At Pola on Quarnaro, that shuts in
Italia and bathes its boundaries,
Thus did they here on every side, except
The mode of it was here more merciless.
For midst the tombs were scattered flames of fire
Whereby so glowing hot were kindled all
That iron itself demands no further craft.
All of the covers over them were raised
And thence there issued violent laments
Of suffering (souls) and injured, well it seemed.

And I: ' Master, what are these people who
' Buried within these coffers make them heard
' With sighs of agony? ' And he to me:
' Here are the master Heretics; with them
' Their followers of every sect; far more
' Are the tombs crowded than thou canst believe;
' Here like with like is buried; more and less
' The monuments are heated.'

Then after he had turned to the right hand
We passed along between the martyred ones
And the high walls.

The far reaching punitive system of the Church, spent
itself for the most part on the dead. Compared with the
vast throngs of souls doomed by the Church in the course
of ages to eternal flames, the number of the antique spirits
who called out vainly in this life for the second death to
ease their pains was insignificant. When Dante contem-
plated the handiwork of the ecclesiastical courts it was a
vision of the dead—their tombs ablaze with the curses of the
Church—that seized on his imagination. Entirely disregard-
ful of conduct during life, the system plunged all independent
seekers after truth and many loyal sons of the Church into a
common tomb, denouncing some opinions more hotly than
others, but owning no distinction in regard to their greater or
less opportunity of acquiring truth. Indeed, the judges were
often too ignorant of history and philosophy to gauge the

trend of the speculations they condemned. None could guess how many had been thus swept into perdition—'more than you would believe' warned Virgil, 'are these tombs laden'. The curses fell indiscriminately purely on account of the theories attributed to the victims, and often attributed to them erroneously.

Dante did not leave the world without a clue to his judgment on the men relegated by the Church to the fiery sepulchres of damnation. He vindicated them once for all from any stain of presumption in their search for truth by setting some of them in the Heaven of the Sun among the great saints of God. Siger of Brabant, cited before his tribunal by a Dominican Inquisitor General of France as ' probably and vehemently suspected of heresy', and subsequently condemned to a lingering death, is set among this illustrious company, and Dante chose Thomas Aquinas, who in his lifetime so ably exposed the unorthodoxy of Siger, to point him out, not so it would seem, without affectionate pride in his intellect, not without a reverent pity for his sufferings. In Dante's student days to be found studying any of the works of Joachim de Flore was sufficient to condemn a man out of hand as a heretic. Yet in the Heaven of the Sun, numbered among some of the great theologians of the world, we find Joachim enthroned, and it is Dominic, founder of the great Order which spent itself in vain against Joachist doctrines, who brings to notice the Calabrian Abbot Joachim ' at my side', and proclaims him in very truth a prophet.

Writing as he did under the shadow of never-ceasing suspicion, Dante was debarred from expressing his contempt for the specious pretences with which the lawyers entrapped the learned and devout. It is abundantly clear that, like Roger Bacon, he himself condemned no man on account of his genuine and disinterested opinions however contrary to his own. His conviction that God does not condemn men because their judgment has gone astray was often implied and sometimes deliberately stated, as for instance in an outspoken passage in the *Monarchy* (III, 4). Here he quotes Augustine's words about 'one who should find in the Scriptures something other than he who wrote them really says', —a typical instance of heresy—and Augustine's opinion, that ' the error of such an one should be pointed out to him ', etc.

Dante adds to this his own dictum authoritatively enunciated with the very formula employed by Christ: ' But *I* say, that if such mistakes are made in ignorance they should be pardoned after careful correction. And if the mistakes are made on purpose we must deal with such as go astray no otherwise than with tyrants who follow not the public laws for the common advantage, but strive to wrest them to their own ends. Oh, the supreme crime, though it were but in dreams, of abusing the intention of the Holy Spirit.'

The words are pointedly directed against the ecclesiastical lawyers who tried to strengthen their privileges by misquoting Holy Scripture, and fabricating arguments out of it to prove the supremacy of the Church over the State.

We learn that the immediate effect upon Dante of contemplating at close quarters the penalties inflicted by the Church for the crime of heretical depravity, was to fasten his mind on the character and motives of those thus condemned. In particular this attention centred on the fate of two modern statesmen, Farinata, condemned for taking arms against the Church, and Cavalcante, the father of his closest friend, condemned for holding heterodox opinions.

The ostensible Hell narrative would seem to have worn a little thin during the obstructed entry to the City of Dis. Damned souls had dropped into the background while the adventures of Dante's mind held the centre of the stage. By the introduction of the Furies as symbols of the travesty of justice exhibited in the ecclesiastical Courts of Law, the satire had begun to take a very perilous direction, especially as it is not improbable that the Inquisition officials had a shrewd inkling of the mode of writing employed by young intellectuals to outwit them. Eugène Aroux believed them fully conversant with it. Hence it was imperative to present for once an unmistakable dialogue with the dead souls doomed to the penalty of undying fire. It was not beyond the powers of Dante to do this, and yet at the same time to keep the allegorical and true subject intact.

Writing after a lapse of many years, at a time when he himself was suffering exile for deeds at least as daring against Florence and against the Church as those for which Farinata had been doomed, Dante painted himself as he had been in old days in the first fervour of Guelf prejudice, in act to interrogate as an antagonist the dead hero, whose burial place he may possibly have been visiting. Between the hour when he stood in fancy before the Ghibelline leader, and the hour when in the *Divina Commedia* he retraced his steps through the blind world, lay stretched a lifetime of blundering, obloquy, disillusion, despair, followed by recovery of the right path. As he stood among the tombs he was an untried youth, seeking for enlightenment about the spirit world, eager specially to peer within the veil which hung over his own future life.

AN ATTEMPT AT DIVINATION

Inf., x, 1-21.

Now goes my Master by a secret path
Between the tortured and the city-wall
And I behind his shoulders.
' O grace and power supreme, that wheelest me
' Throughout these impious circles,' I began,
' Speak as it pleaseth thee, and satisfy
' My wishes. Could the people who are lying
' Within the sepulchres be seen? Already
' The covers are well raised and none keeps guard.'

And he to me: ' They shall be all closed up
' When hither with their bodies they return,
' Which they have left above, from Josaffatt.
' With Epicurus all his followers
' According to this party are entombed,
' For thus they make the soul dead with the body.
' However to the question that thou askest
' Soon, here within, shalt thou be satisfied,
' And also in the wish thou hidest from me.'
And I: ' Good Guide, I do not keep my heart
' Hid from thee save for brevity of speech;
' Thereto, not now alone, thou hast disposed me.'

Dante invokes Virgil to aid him in interrogating the dead.

He assumes that Virgil who had inspired the wish by his poetry is aware of it.

The little play of words between himself and Virgil is very significant. He will not unfold his secret wish, he says, because he desires to be brief, ' and thou hast not only now disposed me to *that*,' viz., the wish to question the dead. It was from Virgil's page that he imbibed both the desire and the notion that it could be gratified. Virgil had set his hero to learn about the future from his father's ghost, and in Paradise

Dante repeatedly interrogated the dead and invited their prophecies.

Many orthodox persons in the Middle Ages practised divination, and there was much to encourage the fancy that the ghosts whose tombs were flaming with denunciations had power to throw light on the future. Yet it was Virgil as pagan poet rather than Virgil as symbol of Reason who led the way on this occasion, and the dialogue ends on that note as Dante turned his steps towards *the antique poet*.

The new theme is linked on to the old one by the spectacle of flames engulfing in a great pit Epicurus and his followers: ' they make out that the soul dies with the body.' This innumerable crowd (*più di mille*) were huddled together in a common tomb, good and bad, Guelf and Ghibelline together, all under suspicion of disregarding orthodox notions about their future state. It was under the heading of Epicureanism that the Inquisition Courts were able to get a handle against Ghibellines, and even against wide-minded Guelfs who could not be fitted into any other category of heresy. Men could take refuge against excommunication either in denial of any future life at all, or in denial of the Papal authority to pass sentence of eternal damnation. Of the two it was less disintegrating in its effects to pillory sceptics for their unbelief in a future state, than to admit the fact that they were frankly incredulous about the future consequences of excommunication. Such offenders were swept into hell promiscuously by the Inquisition under the head of Epicureans, as guilty of the baser but less contagious error, and quite regardless of their actual theories about immortality. Dante held in high honour the philosophy of Epicurus, and evidently did not believe that he denied the immortality of the soul.

He put on record very distinctly his opinion about those who denied the immortality of the soul. ' I say that of all brutalities (bestialitadi) that is most stupid, vile, and pernicious which maintains that after this life there is no other life.'[1] But he also took some pains to distinguish Epicurus and his followers from the number of such base unbelievers. For he declared that ' if we turn over all the writings, whether of philosophers or of other wise writers, all agree in this that there is a certain part within us that endures for ever '. He

[1] *Banquet*, II, 9.

instanced as firm believers in immortality Aristotle and the Stoics, with Cicero in particular, and later, high among the great authorities 'worthy of faith and credence', he mentioned Epicurus, and instead of accusing him of this base and pernicious doctrine he showed irrefutably that his creed was quite other than was vulgarly supposed. Far from advocating gross bodily pleasures on the ground that there is no survival after death, Epicurus taught that, since every living creature as soon as it is born, as though prompted by nature towards its proper end, flies from pain and seeks happiness, this our proper end must be Delight, *i.e.*, Delight without subsequent pain. But all gross pleasures and unjust demands result sooner or later in pain. And he showed that Cicero seems to agree with him in defining Delight as absence of Pain. Further to vindicate the followers of Epicurus Dante quoted the example of his noble disciple Torquatus who, ' surely *not without Divine help* ' set devotion to honour even before the life of his own son (*Banquet*, iv, 6). Dante was in accord with Epicurus in so far as he believed that man was created for Delight; nothing short of the supreme Blessedness can satisfy the pure craving for Felicity which grows in the soul through its Divine seed of Blessedness (*Banquet*, iv, 22). It is important to set the above vindication of the doctrine of Epicurus side by side with the spectacle of the fiery tomb pointed out to him by Virgil. The accusation ' they make the soul dead with the body ' was levelled against those who launched the sentence of excommunication, not against those who without guilt incurred it.

FARINATA DEGLI UBERTI

Inf., x, 22-51.

' O Tuscan that alive art going through
' The City of Fire, speaking thus loyally,
' Thy speech makes manifest that thou wert born
' Within that noble fatherland to which
' I wrought overmuch harm, perchance.'
This sound came forth from out one of the tombs
Suddenly; whereupon I drew in fear
A little closer to my Guide. And he

The Voice of the Dead Hero.

Said to me: ' Turn thee round; what doest thou?
' See Farinata who hath raised him there;
' From the waist upward thou shalt see him all.'

His higher part alone made visible.

205

I had already fixed my eyes on his;
Upright he reared himself, with breast and brow
As though he held th' Inferno in great scorn.
And my Guide's fearless, ever-ready hands
Thrust me between the sepulchres to him,
Saying: 'Behoves thee make thy words precise.'

When I was at the foot-stone of the tomb
He looked on me awhile, then asked of me,
Half in contempt, 'Who were thy ancestors?'

Desirous to obey I hid it not
But laid open before him everything;
Whereat he made a supercilious gesture,
Then said: 'Fiercely were they opposed to me
'To my forefathers and my party also
'For which I scattered them to exile twice.'

'If they were driven forth, back they returned',
I answered him, 'both times from every place,
'But yours have not acquired that art aright.'

Suddenly in Dante's startled ears the sound of Farinata's voice resounded, and the old Ghibelline appeared, raised from the dead full in his sight.

In accordance with the scheme of the *Divina Commedia,* shortly to be expounded by Farinata, the ghosts could read the future though imperfectly and remember the past but were ignorant of the present. Dante is presumed to be ignorant at first of this idiosyncrasy on their part, but it forms the clue to the entire episode. Farinata could not know who Dante was until he knew who were his ancestors, but as soon as his lineage was declared he could pick him out not only in the map of the past, but also of the future which lay unrolled before his eyes. All the deeds of the Alighieri Guelf ancestors lay clear in Farinata's view, and simultaneously he obtained insight into the coming change in Dante's political opinions, his ill-treatment at the hands of the Florentines, and his dateless exile. All unconsciously Dante was standing in the presence of one who was turning a search-light over his entire life, always excepting that period which lay in the immediate present.

But he was first to receive another warning about the future which he was at that moment quite incapable of understanding.

CAVALCANTE DEI CAVALCANTI *Inf.*, x, 52-72.

Then by the side of him there rose to sight
A shade uncovered far as to the chin;
He had raised himself I think upon his knees.
Round me he peered as with a wish to see
Whether some other were not with me; then
After his expectation was quite spent,
Weeping he said: ' If thou art going through
' This prison blind by height of genius
' Where is my son? Why is he not with thee? '

And I to him: ' I come not of myself.
' He who waits yonder leads me through this place
' Which in contempt your Guido held perchance.'
The words he spoke, the manner of his doom
Already had revealed to me his name.
And therefore was my answer thus complete.

Suddenly rising up erect he shouted:
' How sayest thou? He *had*? Lives he not still?
' Does the sweet light not strike upon his eyes? '

When he perceived I made some slight delay
Before I answered him, he fell once more
Supine, nor did he further forth appear.

The friendship of Dante for Guido Cavalcanti was one of the strong passions of his life. Guido, like himself, was a poet. The friends shared the same pursuits, spent most of their time together, and held the same political and philosophic views. Guido alone fully understood the hidden sense of the *Vita Nuova*. His love for Dante dated from the publication of the first sonnet about the year 1283; the book was dedicated to him and it was by his advice that it was written in Italian. He is alluded to several times in the course of it, and Dante called him his chief friend. Guido was some years older than Dante. His father betrothed him while he was still a boy to Beatrice, daughter of Farinata degli Uberti, during the general movement towards a reconciliation which marked the year 1267, and there were two children by the marriage. He began early to take part in public life. In 1280 he acted as one of the sureties in the peace between Guelfs and Ghibellines promoted by Cardinal Latino. Four years later he became a member of the Grand Council in Florence. Here he soon drifted into violent opposition to Corso Donati, and Florence was enlivened by frequent collisions between these two and their partisans. Before long the Guelf party, to which they both belonged, split into opposite camps. Guido's party, led by Vieri dei Cerchi, was called the Whites, and Donati's party the Blacks. It was the aim of a few patriotic Florentines, among whom were Dino Compagni and Dante himself, to reconcile these two factions, but the forces of disunion were too strong. By a most unhappy turn of events Dante was in office as one of the Priors of the city from June to August 1300, at the moment when a crisis occurred which called for stern measures against the rivals. A sharp conflict occurred in the streets of Florence between the Whites with Guido at their head and the Blacks led by Corso Donati. The Priors were compelled by decrees they had themselves made to banish the leaders on both sides. Dante was thus forced into the odious position of banishing his best friend. At the time when the sentence was pronounced it did not appear a matter of great moment. The leaders of the Whites, including Guido, were merely directed to absent themselves from the city and to retire to Sarzana a few miles off. No one imagined the sentence would be for long. But it was a hot unhealthy summer. News came that Guido was attacked by fever. He was brought back to Florence and died within a few days of his return under circumstances which suggested poison to his friends. The tragedy cut Dante to the quick. To be compelled as a judge to inflict humiliation on his friend was in itself a cruel blow. To have sent him to his death was such an intolerable grief as could never be effaced.

The poignancy of this imaginary encounter with the father of his friend may now be apprehended. Although politically a Guelf, Cavalcante was a liberal [1] and a wide-minded patriot,

[1] It was in his house, in 1265, that the celebrated Cunizza, friend of Sordello, manumitted by deed the slaves of her late father and brother. She was alive in 1279 and it seems probable that it was through the Cavalcante family that Dante gained the insight into her inner life which led to his setting her in Paradise, in the Heaven of Venus, with other noted disciples of the Gospel of Divine Love.

as is shown by his consent to give his son to the daughter of the
defeated Farinata. The text reveals the significant fact that
he had died under the ban of the Church.

From the sound of Dante's voice he had evidently recognized him, and he hoped to find that Guido as usual was in his
company. Like Farinata he had instantly obtained a vision
of Dante's future. And written on the page he beheld though
indistinctly, the story of Guido's banishment at the hands of
this very friend who was seeking to peer into the future. With
a sudden rush of senseless hope, Cavalcante knelt [1] before
Dante, forgetting all but the fact that the future judge of his
son was before him, and might perchance be moved to
lenience. The train of thought which Cavalcante followed
was suggested by the words Dante had just uttered. He had
spoken of banishment, and the art of returning from it. Hard
upon this the kneeling suppliant broke out: 'Where is my
son, and why is he not with thee?'

There seems to be a gleam of satire in the reference to the
'height of genius'; Dante points, perhaps, the moral against
himself: inasmuch as this '*altezza d' ingegno*' was to bring
him, first to exile his friend, and next to incur the same sentence himself. In his imperfect vision Cavalcante was ignorant how time was passing, looked for his son in vain, and failing to see him as usual in Dante's company, concluded he had
already met his fate, after a banishment in which Dante had
concurred.

In Dante's answer he naturally went astray from the point.
He had no conception of the old man's meaning, and no
knowledge that he was himself actually receiving that hint
about the future which he had begged Virgil to procure for
him. He defended himself from the accusation of peering into
the future by the light of his own genius, and explained that
the antique poet was leading him through this place (*per qui*),
for which (not 'for whom') Guido cherished disdain. The
suggestion is that, in spite of their common interests, Guido
did not accompany Dante in his present quest, whether because he scorned the notion of looking into the future, or
scorned the flames with which the tombs were decked. The
allegorical and the surface meaning are here almost inextricably intertwined.

[1] *Credo che s'era in ginocchie levata.*

The words used to explain Guido's absence led up to the climax of the scene. The father took up the only word in the sentence which he understood. And pausing a moment while he gained full vision of his son's death, Cavalcante fell back supine, leaving Dante wholly unconscious that the despair he was now witnessing would one day be lived over again in his own person. The very words he put into Cavalcante's mouth may have been those with which Dante himself learned the news of his friend's death.

It is hard to believe that Dante left this episode incomplete. In visiting, as he feigned to do, the realms of the blessed, would he not find somewhere awaiting him with forgiveness the friend whom to his lasting sorrow he had sent to his death?

The first figure whom Dante encountered in Purgatory [1] was that of the friend whom he hailed as ' Casella '. [2] Thrice they vainly stretched out their arms to embrace. Then, following his shade, Dante besought him to speak, and Casella, responding to Dante's unspoken petition for forgiveness, gave him the assurance he desired: ' Even as I loved thee in the mortal body, so do I love thee now I am loosed from it.' Once more they walked in closest communion with each other. Casella used Dante's own words, *'Amor che nella mente mi ragiona,'* to solace him. And the sweetness of Paradise rested upon that hour.

Inf., x, 73-93.   PROPHECY OF DANTE'S OWN EXILE

That other lofty soul, at whose command
My course was stayed, changed not his countenance
Nor did he move his head, nor turn his side.
' And if ', continuing his former words,
' They have ', he said, ' but ill acquired that art.
' 'Tis that torments me far worse than this bed.
' But fifty times there shall not be re-lit

[1] *Purg.*, II, 76 ff.

[2] Commentators have surmised from the text that Casella, whose name occurs in no other place, was a musician. But the name may equally well have been a familiar appellation of Guido. *Caselle* were the squares used in posing mathematical problems, and the expression ' far Casella ' was used for the construction of puzzling phrases or poems designed to conceal the true meaning of the writer. Guido left much verse of this description the key to which is lost.

' The lady's face that ruleth in this place
' Ere *thou* shalt know the hardness of that art.
' And tell me, so mayest thou once more win back
' To the sweet world, why are the people there
' So fierce in all their laws against my kin? '

Then I to him: ' The rout and the great slaughter
' Which caused the Arbia to run blood-red
' Makes such petition heard within our temple.'

Then with a sigh, he shook his head and spoke:
' In that I did not stand alone, nor surely
' Would I with the rest have stirred without good cause.
' But I *did* stand alone, in open view,
' When I defended her where all agreed
' That Florence should be wholly swept away.'

A still sterner picture of the future awaited Dante from the lips of the magnanimous Ghibelline who gave no sign of pity or yielding. The theme was still the art of returning from banishment, and Farinata picked up the thread of the colloquy at the point where it had been broken off by Cavalcante. In doing so he lifted the veil over Dante's future, and foreshadowed two coming events, but in such a manner that while Dante could dimly understand the nature of one prophecy, he remained totally unconscious of having heard a second. Notwithstanding Farinata's relentless attitude his real sympathy with Dante was expressed in no measured terms. The sufferings of the exiles who were to know no return, afflicted him, he said, more than his own curse. Dante himself would learn, he warned him, within fifty revolutions of the Moon, how heavily weighed the art of return from banishment. The gentle warning lends itself to interpretation according to either sense of the poem. In the literal theme it is the year 1300, and Dante in his own person is to learn within four years some of the burdens of exile. In the allegorical theme the year is 1287-8, and within the next four years Dante was to be in arms against the exiled Guido da Montefeltro and his party, and was to be an eye-witness of the desperate condition to which so many of his fellow-citizens were reduced. In describing the Dark Wood and the Burning Sands Dante exposed some of the horrors of exile which came under his observation as a conqueror. This double-edged prophecy was not, however, the weightiest which Farinata had to deliver.

Suddenly he asked Dante why the Florentines were so bitter in relentlessly destroying every vestige of the Uberti property which remained in the city. Dante reminded him in reply of the great battle of Montaperti which took place near the River Arbia in 1260, when Farinata with the victorious Ghibelline party held Florence at their mercy. No wonder, he seemed to imply, after such an onslaught on his native city, that he should be regarded by the citizens as a traitor.

Just as had happened in the case of Cavalcante the Ghibelline warrior, now speaking prophetically, assumed the precise position in which after the lapse of years Dante was to find himself. If we look forward, as Farinata was able to do, to the year 1312, we shall behold Dante also in league with a hostile force against Florence, under the leadership of the Emperor Henry VII. Farinata, now quite plainly on the defensive, bade his hearer remember that he had not moved against his own city without a good cause, and without good company. But among all that band who were approaching Florence with intent to raze her to the ground, it was he alone who spoke in her defence.

A long series of events was to sink Florence deeper and deeper in treachery before Dante found himself standing among those who were clamouring for her destruction. Tradition has it that Dante held aloof when the German force encamped before the walls of his city, and although no certain evidence exists on this matter, it furnishes no slight confirmation of his own patriotic action in the moment of extremity to find him laying stress on Farinata's victory over hate. Well may Dante also have found himself alone in counselling restraint and moderation among the German contingent which took up its quarters under the walls of Florence, elated by the prospect of easy victory. Could he write in later years of Farinata's famous deed of magnanimity without recalling that he himself was set to encounter the same conflict between patriotism and revenge and, like Farinata himself, had found that Florence lay nearest to his heart?

EXPLANATION, NOT OF DIVINE JUSTICE BUT OF
DANTE'S ALLEGORY

Inf., x, 94-120.

' Ah, so may your seed hereafter find repose.'
I prayed him, ' loose for me that knot
' That has involved my judgment in this place.
' It seems, if I hear right, that you can see
' Beforehand that which time is to bring with it
' Yet with the present hold a different mode '.
' We see ', he said, ' like those who have poor light
' The things remote from us. To this extent
' The Guide supreme illuminates us still.
' When things draw near or come to pass, our mind
' Is quite at fault. Save others bring it to us
' Nothing we know about your human state.
' Hence thou canst understand that wholly dead
' Shall be our knowledge from the moment when
' The portal of the future shall be closed.'
Then conscience-smitten for my fault, I said:
' Now therefore would you tell that fallen one
' His son still to the living is conjoined.
' If I was mute before in the response,
' Give him to know it was because my thought
' Still held the error you have solved for me.'

And now my Master was re-calling me;
Therefore more hurriedly I prayed the spirit
To tell me who were they with him. He said

' With souls innumerable here lie I;
' The second Frederic is here within
' Also the Cardinal and of the rest
' I will keep silence.' Then he hid himself.

By the device of conferring second sight on the dramatis personæ the limitation of time to one day in the year 1301 became indefinitely extended.

Dante was still unaware that he had received a warning of Guido's impending death.

The prophetic words passed unnoticed for the moment.
The poet was occupied in trying to discern the limitations of
the ghostly messages he had heard. 'We can see distant
things though in a bad light', he was told, ' but our intellect
fails in interpreting the things which are or which draw near.'
It was a warning meant for the living no less than a comment
on the dead. Not till these things were far distant would
Dante receive power to understand. For the moment he was

ignorant whither his steps were tending, and no clear light shone on the ground he trod. He was still in the depths of that Wood out of which Virgil was hereafter to show him the way. He failed utterly to perceive that his present political opinions were to drop from him. The mirror held up before his face remained dark.

Farinata displayed great reticence in mentioning his fellow heretics. Two conspicuous figures, Frederic II and 'the Cardinal', he brought to Dante's mind. But he would speak of no others. There were many, whether Guelf or Ghibelline, who had drifted into the flames they were told awaited them hereafter, and some denied the resurrection. The misgovernment of the world consequent upon Papal usurpation had weakened men's hold upon spiritual truths. The misuse of excommunication had driven both partisans and enemies to doubt; the thunders had been overdone. Farinata gave no hint of holding heterodox doctrines. On the contrary we find the man who was supposed to deny the continuity of human personality eternally living over again the past, tormented by the harsh judgment of his countrymen, clinging to the memory of his city and sensitive in the grave itself to the sound of the Tuscan tongue.

It is hard to imagine any figure less like a damned spirit than Farinata of the great soul. Quite plainly he alluded to illumination vouchsafed to him in the tomb by the Supreme Ruler. Quite obviously the griefs which oppressed him were those of his native city hastening to ignominy, and had no reference to the contemptible flames with which his burial place had, as it were, been strewn. His curious observation that when eternity has swept past, present, and future away he would no longer be able to see into the future, is one of those subtle strokes of irony with which Dante from time to time enlivened his survey of ecclesiastical penalties.

The entire episode stands out as the spontaneous vindication of a great Florentine statesman cruelly misjudged by the men of his own generation.

Inf., x, 121-136.

FORECAST OF ENLIGHTENMENT THROUGH
BEATRICE

I turned my steps towards the antique poet,
That speech revolving that seemed adverse to me.

And he moved on. Then going forward thus
He said to me: ' Why art thou so distraught? '
And at his question I revealed my thoughts.
' What thou has heard against thee ', bade that Sage,
' Let memory retain.' He raised his finger.
' When in the sweet radiance thou shalt stand
' Of HER whose glorious eye beholdeth all
' From her thou'lt learn the journey of thy life.'
Thereupon towards the left he turned his feet.
We left the wall and wound towards the middle
By a path which led us down into a valley.
Its fetor even above caused us annoy.

Virgil supplies the true key to the future.

Farinata's prediction lingered in Dante's mind with a sense
of discomfort. To what extent the scene is wholly imaginary,
and to what extent founded on musings amid the tombs of the
Warriors, it is impossible to say. Possibly the rapid mutations
of parties, to which the sight of these graves had given prominence, may have suggested some presage of an approaching
epoch in his life when he too might be counted as an enemy
to his country, and wander forth as an exile. But in this hour
of foreboding, Reason brought him comfortable assurance of
a divine light one day to be shed over every step of his way.

Hard upon this vision of Beatrice, for it was no less though
guardedly referred to, Dante turned his steps sharp towards
the left. The reek of bloodshed was in the air. The valley
through which flowed the river of boiling blood was in sight.
Before surrendering himself to the warfare he lingered still to
ponder in his own heart the nature of sin and God's judgment
on sinners.

CHAPTER XIII

VIRGIL CONDEMNS THE ECCLESIASTICAL CODE OF MORALS

[*Inferno XI*, 1-27; 67-93]

Dante finds a refuge behind the tomb of the excommunicated Pope. The significance of Virgil's rôle as arbiter of Morals. He defines sin as an injurious act committed against self, against man, or against God, and relegates five of the Deadly Sins to a lighter category. On Brutishness.

Period covered: 1287-8.

Corresponding hour: 2.40 to 3 a.m.

THERE WAS a time in the course of Dante's studies, so he tells in the *Banquet* (Bk. IV, c. 1), when he discontinued trying to find out what is meant by primal matter, a dreary speculation popular with the Schoolmen, and, conscious of a sense of estrangement from his Lady (the Church?), set himself to consider the problem of human imperfections. He had already exercised his mind on the corresponding problem of human goodness, and had reached the conclusion that almost every one was possessed by a totally wrong idea about goodness or the Nobility sown in us by Nature. He had come to recognize that this error led to a far-reaching chain of evil consequences, and he states that it was with the aim of rectifying it that he composed the Ode beginning ' The gentle rhymes of Love ' (*Le Dolci Rime d'Amore*). This beautiful Ode, amplified and interpreted in the Fourth Book of the *Banquet*, was ostensibly designed to correct the popular notion that the possession of either riches or ancient lineage is essential to the making of a gentleman,

But although laying stress in certain passages on this harmless and rather well-worn thesis, the Ode, as explained in the *Banquet*, soon passed far beyond its bounds to demonstrate that the entire human race unreservedly—pagan, Roman, and Greeks, specifically, and by inference Turks, infidels, and

216

heretics no less—were born *good*, and being endowed with a Divine germ are thus potentially virtuous. It was not true that they were created in God's wrath; they were created in his Love to reflect His Divine Image. Hence from Adam downwards the entire race of man is noble. Nothing could be more definitely Pelagian in tendency, or more clearly opposed to the ultra-Augustinian doctrine of Original Sin which in the thirteenth century was insisted upon as orthodox. In further refutation of the ecclesiastical dogma of perdition, so heavily stressed by the ' Carnal Church,' the Fourth Book of the *Banquet* proceeds to illustrate from Greek and Roman history the height of virtue to which man in his natural state, long before the Redemption, had been able to attain. The theory of the inherent baseness in man's nature is overthrown with scorn, and the book ends with a sublime exposition of the true glory of Christianity.

In retracing the more significant moments of his life in the *Inferno* narrative, Dante found a place for the pregnant season of deliberation, during which he adopted the above theory of good and evil, a theory more in accord with reason than that imposed by ecclesiastics. It was impossible for him to expose it openly, and dangerous even to hint at it, but it seethed within him and found expression in the exquisite Ode which, some years later, he ventured to interpret, also in enigmatic language, for his inner band of disciples.

He threw his abstract meditations as usual into the form of a dialogue between himself and Virgil.

THE SIGNIFICANCE OF ANASTASIUS

Inf., XI, 1-15.

On the extreme edge of a lofty bank
We came above a still more cruel throng.
And here by reason of the foul excess
Of stench which the profound abyss threw up
We sheltered, drawing near behind a lid
Of a great sepulchre on which I saw
A writing which declared: ' I hold the Pope
' Anastasius, whom Photinus drew
' From the right way.'

The excommunicated Pope.

' Our downward course we must delay until
' Our senses first become a little used

Reason
counsels
delay and
deliberation.

' To the evil blast—then we shall heed it not.'
Thus (spake) the Master, and I said to him:
' Some compensation find, so that the time
' Pass not in vain.' And he: ' Look you, on that
' I ponder.'

When Dante turned to the left and climbed the shattered
battlements of the City of Dis, he came out on a plateau from
which he was able to survey in the distance the region of warfare through which he had to pass. Very vividly he perceived
that his path was to lead him into association with the bloodthirsty. His nostrils were filled with a fetid odour; a shrink-
ing from blood-lust possessed his soul. And he paints himself
in act to pause, as in the *Banquet* he revealed that he actually
did at this time in his life, in order to undertake a philosophic
investigation into the nature of sin. Dry as the eleventh
canto of the *Inferno* may appear in the eyes of those who merely
seek to trace in it the extent to which the author displayed his
indebtedness to Aristotle, Cicero, and Aquinas, it sheds a
flood of light upon the allegorical theme, and forms the
natural climax to the scenes narrated within the City of Dis.

The *Inferno* has become so familiar a locality that it is
seldom the reader calls in question any detail he finds described there. It is taken for granted that when Dante took
shelter under cover of the tomb of Pope Anastasius, he did so
because he found that particular tomb just in the right spot,
and was able to make use of it for the strange purpose of pro-
tecting him from the stench which ascended from below. Yet
since it can hardly be disputed that every detail has its purpose in the allegory, Pope Anastasius and his opinions plainly
become a matter of considerable moment. Why did Dante
take refuge behind this tomb when he began to examine into
the nature of sin and its punishment by the help of his own
reason? Pope Anastasius was condemned, or believed to have
been condemned (for the details are obscure), on a charge of
heresy, for supporting Photinus in throwing doubts on the
damnation of Bishop Acacius, who had been excommunicated
by Pope Felix in the year 484. This Pope was, therefore, a
powerful shelter behind which a man might find refuge who
denied the validity of the excommunications launched by
Papal lawyers against their political enemies. Anastasius was

a standing lesson that it was not merely heretics and Ghibellines who doubted the efficacy of Papal curses, but God's Vicar, a lawfully-elected Pope, with power and courage to reverse the sentence of damnation. The size of the tomb (*grande avello*) bore witness to the multitude of those who followed his example in ' doubting the validity of the damnation' of those condemned by ecclesiastical authority to eternal flames.

Dante's struggle to emancipate his reason from discordant authorities had brought him to understand that the estimate of sin held by the Papal lawyers by no means accorded with the judgment on sin exposed by pagan philosophers, revealed, moreover, in Holy Writ. It was a violent awakening which did not instantly shake his political creed. He remained for many years a Guelf. Yet his perception that the Carnal Church had fallen into gross errors about sin seems to have been the first step towards the complete liberation of his intellect. The immense gulf which separated the morality of the Papal lawyers from true ideals of righteousness became at once apparent when the lives of men whom the Church delighted to honour were examined. Thus after witnessing the flames which hovered over the tombs of men vindictively condemned as heretics for political reasons, Dante determined to exercise his own reason about what was sin and what was not. And in the endeavour to do so, Pope Anastasius, who had declared that a man was not necessarily damned because he had been excommunicated, gave him great support.

The conclusions which Dante reached about original sin are decisively expressed in the *Banquet* and in the treatise on *Monarchy*. The demonstration of them lies outside the scope of the *Inferno* and is not here introduced. They must be examined later. But the whole fabric of society, no less than that of Hell, hinged on the question whether man was created in love, endowed with ability to lead a virtuous life, well pleasing to God, or whether he was created in wrath, doomed to undying flames, unless rescued by the ministrations of the Catholic priesthood.

Dante dealt with the matter dramatically and discovered thereby with subtlety, but quite definitely, on which side of the controversy he stood. In order to expound the highest ideals of right conduct he chose out a pagan, and set him to draw a pointed contrast between the pure morality esteemed and followed by reasonable men before the Christian era, and the corrupt morals of priest and laity condoned by the Carnal Church. Among all the significant anomalies which have grown familiar to Dante students, none is more arresting than this choice of a pagan to set up a right standard of morals for fourteenth-century Christians. Virgil is the pivot on which the whole philosophy of the *Inferno* and *Purgatorio* may be seen to turn. He is the witness of God in men's minds. Though not himself divine he is the recipient of Divine inspiration, the vehicle through which in the beginning Beatrice was able to make herself understood. He stands for Reason in its highest sense assuming ever more definitely an Imperialistic hue. Although, as will be shown, he is liable to error, he typifies the standard of righteousness to which natural man can attain, assuredly not without a power bestowed of God. Virgil is in fact saturated with the spirit of God's will, and exposes the beauty of God's natural creation. In his own person, stripped of allegory, Virgil is set before the reader as the noblest of mankind, created for the glory of God, uncorrupted by the errors of the vulgar, a philosopher, poet, and teacher to be revered and imitated, a great force in the world's history.

To realize all this, and in no particular have these aspects of Virgil ever been controverted, and to assert that Dante, immersed in medieval tradition, gave Virgil his portion in the realm of darkness, under the dominion of the devil, however benignly screened from bodily torture in a kind of suburb of hell, is the cardinal error of the Dante tradition. When this traditional point of view has been abandoned, it will be discovered that the damnation of Virgil was the crowning crime, if it were not rather to be considered the crowning absurdity, of the whole ecclesiastical system of rewards and punishments, exposed in the *Divina Commedia*. These false Popes, depraved Cardinals and Bishops, usurping sovereigns, vicious priests, treacherous nobles, bloodthirsty tyrants whom we are to behold, all died in the odour of sanctity. Did he, indeed, believe they were wafted by purchase in their last hour to inherit eternal bliss, while such men as Aristotle and Virgil, the guides of the human race, were relegated to perdition? Was this morality? Was it the judgment of God? Could it be held by sensible men? It presents such a plain contradiction of the philosophy enunciated in the *Divina Commedia* that nothing but a petrified theory of Dante's mind could have brought men to accept it as a part of his plan.

Suppose that Dante, revolting, as we know he did, against the narrow conception of Divine Love held by Churchmen, had desired to bring into high relief the contrast between the men they damned and the men they sanctified, could he have done better than select a heathen for a specimen of righteous man, and set him to pass judgment on the figures contemporary with himself whom the Church approved?

Dante has taken the greatest possible pains to rescue the figure of his hero from the ignominy which covered it in the Middle Ages. In *Inferno* xx Virgil is vindicated once and for all from the imputations of sorcery which then soiled his memory, and helped to earn him his reputed place in hell. In *Purgatory* xxii he is vindicated from false notions of worship, and is revealed through the lips of Statius as the forerunner of Christianity, the seer who proclaimed:

> ' Secol si rinnuova
> Torna guistizia e primo tempo umano
> E progenie discende dal ciel nuova.' [1]

Statius declares with no uncertain sound that his own conversion to Christianity was due to Virgil:

> ' Per te poeta fui, per te Cristiano.'

This was to bestow on Virgil an incontestable passport to Heaven, for Dante brings St. Bernard on the scene to demonstrate that while half of Paradise was reserved for those who believed in Christ after his coming (*Christo venuto*), the other half was occupied by the hosts who had looked forward to the birth of a Messiah (*Christo venturo*). [2]

It was surely not without some flash of humour that the Roman poets meeting in Purgatory contrasted their very different fates. ' If God deigns not you shades on high ', says Statius, as he and Virgil and Dante moved forward at a powerful pace, ' who has escorted you so far up His stairs? ' And Virgil observed that since Dante could not come alone ' I was brought forth from the wide jaws of Hell to guide

[1] *Purg.*, xxii, 70.   [2] *Para.*, xxxii, 22 ff.

221

him'. [1] A marvel, indeed, surely not thus emphasized without intention, that a damned soul had to be brought out of the very jaws of Hell to show a thirteenth-century Christian the lost way to Heaven.

Whether as a damned soul claiming Divine authority to reveal the judgments of God to a Catholic, or as human Reason bearing witness to the highly moral standard of pre-Christian days, Virgil's pronouncement on the subject of sin, accepted without reserve by his disciple, reveals itself as a definite challenge to orthodox opinion and practice.

Inf., XI, 16-27.

VIRGIL'S DEFINITION OF SIN

' My son ', he then began to say, ' there are
' Three lesser Circles down from grade to grade
' Within these rocks, like those that thou art leaving.
' Full are they all of spirits that are accurst;
' And, so that sight of them alone suffice thee,
' Understand how and why they are imprisoned.
' In every sin that incurs hate in Heaven
' Injury is the object aimed at, and
' Every such object doth aggrieve some other
' Whether by violence or fraud.
' But because fraud is man's peculiar sin
' It more displeases God; hence lower down
' The fraudulent are set and greater pain
' Assails them.'

Virgil proceeded to distinguish three categories of Violence and ten categories of Fraud, concluding with a reference to the Inhuman or Bestial category of Fraud known as Treachery. [2] Since these misdeeds only came under Dante's observation by degrees on his way through life they need not in this place be enumerated.

Virgil began by asserting the principle that the crimes abhorred of Heaven are such as inflict injury, whether by violence or fraud, on other people. Wilfully to harm others is to reverse the Divine Law of Love, and bring about that fatal condition of ruin and despair in the world of living men which forms the theme of the *Inferno*. It was a principle ignored in practice, if not in theory, by the Papal Government

[1] *Purg.*, XXI, 19 ff.   [2] Note on Brutishness at end of Chapter.

which was gradually superseding, in many directions, the civil administration. In the artificial code of morality observed by ecclesiastics in this debased period, sin had come to be regarded primarily as an offence against ecclesiastical regulations. Actions came to be regarded as blameworthy because prohibited by the Church and, as the Church prohibited much that was not in itself sinful, the standard of morality tended to become blurred. Clerical offenders, not only priests but men who had registered as ' clerks ' and wore the tonsure without intending to take orders, were entirely sheltered from civil condemnation, and were continually protected from the consequences of their misdeeds by episcopal authority. Thus it came about that criminals guilty of rape, robbery in arms, murder, rebellion, or treacherous conspiracy were often suffered to atone for their wicked deeds far more easily than persons convicted of evading some vexatious ecclesiastical regulation.

With unerring discrimination Dante proceeded to lay his finger on the crucial defect of the ecclesiastical system of jurisprudence. Virgil's pronouncement that the crimes detested of God are such as aim at inflicting injury on others was no mere trite scrap of morality, meant to elucidate the topography of Hell, but a truth consistently ignored in the practice of the ecclesiastical courts when they burnt a man alive for reading the Gospels in translation while they let off a murderer with a fine.

SINS WHICH THE CHURCH CALLED DEADLY   *Inf.*, xi, 67-
                                                         93.

And I: ' Most clearly Master, thy discourse
' Works out, and very well distinguishes
' This chasm and the people that possess it.
' But tell me: Why are those of the rank marsh,
' Those whom the wind drives, those whom the rain flogs,
' And who encounter with such bitter tongues,
' Why are not *they* chastised in the Red City
' If God holds them in wrath? If He doth not
' Why are they in such plight? '

And he to me: ' Why goes thy mind astray
' So far beyond what it is wont to do,

Virgil, like
Aristotle,
calls them
childish sins.

' Or are thy thoughts fixed on some other (teaching)?
' Rememberest thou not the words wherewith
' Thy Ethics carefully define the three
' Dispositions (of mind) which Heaven wills not,
' Incontinence, injustice, and the vice
' Of brutes insensate—how incontinence
' Offends God less, and a less blame incurs?
' If thou consider this conclusion well
' And callest back to memory who they are
' That penance undergo, up there, outside—
' Why they are separated from these below
' Thou wilt clearly perceive, and also why
' Justice divine hammers them with less wrath.'

' O Sun, who hatest every clouded vision,
' When thou dost solve my doubts thou dost content me
' So utterly, it pleases me to doubt
' No less than to acquire knowledge (of truth).'

Virgil's attitude towards the sins already observed by the
young Dante, examples of anger, illicit love, greed, love of
money, etc., is remarkable. Stress is laid on this by the device
of setting Dante to inquire why they are not included among
the sins specially detested by Heaven. The reader has already
perceived that these are some of the sins classified by the
Church as mortal, although as a category of the Seven Deadly
Sins they come short of Envy and Pride, which are only
hinted at among the occupants of the Styx, and were presumably too grave to be reckoned among youthful transgressions.
Virgil, not without a hidden intention, made very light of so-
called Deadly Sins. These, he reminded his disciple, were
transgressions classed by Aristotle as properly speaking childish (sins of *akrasia*), arising from unrestrained natural instincts
of passion or incontinence. As such they are far less offensive
to God than the sins which injure other men. In fact Virgil,
curiously enough, rebuked Dante for expecting to find the
Deadly Sins punished with the severity incurred by fraud and
violence. ' Why goes your judgment more astray than usual ',
or, as another rendering has it, ' On what *elsewhere* is your
mind fixed? ' It was the express intention of Virgil to expose
iniquity by stating the law marked out by Reason. The im-

plication then is that Dante had left this clearly marked furrow [1] and had adopted the code of morality taught by ignorant Confessors and enforced by law.

There can be no dispute about the execrable tone of morality inculcated, not of course by the great doctors of the Church, nor by the faithful priests whom the Church never lacked, but by countless ill-instructed and greedy Confessors. In particular morality was ill served by the orthodox practice of grading every kind of transgression as a manifestation of one or other of the Seven Deadly Sins. This offered an obvious way of escape for the host of ' penitents ' who craved for the security of absolution, but not at the price of abandoning their evil courses. For by classifying the most heinous offences against others under a heading used also to include unpremeditated acts of impulse or desire, the distinction between aggressive deeds of violence and fraud, as compared with lighter offences involving injury to none, dropped out of sight. The Deadly Sins were in effect unlawful passions, but the degree of guilt attaching to them depended, so Virgil pronounced, on the actions to which they gave rise. As for instance the Lust of the second Circle is the purely personal passion which links lovers who are cut off by fate from lawful union. The Lust exhibited in Malebolge is the passion which outrages for gain and then deserts an unprotected woman. The impetuous passion for gain of the gambler bears no comparison with the sacrilegious Avarice of Popes who confiscated for their own private treasury pious offerings for the recovery of the Holy Sepulchre.

Virgil then rejected with intention as plainly insufficient the classification of sins adopted by the Church. His code owed nothing to revelation or tradition. The Masters he followed had learned the truth about sin from Reason and Reason alone. The implication throughout is that Reason, which could throw a searchlight on the errors of mankind was, moreover, the Divine instrument by which they could be avoided.

Virgil's scheme of transgressions contained no mention of rebellion against orthodox opinions, though Dante was plainly aware that heterodox opinions existed long before

---

[1] ' *Perche tanto delira* ' means literally ' why have you so completely left the furrow? '

Christianity. He pointedly omitted from his catalogue the heterodoxy for which Epicurus and his supposed followers were plagued with flames.

In Virgil's vision of God's judgments, men were punished solely for their vices and the injuries they inflicted on others, never for the transmitted guilt of their parents, never for the ' place and time and the origin of their seed and their birth ' as in that glimpse at the inexpressible horror of the supposed curse on all mankind vouchsafed to Dante at the outset. The groups of philosophers and poets set in Limbo may seem to stand as an exception. But it is not really so. The doom of these souls was contentment, and their dwelling-place is the Elysian fields—a conception poles asunder from the orthodox notion of their eternal torment.

An interesting feature in Dante's scheme of sins is the extent to which it is grounded on the teaching of Thomas Aquinas.[1] It was by no means at once, as has been shown, that Thomas stepped into the position of authority and ultra-orthodoxy he was to occupy in the Roman Church, for he narrowly escaped condemnation as a heretic in the years immediately following his death. This would greatly stimulate the demand for his works, and it is probable that by 1287-8, when Dante was pondering over the problems of sin, copies of the *Summa* were accessible in the more important Monastic libraries. Thomas was incalculably the most live and profound exponent of pure Catholic doctrine in his generation. Certainly he ranked from the first as founder of a new school, and the effect of his teaching on Dante's mind was immediate and lasting.

ON BRUTISHNESS

In order, however, to understand the sense in which the term Brutishness (*Bestialitade*) is here used it is necessary to search the pages of Aristotle, for the modern ideas of Brutish-ness, as synonymous with violent lust, is as far akin from the conception Dante meant to convey, as is the modern idea of incontinence from Aristotle's picture of a miser. Referring to Aristotle we find that he ascribes the word Brutish to ' vice carried to a great pitch ', and applies the name, irrespective of the particular kind of crime, as a term of reproach to all ex-

[1] This is lucidly demonstrated by Dr. Reade in his *Moral System of Dante's Inferno*, Oxford, 1919.

tremes of wickedness in whatever direction it may be exhibited. Aristotle's words are: ' The brutal character is rare
among men . . . we apply the name as a term of reproach to
those who carry vice to a great pitch.' ' Even folly and
cowardice, and profligacy and ill-temper, whenever they are
carried beyond a certain pitch, are either brutal or morbid....'
' Brutality is less dangerous than vice but more horrible, for
the noble part is not corrupted here, as in a man who is
merely vicious in a natural way, but is altogether absent.' It
was open then to Dante, in completing his scheme of hell by
including a region tenanted by wretches who had altogether
lost their noble human quality, to place in it any class of
criminals provided he made it clear that they carried their
vice beyond bounds. The essence of brutality is ' vice carried
to excess ', and Aristotle says that even timidity can be carried
to such an extent that it becomes brutal. In order to make it
plain that the particular kind of crime stigmatized as ' Brutal '
satisfied Aristotle's definition,[1] Dante was clearly constrained
to display the crime, first in its ordinary human manifestations, and then in its inhuman extremes. For this purpose he
selected the vice of Fraud. Taking ten divisions of ordinary
fraud, the fraud of which he says every conscience is smitten,
he shows these forms of fraud as phases of injustice, and exposes the condition of such as practise them. Then—still
keeping the reader's attention fixed on the subject of Fraud—
he shows the deep gulf which separated this kind of Fraud
from that which the traitors used in their betrayal of friends,
guests, and benefactors. Here is ' vice carried to an extreme
pitch '. Here is a total lack of humanity, without which man
is reduced to the level of the beasts. In a word the Traitors
are exhibited as men in whom the noble part is altogether
absent. The Fraud of the Malebolge is distinguished from the
Fraud of the Pozzo by every device of which Dante was master.
There is the deep descent. There is the separate group of
Guardians, proclaiming their extra human office as plainly as
it was possible to do by their size and attributes. There is the
brutal or *in*human nature of the crime exposed in the narra-
tives of the offenders. Lastly, there are the brutish characteristics, gradually more marked as the human features in the
traitors become, with excess of crime, more entirely obliterated.

[1] *Ethics*, vii, 5.

They chatter like birds, they bark as dogs, they rend and gnaw.

It is generally assumed that Dante did not adhere to the order he laid down in this canto, and has unaccountably omitted Brutality altogether from his scheme. And yet Dante took some pains to make it clear that he was going to exhibit in the Pozzo not Violence but Fraud, carried to such an extreme pitch as should constitute Brutishness. That he chose extremes of Fraud, rather than extremes of Violence, to illustrate Brutishness accounts for the somewhat garbled arguments of which he made use to justify him in placing Fraud lower in the scale of crime than Violence. Dr. W. H. V. Reade [1] has been at some pains to demonstrate that in setting Violence above Fraud, Dante ' contradicts the judgment of St. Thomas upon Fraud and Force, distorts the meaning of Cicero, and hints at a doctrine of *malizia* which we cannot believe him to have held '. Dr. Reade concludes by asking ' Can such behaviour have been accidental, or was it inspired by some special design? ' We answer without hesitation that it was inspired by special design, that the design was to pillory in the Pozzo men guilty of so monstrous a Fraud as to obliterate every human quality, Traitors who had betrayed their country, Traitors who had baffled the designs of the Emperor Henry VII, and plotted his assassination.

[1] Dr. W. H. V. Reade, *Moral System of Dante's Inferno*, p. 335.

CHAPTER XIV

IN ARMS ON THE GUELF SIDE

[*Inferno XI*, 112-115; *XII*]

Time Reference. Dante takes part in the Campaign against the Ghibellines in 1288-9. The Minotaur as a figure of the Guelfic League. First impressions of military operations. Dissection of motives. The Centaurs (*a*) as martial Instincts (*b*) as prominent Guelf Captains. Guy de Montfort.

Period covered: 1288.

Corresponding hour: 3 a.m.

AMONG THE facts of Dante's life for which there is documentary evidence one of the most prominent is his share in the campaign undertaken by the Guelfic League in 1288-9 against the Ghibellines of Arezzo and the surrounding district. The twelfth canto of the *Inferno*, which describes the travellers' adventures in crossing the River of Boiling Blood, and depicts Dante on his way through the Bloodthirsty, brings this campaign forcibly before the reader, for it mentions under their own names some who took part in it, and glances at others who were present, under a veil of historical allusions. Moreover, Dante prefaced his descent into the valley of warfare with a highly significant Time Reference which, by noting the hour, gives a sufficient clue to the date at which the occurrence took place.

TIME REFERENCE

(Virgil speaks:)

' Follow me now for I would fain move on.
' The Fishes swim up to the horizon;
' And wholly over Caurus lies the Wain.
' Yonder far onwards we descend the cliff.'

Inf., XI, 112.
Time about 1288.

229

The rising of the Constellation of the Fishes begins about 3 a.m. and takes about two hours. At three o'clock[1] when this movement began Dante had spent eight hours over the journey of his life, having entered the *Inferno* about seven p.m. Reckoning three years for each hour (in order to bring the twenty-four hours of the day into relation with the average seventy-two years of man's life on earth) it will be seen that about twenty-four years had now elapsed. Born in 1264-5, Dante had reached the year 1288-9, which synchronizes with the date of the campaign now to be described. He was about to become an eye-witness of the offences committed in the first Zone of the Seventh Circle, and be compelled actually to take part in them himself. In his own person he was to be numbered among ' the homicides and all who strike harmfully'. Moreover, he was to share in their handiwork: ' death by violence and grievous wounds perpetrated against one's neighbour; and destruction, incendiaries and hurtful exactions against his substance.' The Time Reference coincides remarkably with the events in his own life. With this clue in mind, the strange antics of the Centaurs and the hot blood of Phlegethon assume a new significance. They are presented as they were transmuted in the mind of the poet in years to come into a species of allegory, neither far-fetched nor difficult of interpretation according to the mode of the times. Alive with many flashes of intimate self-revelation, the narrative takes its place as the *apologia* of the mature Ghibelline statesman for the part he played as a youth in arms on the Guelf side.

The immediate cause of the campaign in which Dante was called to take his part was the revival of Ghibelline influence in Pisa and Arezzo. It was in this year, 1288, that Ugolino, the Guelf tyrant of Pisa, was overthrown, and left to starve with his grandsons, by the Ghibelline Archbishop Ruggiero. All the Guelfs were banished from that city. The Ghibelline exiles flocked back to their forfeited homes, and the whole country was in a blaze. The newly banished Guelfs appealed for help to Charles II of Naples and a great rally of the Guelfic League ensued.

[1] *Che i Pesci guizzan su per l'orizzonta.* Guizzare is properly to swim and the line implies they are beginning their approach which would mark the hour of 3 p.m.

THE MINOTAUR—FIGURE OF THE GUELFIC
LEAGUE

Inf., XII, 1-45.

The place we came to, where we might descend
Over the brink, was Alpine, and the reason
Of what was there besides, of such a kind
That every eye would shun it.
Of such a sort it was as the landslide
Which struck the Adige on this side Trent
In flank, from earthquake or defective prop.
For from the mountain summit, whence it moved,
Down to the plain, the rock is shattered, so
As might afford some path to one above.
Into that chasm such was the descent.
And on the broken cliff—the very top—
There lay outstretched the infamy of Crete,
That was conceived in the adulterous cow.
When he caught sight of us he gnawed himself
Like one whom anger inwardly consumes.

> Country
> devastated
> by civil war.

> Challenged
> by the out-
> posts.

My Sage cried towards him: ' Dost thou think perchance
' That (Theseus) Duke of Athens may be here
' Who in the world up there did bring thee death?
' Monster, begone, for this man cometh not
' Instructed by thy sister (Ariadne).
' He passes on to see your punishments.'

> Dante is no
> Imperialist
> yet criticizes
> the Guelf
> tactics.

Th' Minotaur, like a bull that hath broke loose
Just when he hath received the mortal stroke,
I saw do thus—forward he cannot move,
But plunges now on this side, now on that.

' Run to the passage ', cries the wary one;
' 'Tis good while he is in frenzy, thou descend.'

Thus down over those hills of rock discharged
Which, open from the unaccustomed weight,
Gave way under my feet, we took our path.
I went on musing; and he said, ' Maybe
' Thou ponderest on this ruin, guarded by
' That brutal fury which I quelled but now.
' I would thou knowest that the other time
' When I came down, here to the deep Inferno,

> Fortress of
> error and
> hatred
> shattered by
> Christ.

Allusion to
the Fourth
Eclogue.

' This rock had not been yet broken asunder.
' But, if I well discern, short while before
' He (Christ) of the celestial Circle came [1]
' Who carried off from Dis the mighty spoil,
' 'Tis certain that the valley deep and foul,
' On all sides trembled in such wise I thought
' The Universe was moved by Love—whereby,
' So some oft-times believe, the world has been
' Thrown back into confusion. Then both here
' And elsewhere was that ancient rock o'erthrown.'

Descending from abstract cogitations on sin, Dante embarked on a dangerous pathway, and found the ground often giving way under his feet. It would seem that on his way to join up as in duty bound with the forces of the Guelfic League, Dante was horrified at the scenes of desolation and ruin which met his eye on all sides.

Soon he was confronted by the power which guarded the devastated district, in the likeness of a fierce sprawling monster, spreading universal dismay. Under the symbol of the Minotaur, it would seem we have a presentment of the Guelfic League.

The combined Guelf army was made up of 2,600 horse and some 12,000 foot soldiers. Dante alluded to it as ' infamy of Crete ', and the symbol serves its purpose in many unexpected particulars as symbols are apt to do.

Crete was the cradle of Jove who administered his laws from Mount Ida. Hence in the poem Crete stands for Rome, traditional seat both of Imperial and Papal authority, and the army which fought for Papal dominion brought infamy by its cruelty on its own cause.

The new policy of exalting every expedition undertaken at the behest of the Papal party into a Holy War was as detest-

[1] The passage is worded in such a way as to suggest the usual rendering: ' Before He came Who carried off from Dis the mighty spoil of the upper circle.' But it was a very common device in double writing to detach some significant clause from its context (as is strictly permissible in Latin verse) and thus present two very different meanings between which the reader may take his choice. To limit the spoils of Christ, as the medieval Church did, to the scanty number of chosen Israelites, by whom Limbo was exclusively tenanted, was curiously out of keeping with the Virgil of the Inferno.

able to the devout Guelf as to the Ghibelline. Never had worse excesses been committed against defenceless cities than since the Popes had offered indulgences to all who served under the Guelf banners. Armies raised under such promises and tricked out as though going to a Crusade [1] might well be reckoned as the most disgraceful feature of the usurped Papal power. The Minotaur then represented that very force of allied Guelf towns under which Dante was about to fight. For the creature was the offspring of Minos, who, under this aspect seems to symbolize Monarchy, in unholy wedlock with the '*falsa vacca*', Anti-Christ, the Carnal or usurping Church. On one side the monster partook of a semi-divine nature, completely blotted out by a bestial heritage.

Athens is a synonym for Florence. The Florentines were wont to boast in their pride of being the new Athenians, and Gacciaguida warned his descendant in Paradise [2] that the Athenians would banish him from their city as they had banished Hippolytas before him. From Florence a yearly toll of the citizens was exacted to this Guelfic League, and few indeed were those who returned safe home from the jaws of the Monster. Ariadne, the Monster's sister, stands perhaps for the opposing Imperial or Ghibelline army. For these were the legitimate offspring of Minos or Monarchy, and hated the misbegotten enemy with its lust for blood. None but those who had learned the labyrinthine art of war in the school of the Imperialist could hope to conquer the Monster. Such seem to be the implications of the allegory. On behalf of the young recruit who was one of the selected victims of the Monster, Virgil disclaimed any hostile intent. For the moment Dante was marked out by fate for the rôle of critic rather than opponent.

As he journeyed towards the seat of war he meditated, presumably on the handiwork of the most Christian army, while Virgil, resuming his personality as ancient Roman poet,

---

[1] *Para.*, xxvii, 46. *Cf.* St. Peter's denunciation of this practice.
' 'Twas not our purpose that on the right hand
' Of our successors, part of th' Christian folk
' Should sit while on the left hand were the others,
' Nor that the Keys given in grant to me
' Should turn into an ensign on a standard
' To undertake war against the baptized.'
[2] *Ibid.*, xvii, 46.

went back in memory to the days immediately preceding the Christian era. The great fortress of error was then intact. The curse of the law which the Apostle summed up as ' the enmity', kept all but the children of the promise aloof as strangers and foreigners. Then came ' He of the celestial Circle ' and carried off the mighty spoil from Dis. The rocks were rent; [1] the middle wall of partition was broken down and a way of approach was made for them that were afar off. [2] The ruin in fact of the jurists' stronghold had made the exit from it practicable. The iron walls were shattered in such a way ' as might afford some path to one above'. Virgil's parable is in effect a simple one. The broken rocks furnished a means of escape. For the *Inferno* as the scene of man's probation on earth was the appointed road which, in spite of all the horrors yet to be encountered, led in the end to God. Whatever removed obstruction was divinely planned.

And here Virgil made a very interesting reference to his own fourth Eclogue. [3] He told Dante that just before the birth of the Holy One on high, he had been distinctly aware of a movement towards harmony in the world, fouled as it was with sin and hatred, a vibration of the universe as though it were inspired by Love. [1] And yet (he added in parenthesis) there be who believe that it is by Love that the world has often been turned to chaos—a doubtful allusion to Empedocles, whose doctrine was far otherwise, but intended, more probably, to stigmatize ecclesiastics who rejected the Gospel of the Divine Love and persecuted all who grounded on Love their faith.

<table>
<tr><td>

Inf., xii, 46-139.

The fever of war.

</td><td>

THE BOILING STREAM OF BLOOD LUST

(Virgil continues speaking:)
' But fix thine eyes below; the River of Blood
' Is drawing nigh, in which are boiling those
' Who injure other men with violence.'
O blind cupidity, wicked and mad,
That doth incite us so in our short life
And then so ill immerses us for ever.

</td></tr>
</table>

[1] St. Matthew, xxviii, 51.   [2] Ephesians, ii, 13-19.
[3] Ecl. IV, 50. Look how the world with convex weight moves with assent, the land and regions of the sea O heaven sublime. Look how all rejoice at the coming age.

I saw a wide-spread fosse, curved like a bow,
Being such that it encircles all the plain
As in accord with what my Guide had said.
Between the bottom of the cliff and this
Centaurs were galloping in single file
Armed as men in the world are wont to go
With arrows to the hunt.

Perceiving us descend, each one stood still;
And from the band three issued forth with bows
And with long arrows picked out in advance.
And one cried from afar: ' What cruel death
' Dost thou approach, that comest down the coast?
' Speak out from there. If not I draw the bow.'
My Master said: ' To Chiron, at close quarters,
' Our answer we will make. Thy will was ever
' In thy rashness evil.' Then he touched me
And said: ' That one is Nessus, and himself
' He wrought the vengeance (taken) for himself.
' He in the middle, gazing at his breast,
' Is the great Chiron who brought up Achilles;
' Pholus, that was so filled with rage, that other.
' Around the fosse they go in myriads,
' Piercing whatever soul may wrench itself
' Farther from blood then guilt allots for him.'

Together we drew near these rapid beasts.
An arrow Chiron took and with the notch
Combed back his beard behind his jaws, and when
He had uncovered his great mouth, he said,
To his companions: ' Have you taken note
' That what he has on hand perturbs that one
' Behind. Not in this fashion go the feet
' Of dead folk.' My good Guide who was already
Where the two natures are conjoined—the breast—
Replied: ' He is indeed alive and I
' Am bound thus solitary to display
' The gloomy valley to him. He is brought
' Not by delight hither but by compulsion.
' He who hath charged me with this novel office
' Cometh direct from singing Alleluia:
' No robber he; nor I a thievish spirit.

235

' But by that Power through which I move my steps
' Along so wild a road, do thou accord us
' One of thy band to whom we may adhere
' That he may show us where to cross the ford
' And carry this one over on his croup:
' His is no spirit which dissolves in air.'
On his right breast Chiron turned him about,
Saying to Nessus: ' Turn and guide them then;
' If other troop come on you, keep it off.'

Dante per-
ceives differ-
ent degrees
of blood lust
in past and
present
warriors.

Under the trusty escort on we went
Along the border of the crimson boiling
Where those whose blood was boiling shouted aloud.
I saw folk to their eyebrows sunk in it;
And the great Centaur said: ' Tyrants are these
' Who steeped themselves in blood and plundering;
' Here they lament their merciless misdeeds.
' Here there is Alessandro and with him
' The cruel Dionisio who brought
' On Sicily long years of misery.

Azzo d'Este
already plot-
ting to slay
his father.

' That brow with hair so black is young Azzo:
' That other, who is fair, Opizzo is
' Of Este who in very truth was quenched
' By his unnatural son up in the world.'

Reason gives
place to
martial
instinct.

Then I turned to the Poet and he said:
' Let him be first, I second, now to thee.'

A little further on the Centaur paused
Beside a crowd that seemed far as their throats
From out that boiling stream to be emerging.
A shade he showed us, on one side, apart,

Guy de
Montfort.

Saying: ' 'Twas he that, in God's bosom, pierced
' The heart still venerated on the Thames.'

Gallant sol-
diers known to
Dante.
Dante's own
feet stained
with blood.

Then saw I folk who kept their head and even
Their breast entirely out above the stream.
And among these many I recognized.
Thus more and more shallow that blood became,
Until it seethed the feet alone—and
At this point was our passage of the fosse.

' Thou seest that the boiling stream grows less
' Continually on this side, whereas,'
The Centaur said, ' I would have thee believe
' That on that other, more and more its bed
' Sinks till it comes again where tyranny
' Is doomed to groan. Here Divine Justice stings
' That Attila that was a scourge on earth,
' Pyrrhus and Sextus too, and draws for ever
' The tears which by the boiling it unlooses
' From Rinier of Cortona and Rinier Pazzo
' Who on the highways made such open war.'
Then he turned back and crossed once more the ford.

Unidentified
figures.

Prior to the pitched battle of Campaldino which decided
the war in favour of the Guelfs, the campaign was carried on
in the usual manner, some forty castles having been stormed
and razed to the ground on Aretine territory, and the whole
district completely laid waste according to the most approved
methods of warfare. Subsequent reprisals made by the
Ghibellines on Florentine territory worked up the war spirit
of the Commune, and each party, becoming aware that a
crisis was approaching, organized their respective armies with
a view to striking a decisive blow. The Pisans appointed
Count Guido da Montefeltro Captain of their force. He had
been released from excommunication two years before, but
could not resist the call to arms with the certainty of incurring
a fresh curse. The Guelfs had no such distinguished com-
mander on their side, and the Florentines therefore approached
Charles II, the newly liberated King of Naples and Sicily,
and asked him to lend them an experienced soldier. Charles
was at this time passing through Florence on his way to Paris,
and he appointed a gallant young officer, Amerigo de Nar-
bonne, to be commander-in-chief. In view of the youth and
presumable rashness of Amerigo, the veteran William de
Durfort, who had distinguished himself throughout the Sicilian campaign, was appointed to act as his ' *balio* ' or governor,
it being the custom of the times to make a man of high rank
commander-in-chief, irrespective of his qualifications, and give
him in charge to an older officer with experience in the field.
Among those who commanded the cavalry in the Florentine
army was Corso Donati, and there is a tradition that Dante

was attached to this wing, though apparently not in the battle of Campaldino.

The stirring panorama of the Centaurs may well have been Dante's early impressions of this campaign. It started with the triumphant march towards Siena of the newly crowned Charles II from a plain near Florence, accompanied by the flower of the citizens of Florence and of the mercenaries who were in the city. A body of 800 horsemen and 3,000 foot escorted the Prince on this occasion, and there are hints which certainly suggest that he himself, with the principal personages in his train, finds a place among the occupants of the River of Boiling Blood.

The operations of the Centaurs who seem to have held the place of staff officers and Provost Marshals correspond with what might take place at such a muster of the forces. The Centaurs had many under them charged with the duty of keeping it up to full strength and punishing deserters who were an ever-present danger. Their office was to keep order and assign each contingent its proper place while themselves making part of the procession.

The spectacle, as Dante descended the incline towards the river of Phlegethon, was animated in the extreme, especially when contrasted with the scenes encountered among the doleful tombs of the heretics. The long indecision which had held him questioning on the summit was over. The moment for action, whether for right or wrong, was at hand, and Reason itself concurred in the forward impulse. The hideous nature of the stream was hidden at first sight from view. It lay curved like a bow, stretching far out of sight right and left, and in fact embraced the entire plain, for no part of Italy was free from strife. Between the cliff on which the poets trod and the rolling river below lay a broad tract of level ground crowded with eager figures. In a long line by the side of the banks the Centaurs rode, armed with arrows which they discharged at any who showed a disposition to disobey orders. Instantly as he came within the sphere of the Centaurs Dante was challenged by three of the number who separated from the throng and advanced towards him.

We shall be prepared to find that the moral aspect of the allegory takes a place of special importance in this canto. In later years Dante must often have reviewed the circumstances which set him fighting on the Guelf side, and severely scrutinized his motives. In building up the moral symbolism of the Centaurs he seems to have aimed at laying bare his youthful impulses, right and wrong, at this juncture.

The Centaurs typify the 'irascible appetite'. In the *Banquet* Dante compares this appetite to a horse, and selects it as one of the particular instincts characteristic of the season of youth. When curbed by the bridle of temperance it is wholly noble, but when ill-guided the horse leads the rider far astray. Aristotle's definition of this irascible appetite as courage was plainly in Dante's mind when he described the three Centaurs. While all are occupied in ' chasing and flying ' [1] three are more particularly brought under notice, and answer to the three kinds of courage which Aristotle describes.

Dante did not condemn himself for the part he played, for Reason was by his side, and in the character of his conscience could sincerely declare, ' Necessity drives him and not delight'. But neither had he any illusions concerning the instincts which were at work within him at this moment of his career. It would seem that none of the Centaurs answer to that noblest form of courage which has in it nothing of the animal instinct but is wholly rational. Aristotle asserts, however, that there are other kinds of courage 'so called', and one of these he specifies particularly as ' the kind which inspires Homer's characters'. It may be safely concluded that it was on this that Achilles was nourished, and hence we may easily identify Chiron the leader of the whole band as personifying this kind of courage. Aristotle says it is most like of all the inferior kinds to the true courage, ' because its impulse is a virtuous one, viz., a sense of honour and desire for a noble thing (glory) and aversion to reproach '. When Chiron drew near to Dante he was gazing at his breast where the higher or human side of him stood revealed, and it was on this side that Dante approached him.

There are two other kinds of so-called courage. The one is to be identified with Pholus, ' *che fu sì pien d'ira* '. For Aristotle says: ' People sometimes include rage within the meaning of the word courage . . . because the courageous man also is full of rage . . . being driven to face danger by rage or pain is not courage proper.' And again: ' The act of re-

---

[1] *Banquet*, IV, 26. *Questo appetito mai altro non fa che cacciare e fuggire. . . .*

venge is pleasant, but those who fight for these motives may
fight well but are not courageous, for they do not act because
it is noble to do so, or as reason bids, but are driven by their
passions.'

Pholus seems to typify the wrathful and Nessus the revenge-
ful passion which drives men to warfare and tortures them
when they have yielded captive their will. The martial impulse, animating in its first effects, as the gay scene Dante beheld before the real inwardness of war became apparent to
his nearer view, was not the noble courage described by
Aristotle as the attribute of a high-minded man, but neither
was it altogether ignoble. It was partly animal no doubt, but
it was unattended by the myriad wild and fierce instincts
which he could behold tormenting those who loved bloodshed. It was threefold in its nature. The guiding spirit was
that laudable ' political courage ', as Aristotle called it, which
was the quality of citizens who ' often faced dangers because
of legal pains and penalties on the one hand, and honours on
the other '. He fought because he was ' called out ', with no
particular enthusiasm, but with the ambition to acquit himself well. Once in the fray, however, he was borne along more
by the sense of retaliation, the desire to give as good as he received in the way of blows, than from this measured kind of
calm courage, although he acted always under the orders of
Chiron, and kept Pholus, whose part was not conspicuous,
in the background. Such seems to be the psychology of the
canto.

Dante and Virgil now drew near to the 'fleet beasts.' By
uncovering his great mouth with the reverse end of the arrow,
Chiron revealed the human feature which redeemed his
figure. The mouth was the classical symbol for eloquence, and
its mention leads the reader to expect wisdom from his utterances. His first remark exposed his perception of more than
met the eye. ' Have you perceived that what he is about
(what he touches) perturbs (causes emotion in) that one behind? ' This permissible transposition of the clauses lends a
new complexion to Chiron's remark. He could divine from a
glance at the sensitive new recruit that bloodshed meant to
him a very different thing from what it meant to the hardened
soldier dead in intellect.

Dante's vindication of himself from blood lust lies in Virgil's reply. He fought because he was compelled to do so and he came thither straight from the worship of God. In the obvious sense ' *tal* ' stands for Beatrice who withdrew from singing Alleluia in order to dispatch Virgil to Dante's assistance. But actually in the allegorical sense the pronoun stands for Dante himself, victor in the long conflict with the forces of incredulity, who interrupted his thanksgiving to charge his Reason with the new office of affording restraint in scenes of bloodshed. Thus Dante freed himself to his inner public from all taint of lust for blood or plunder. He was no robber, nor was the spirit which animated him a guilty one.[1]

Reason alone, however, cannot carry a man forward on the battlefield. Close behind Chiron, representing the quality of ' political courage ' which ruled the field, followed the spirit of anger and retaliation. Wheeling about on his right breast, a sign that the highest motives were uppermost, Chiron selected Nessus to be Dante's guide, for the principle of revenge seems to have been a leading feature in animating the Florentine army to undertake reprisals against the Aretines, who had recently laid waste their countryside. Nessus, therefore, led the way. And Virgil drew back to give him place for, in the moment of approaching warfare, Reason submits to yield to warlike instincts.

The clues supplied in the text, read in the light of historical records, render it possible to guess at the identity of the three Centaurs who personified warlike impulses. In the great Chiron, a commanding personality, we may surmise the poet hid the venerable figure of William de Durfort, the Guelf Commander-in-chief, killed at the approaching battle. William de Durfort was a man of high character, learned in the law no less than in battle. He is represented fixing his eyes on his breast in token that the things of the mind engaged his attention. It is recalled of him as his principal title to fame that ' he brought up Achilles '. Now Achilles, bravest of all the Greeks, stands in the *Divina Commedia* for Charles Martel, whom Dante loved and whose early death he

---

[1] The omission of the pronoun in the line ' non e ladron ' marks out ' tal ' as the subject. The words are spoken of the same person:

> ' Tal si partì da cantare alleluia
> Che mi commise quest'uficio nuovo—
> Non è ladron. . . .'

mourned. Charles Martel had been lately Vicar-General in Naples during the time of his father's imprisonment. William de Durfort was his principal adviser, and doubtless had his part in the moulding of his political outlook so heartily approved by Dante.

The Centaur Pholus 'who was so full of wrath' may possibly stand for the young hot-headed knight Amerigo, whose rashness the Florentines feared. In Nessus there is ground for suspecting that the figure of Corso Donati is glanced at.

The allegory which connects Nessus with Corso Donati is extremely Dantesque. Dejanira is Florence; Hercules the Empire to which she belonged. The poisoned shirt is conspiracy. Nessus attempts to violate Dejanira and falls a victim to his unholy passion for her. Dying he bequeaths, through her, a legacy of fatal poison to Hercules. So did Corso set out to seduce Florence to his own purposes. Slain as a consequence of his fatal lust to dominate his native city, he bequeathed that Nessus shirt of treachery which brought ruin to the Imperial cause.

When Nessus beheld Dante joining his troops he challenged him; and there was a prophetic note in the words he used: 'To what martyrdom (martirio) are you advancing, who descend the cliff side?' All the insults and injuries comprised in Dante's long exile are foreshadowed in this inquiry. And Virgil's retort, '*Mal fu la voglia tua sempre si tosta*,' is no less prophetic, for it holds within itself the long series of Donati's rash deeds which brought discredit and disgrace on Florence and were crowned by his own assassination.

It is possible to identify many of the occupants of the Phlegethon as warriors actually engaged in this campaign.

Alessandro. Neither Alexander of Macedon nor Alexander of Pherae quite fit in here. We suggest that the Alessandro referred to was the celebrated Count of the Romena branch of the Guidi, who was notorious in his disdain for law and honour. Alessandro figures here among the bloodthirsty as the recent Captain of the Guelf Taglia and the hero of many a savage raid. In particular he was in command, defeated, and put to flight in the ambush on the ford of the Toppo, which took place in this very year. A striking allusion to this exploit occurs in the next canto.[1]

[1] *Inf.*, XIII, 121.

Dionisio. The Dionysius who caused Sicily to have years of misery is an easy disguise for Charles II, recently liberated from his Sicilian prison after years of strife on his behalf. The younger Dionysius was expelled from Sicily and lost the crown of his father. This younger Charles, whose misfortunes paralleled those of the former Sicilian King, visited Florence, as mentioned above, just before the battle of Campaldino, and took an active part in promoting the Guelf interests.

Azzolino and *Opizzo d'Este.* These are son and father. Opizzo, the notorious Marquis of Ferrara, to whom Modena and Reggio submitted, not without much bloodshed, in 1288-9, was nearing the end; he died in 1293, and his son Azzo, who succeeded, and perhaps in vices excelled him, was believed to have murdered him. The contrast in complexion between him and his father is emphasized, as with a view to throwing doubt upon Azzo's parentage, and the expression applied to him '*figliastro*', or stepson, glances at the same idea. Azzolino is usually taken by commentators for the tyrant Eccelino, who died in 1260, and of whom monstrous atrocities are related. But in Dante's survey of the Guelf promoters of strife at this moment the more obvious figure is Azzo the less, the cruel son of a cruel father; both were immersed in blood and the one already plotted the murder of the other. Then Nessus pointed out a conspicuous figure, distinguished from the rest, and briefly alluded to him.

Guy de Montfort. Few of its adherents had brought greater scandal upon the Papal Curia than this Englishman. He was the son of Simon de Montfort, who was defeated and slain at the Battle of Evesham by Prince Edward; six years later, in 1271, under pretext of avenging his father, Guy, who was deputy of Charles of Anjou, the Papal Vicar in Tuscany, horrified the whole of Christendom by stabbing his cousin Henry in the Church of San Silvestro in Rome, at the moment of the elevation of the Host. The astonishing thing about this brutal deed was its acceptance as a reasonable act of filial vengeance both by his friends and by the Church. Not only was Guy left unmolested and accorded speedy absolution, after a purely spectacular penance, but he was actually employed by Martin IV soon after to oppose Guido da Montefeltro and subdue the Romagna to the Pope. By thus placing him, undisguised, in Phlegethon as a damned soul, Dante entered a powerful protest against the use of such instruments by the Papal Curia, and deliberately repudiated the efficacy of the Sacrament of Penance.

Among those less deeply immersed in blood, Dante recognized many whose names he does not recall, for they had fought by his side. He dipped his own feet in that flood, and he does not spare himself the inference of having incurred a kindred guilt.

Thus the poet passed in review the men with whom he was associated in 1289-1290, fighting without motives of patriotism, moved merely by desire for plunder or revenge. All were fighting under the banner of the Church and the Angevin. The instincts which pricked them on were their penalty, and the blood which they shed was their only guerdon.

CHAPTER XV

DEFEAT OF THE GHIBELLINE EXILES AT CAMPALDINO

[Inferno XIII ; Seventh Circle]

Allegorical presentment of the battle of Campaldino. The exiles, spoiled and harassed by legal exactions, seemed themselves but mere worthless stocks hidden behind the impenetrable barrier of thorns and stakes thrown up to check the Guelf onslaught. Dante depicts what he did and saw on his way through the thicket, pausing now and again to comment, from his later standpoint as a Ghibelline exile himself, on the incidents of the day.

Identification of the unnamed Thorn with Guido da Montefeltro. Reasons for inferring that it was Dante who killed Buonconte in this battle. Introduction of Talano Adimari under his own name fixes the occasion and the date. The fate of the Bishop of Arezzo.

Period covered: 1289.

Corresponding hour: 3 to 3.20 a.m.

In Villani's account of the battle of Campaldino[1] he mentions that the Ghibellines had carefully prepared the ground on which they made their stand, and that they sheltered themselves behind a thick entanglement of stakes and thorns to receive the charge of the Guelf cavalry. Hence, so it would seem, arose the strange transition in the narrative from the River Phlegethon to the Pathless Thicket. Dante depicts himself dashing over as it were in hot ardour, born by a martial spirit of retaliation, stained with blood-lust, to be pulled up suddenly before an impenetrable thicket bristling with hidden foes. Regarding them as enemies of their country he esteemed them mere poisonous growths. In his eyes they had no human semblance. It came to him later with a shock of horror that they had like feelings with himself. Moreover, he was to realize many years later in what way men, banished from their homes and native city, were comparable to spirits imprisoned within such worthless stocks and briars as those

---

[1] Villani, Bk. VII, c. 131.

through which he pushed his way. They could offer stubborn resistance it is true to their enemies, but this resistance was weakened by the many foes who preyed upon them at all times. Everything he saw and heard and did on this memorable occasion furnished material to feed his unerring instinct for allegory. This mournful Wood of battle reappears again in the *Purgatorio*,[1] when Dante exposed the treachery of the Podestà responsible for his condemnation. In that passage the battle-ground was Florence itself. From this sad Wood, Fulcieri da Calboli came forth stained with blood. The trees he hacked down were the old Ghibelline stocks, so drastically rooted out that not within a thousand years could Florence hope to be renewed to its pristine state of felicity. Moreover, the same imagery is employed for the promising youths or *scions* which spring from the parent tree.[2] It is a familiar figure to all in prose and verse.

<table>
<tr><td>Inf., XIII, 1-15.</td><td>RUINED GHIBELLINES</td></tr>
</table>

Inf., XIII, 1-15.

RUINED GHIBELLINES

Not yet had Nessus reached the other side
When we, into a thicket cast ourselves
Which by no path whatever was marked out.

Exiles transmuted to barren stocks.

Not green the foliage but of dusky hue;
Not smooth but gnarled and tangled were the boughs;
Not any fruits were there but thorns with poison.
Those savage beasts that hate the cultured tracts
Between Cecina and Corneto, hold
No brakes so rugged or impenetrable.

The lawyers prey upon them in likeness of Harpies.

Here do the loathsome Harpies make their nests,
Who chased the Trojans from the Strophades
With dismal augury of future woe.
Broad wings they have, with human necks and faces
Their feet with claws and the huge belly feathered;
They utter mournful cries on the weird trees.

Then the kind Master thus began to say:
' Before thou enter further, know that thou art in
' The Second Round, and there shalt stay until
' Thou comest out on to the dread Arena.
' Therefore look well around and thou shalt see
' Things which might rob belief from my discourse.'

[1] *Purg.*, XIV, 64.   [2] *Ibid.*, 102.

On first coming into contact with them the impulse was to
hew and hack as the only way to struggle through. Armed
with sharp spears they offered an unbroken front of resistance.
More savage than the bandits who infested the countryside,
they were utterly useless to the commonwealth, and fit only
to be exterminated. The Harpies (fit emblem of the rapacious
ecclesiastical lawyers) did what they could to discourage and
embarrass the exiles on whom they battened, for ever dinning
their doom of eternal damnation into their ears, injuring
their property, and paralyzing their energies.

The reasoning which follows must be taken as the swift in-
rush of perceptions hardly realized at the moment till in later
years they assumed significance. In among the serried ranks
of men, who for him had no human semblance or feelings,
Dante plunged, bent only on getting through. Most of the
rugged stocks among which he struggled were Florentines
actually fighting against their native city and, from the
patriotic point of view, they were one and all like suicides,
dead as citizens by their own act. Such was his first impression
of the enemies he had been called out to oppose.

DANTE'S DEED OF VIOLENCE

I heard groans uttered upon every side
But saw no person who was making them
So that in blank amazement I stood still.
I think that he may have thought that I might think
That all these voices in the branches came
From persons who were hiding them from us.
Thereat the Master said: ' If thou dost break
' From off one of the plants some little shoot
' The thoughts thou holdest will be all cut short.'
Forward a little then I stretched my hand
And plucked from a great Thorn Tree a small branch.
' Why dost thou tear me? ' it began to cry.
' Hast thou no spirit of pity whatever?
' Men were we once and now are turned to stocks.
' More pitiful might well have been thy hand
' Had we been souls of serpents.'

As a green brand that at one end is burning
And from the other sap exudes, the while

Inf., XIII, 22-45.

The
Ambush.

Dante de-
stroys the
scion of a
great stock,

hears the
father's
shout of
anguish

and is pene-
trated with a
sense of
blood guilt.

247

It hisses with the air that is escaping,
So from the broken splint came forth together
Both words and blood. Hence I let fall the top
And stood still, like a man that is afraid.

Leonardo Bruni, who had seen a letter from Dante with a plan and account of the battle of Campaldino, related that Dante

' fought vigorously on horseback in the front rank where he was exposed to very grave danger; for the first shock of battle was between the opposing troops of horse, in which the Aretine cavalry charged the Florentine horsemen with such fury, that they were borne down, broken and routed and driven back upon the foot soldiers '.

This account of the battle may be pieced out by Villani's story:

' So great was the shock that the most part of the Florentines' forefront was unhorsed, and the main body was thrust back some way across the field, but for àll that they were not dismayed, nor thrown into confusion, but received the enemy steadily and bravely; and with the foot-soldiers drawn up on either flank they closed in on the enemy, fighting desperately for a good while.'

The curious occurrence in the Wood suggests that, notwithstanding more than one hiatus we have here a picture of Dante's own deeds in the famous battle. His first actions were plainly violent and pitiless, even if they were prompted by Reason. He rushed in among the poisonous growth which confronted him regardless what damage he did. All round him sounds of anguish were filling his ears. There would be cries for mercy, horrible groans from those wounded in the first onslaught, fierce shouts from those who dashed upon each other; all plainly audible in the strange hush of battle before the introduction of gunpowder. That those against whom he hurled himself were sentient beings like himself never entered into the head of the meditative student now for the first time engaged in hand-to-hand strife. Some indistinct idea crossed his mind that the sounds all round meant that he had fallen into an ambush; and while his imagination was fired with

248

the apprehension of a hidden foe rushing up to overwhelm the squadron in which he was fighting, Reason prompted him to strike out and slay. The ambiguity of the expression '*Io credo ch'ei credette ch'io credesse*' suggests the effort of the mind to account for action committed in a moment of intense excitement. With a deliberation which it filled him with shame to reflect upon he broke off a bough from a great thorn-tree confronting him. In other words he aimed a mortal blow at a scion of one of the great Ghibelline families. He saw the blood gush out. He let go his hold upon his adversary. And in a moment the full meaning of war rushed over his soul. What no reasoning could ever have done, what no poetic description of battles even in the words of Virgil himself had been able to effect, the first sight of blood shed by his own hand had brought to his inner perception. He realized instantaneously that the dense thicket of enemies was composed of men of like passions with himself. The tumult of the battle rolled on afar. But we do not at once follow its course. In a flash the stage is cleared, and we behold merely the figure of the Great Thorn for whose sake the drama here pauses while he clears his reputation.

THE VINDICATION OF GUIDO DA MONTEFELTRO   *Inf.*, XIII, 46-78.

' O wounded Soul', my Sage replied, ' had he
' Been able to believe at first that thing
' Which only in my verse he has beheld
' Against thee he would not have stretched his hand.
' The thing incredible it was that made me
' Incite him to the deed, which grieves myself
' But tell him who thou wert, so that in lieu
' Of other amends he may revive thy fame
' Up in the world, when he is let return.'

Then said the Trunk: ' Silence I cannot keep
' Thou so allurest me with gentle speech.
' May it not burden you if I become
' Somewhat involved in making out my case.
' I am the man who guarded both the keys
' Of Frederic's Heart, so softly turning them
' In locking and unlocking, I drew forth
' From his retirement almost every man.

Guido had charge of the Capitol for Corradino.

249

Papal
emissaries
sowed discord
between him
and his
master.

' Faith in the glorious office I maintained
' So firm I lost thereby both sleep and vigour.
' The Harlot, common Death and vice of Courts
' That never lifted her adulterous eyes
' From Caesar's house, inflamed all souls against me;
' And they that were inflamed did so inflame
' Augustus that his joyful honours turned
' To bitter griefs.'
' My soul in its disdainful inclination
' Thinking to shirk disdain with Death no less

He sur-
rendered
the Capitol,
but declared
himself loyal
in spite of
appearances.

' Made me though just, unjust against myself.
' To you I swear by the young roots within
' This Tree, I never broke faith to my Lord
' That was so worthy honour. And if one
' Of you into the world return, let him
' Refresh my fair fame that lies prostrate still
' Beneath the stroke that Envy dealt on it.'

The incident is grounded on a passage in the *Æneid*,[1] relating how Æneas, after tearing a myrtle from the earth, dis-
covers it to be bleeding and learns that it holds the transmuted figure of his intimate associate Polydorus, who was
foully assassinated and lies under the imputation of betraying
his country for gold. In the hands of Virgil the story became
intensely personal. Polydorus is greatly concerned to warn
his friend of approaching danger, while Æneas, smitten with
anguish at the false accusation under which Polydorus is
prisoned, takes immediate steps to bring rest to the tortured
soul and vindicate his memory.

The unnamed figure from whose rugged stem Dante broke
off a shoot has always been identified by commentators as
Pier de la Vigna, Chancellor of Frederic II. Pier was accused
of plotting with Pope Innocent IV against his Master. His
eyes were put out and it appears (although the stories about
him by no means agree and may possibly be glosses on Dante's
text) that he committed suicide. His description of himself
in the text seems *to suggest* this disgraced statesman who died
in 1249. But there is room for conjecture that Dante used his
story as a screen for that of a personage infinitely more interesting in his eyes, the Commander-in-chief of the Ghibelline

[1] Bk. III, 22 ff.

army at Campaldino, Guido da Montefeltro. There was no such personal link between Dante and Pier de la Vigna as could account for the amount of space devoted to the episode and to the intense emotion it evoked. But with Guido da Montefeltro it was otherwise; Dante's own exile and the calumny heaped upon his name, rendered him very sceptical about the crimes imputed to Ghibellines, and eager to exculpate from blame any whom in his unregenerate Guelf days he had in any way injured. One incident in Guido's career shows a curious parallel with the tale of Pier de la Vigna as abridged in the elliptical narrative of the text. Pier was the trusted minister of Frederic II; Guido held the same post of confidence with Frederic's *Heart*—his grandson, *COR*radino, such a play on the name as could not escape medieval attention. Both men were exposed to obloquy for crimes they had not committed. Both maintained in the teeth of adverse evidence their abhorrence of treachery, their loyalty to their Imperial Masters.

It was easy to frame the confession of the unnamed victim in such a way that only points coinciding with the careers of both statesmen were brought forward.

Examined as part of Dante's autobiography the story assumes an entirely new aspect. Dante is beheld face to face with one of the great figures of his own day, disguised under the figure of a Thorn Tree, because it was his unhappy destiny to rend and destroy instead of bearing the wholesome fruits of statesmanship. Like Æneas in the presence of Polydorus, Dante was not only to listen to a tale of bitter wrong endured, but, alas, to receive a warning of impending disaster; like him he was to make such reparation as lay in his power to a man he had deliberately injured.

To identify the Thorn Tree with Guido da Montefeltro is to perceive at once the true import of the injury involved in breaking off the shoot from the parent stem.

Guido da Montefeltro had a long and chequered career. He was by far the greatest warrior in the Ghibelline party, feared even more than he was hated by the Papal party, and unrivalled in stratagem and daring. But for all his fame he lay, even for his own side, under a dark cloud. His prowess stretched back to days before Dante was born. When, in 1267, Corradino at the age of sixteen made his bold descent into Italy, and, as the grandson of Frederic II, attempted to wrest Sicily, his lawful inheritance, from Charles of Anjou, Guido da Montefeltro, already famous, was at his side. The Sicilians at once proclaimed Corradino their king, the City of Rome declared for him, and the Capitol under the Senator Don Arrigo of Castile was fortified to serve as a base of operations. Guido da Montefeltro ' esteemed the greatest general of his age ' succeeded to the high dignity of Don Arrigo's Vicar, and was entrusted with the custody of the Capitol.

Astonishing success attended Corradino in his first advances. The Roman City was completely subdued to the Ghibellines and there seemed but a step between Frederic's grandson and the Empire. Then followed the disastrous defeat of Tagliacozzo, 23rd August 1268, and Corradino with a scanty following fled to Rome. Guido da Montefeltro, as Vicar of Don Arrigo, still held the Capitol; thither the fugitives directed their steps. They were refused admittance, and the Capitol fell into the hands of Charles, who captured Corradino and put him to death. Guido da Montefeltro at once made his peace with the Church, and incurred suspicion of having taken bribes to surrender the last stronghold.

In the vindication of Guido which Dante ' to make some amends ' dramatically supplied from the lips of the culprit himself, there is confession of cowardice but denial of treachery. Both Keys, Guido declared, he held of Frederic's Heart, which in very truth was no other than his son, born the year that Frederic died. At first so well did he fulfil his duty that he succeeded in drawing almost every one from his retirement (*secretum*) so that all the hidden Ghibellines openly espoused the cause of Corradino. In fidelity to his glorious office he dedicated himself body and soul to the service of the Emperor-elect. Then arose the Harlot, that Whore of Babylon, under whose figure the Papal Curia is frequently alluded to in the *Divina Commedia*. Ceaselessly active in their machinations at the Imperial Court, the Papal agents, ' common Death and source of vice ' in all the courts of Europe, set about sowing discord. The measure of their success may be gauged by the contrast between Rome on 24th July 1268, crowded with enthusiastic Ghibellines to welcome Corradino, and Rome a few weeks later completely hostile, affording no spot of refuge to the popular hero. All minds were inflamed against Guido, and no less against the unhappy Conrad Augustus, now doomed to behold all his joyous honours turned into anguish and dismay. The text seems to suggest that Guido had been beguiled by a promise on the part of the Papalists which had not been kept. Probably he had been assured of honourable terms for his Master no less than for himself whereby they might escape dishonour with death, if the untenable fortress were surrendered. The step proved fatal. Corradino was butchered. Guido, perceiving that all was lost, made submission and, although loyal at heart, assumed an appearance of disloyalty.

Dante evidently believed that, spite of appearances, Guido had remained true to Corradino. He set himself to open up the truth just as Virgil had done in the case of Polydorus, and leaves us the picture of the calumniated veteran solemnly swearing by his ' new roots ' that he had not played his Master false. It is characteristic of Dante's judgment on sinners that he should have chosen for his typical suicide one who had preferred dishonour to death. But what injury, it must be asked, had Dante done to Guido da Montefeltro that he should feel impelled to undertake the justification of the Ghibelline Captain, in order ' to make amends '? A curious chain of reasoning connects the whole episode with the campaign of 1289 in which Dante took part. Under the parable of the great Thorn a human personality is visible. To break off from it a shoot or scion can hold no other significance than to slay one of his sons. Such a deed could not honourably be wrought save in battle. And it was in battle, on the field of Campaldino, that Guido's son Buonconte was killed. The inference that Dante allowed his inner circle of readers to make was plainly that he himself was responsible for the death of Buonconte, and we surmise that he delayed his narrative in order to set the vindication of the father in juxtaposition with the deed.

The place which this engagement occupied in Dante's mind and the extent to which every incident in the day, the disposition of the ground, and the fluctuations of the weather even, were imprinted on his memory, are graphically displayed in the fifth and sixth cantos of *Purgatory*. Before the Gate of Purgatory, among the late repentant, violently slain, the poet encountered many who had been killed at

Campaldino, and was followed by them much as the winner of the game, he says, may be followed by those who have lost their cast. They were all transfigured, so that he could not recognize them for what they had been when disfigured by violent passions. One in particular hailed him, adjuring him ' by that desire which draws thee up the lofty mount'. It was Buonconte da Montefeltro. Instead of at once giving him the required assurance of his prayers, Dante asked ' what force or what chance made thee stray so far from Campaldino that thy burial-place was never known? ' The question betrays a whole cycle of anxious suspense. It is the continuation of that scene in which the broken bough was seen to fall from Dante's hand, when with the gaping wound in his throat Buonconte fled from Dante's weapon. The minute details given by Buonconte of his subsequent adventures seem to represent the preoccupation of many a remorseful hour. There were two things the poet could do for the man he had killed. The first was to pray for him, the second to vindicate him from the dread implication of being eternally damned, for, according to the cruel proclamation of the Pope, all who died fighting against the Angevin banners were *ipso facto* excommunicate and eternally damned. This was why Buonconte is displayed uncheered, ' with downcast brow', since those who loved him best believed it mortal sin to pray for him. Dante set his vindication in dramatic form, knowing that none would ever doubt Buonconte's salvation who read how he crossed his arms on his breast, ' ended speech with the name of Mary ', and was received in the angel's arms. Is there any finer scene in *Purgatory* than that in which the angel of God contends against the emissary of Anti-Christ, and bears the penitent soul, in the teeth of the Papal sentence of damnation, to the abode of peace? With Buonconte thus vindicated, ' Giovanna and the others ' would no longer scruple to pray for the peace of his soul. The episode of Campaldino closes with Dante's beautiful reasoning on the subject of intercessory prayer which expresses his own faith and practice, and incidentally betrays that here was his refuge when the faces of those who had been violently slain by his own act and that of his comrades in arms crowded round him with beseeching looks.

ANOTHER WARNING OF EXILE

Inf., XIII, 78-180.

He paused awhile, and the poet said to me:
' Lose not the moment since he holds his peace,
' But speak and ask him, if you would know more.'
Whereat I said: ' Do thou ask him again
' Of that thou dost believe will satisfy me;
' For I could not—such pity wrings my heart.'
Then he began again: ' So may the man
' Freely accord thee what thy speech entreats,
' Imprisoned spirit, may it please thee yet
' To tell us how the spirit gets entangled
' Within these knots, and tell us if thou canst
' If any is ever loosed from such like members.'

Then blew the Trunk with force and soon the wind
Was changed into these words: ' Briefly shall you
' Be answered. When the soul relentless quits
' The body whence it hath itself broke loose
' Minos dismisses it to the Seventh Gulf.
' It falls into the Wood, nor is there place
' Allotted it, but where chance launches it
' There like a grain of spelt it germinates.
' A sapling it shoots up and a wild plant;
' Later the Harpies feeding on its leaves
' Cause grief and for the grief an opening.
' We shall come, like the others, for our spoils,
' Yet not that any be re-indued therewith;
' It is not just, forsooth, a man should have
' That whereof he deprives himself, again.
' Here we shall draw them—through the dolorous Wood
' Our bodies will be hung, each on the Thorn
' Of its tormenting shade.'

The inevitable fate of him who contends against his own country is to become a worthless stock.

He has no chance of ever recovering his former possessions.

While yet in consternation at his own deed, the first, probably the only, mortal blow he ever struck, Dante paints himself in the act to receive one of those cryptic warnings about his future which appear at intervals throughout the earlier part of the *Inferno*.

The governing class in Italy at this time was sharply divided into those who held possession and those in exile. Speaking to Guido, the exile, ' How does the soul become tangled up in these knots,' asked Virgil, ' and do any ever get free from them? ' The answer was not encouraging. When the war-like spirit quits the body (of the orthodox Church) from which it has torn itself, he is driven (by excommunication) forth to this seventh gulf where men herd who reckon as ' destroyers of themselves ' because they have taken arms against the Church. He falls back haphazard into the world of exile, where no special place is assigned to him, and wherever fortune flings him there he must linger like some worthless seed incapable of producing fruit. Always, however brave and lusty as a stripling, he is but a wild growth, of no use to any man. The lawyers feed upon his substance, and create endless vexations for which, if for no other cause, the exiles are continually complaining. Like the others (the Guelfs were once exiles too) these exiled Ghibellines will return for their spoils, and it was for that purpose, indeed, that they were in arms at that moment. But Guido had no illusions about their ever obtaining possession of the lands and goods of which they had been robbed. He realized that there was no Justice in seizing, of his own act, on property without legal mandate. Always their doom would be to drag their bodies about in that Wood of exile in which Dante's own feet were one day to wander; here each one of the exiles would feel the torment-ing shadows of the past. Such was the warning that Dante in after years realized that he might have taken to heart from the spectacle of the great Count fighting without hope, stripped of all his great possessions, reduced to ignominy. His after career was full of vicissitudes. Finally he procured re-lease from excommunication and retired to end his days in a Franciscan monastery. Dante spoke with admiration of his intention to turn his last thoughts to God, calling him ' our most noble Latin Guido of Montefeltro '.[1]

Inf., xiii, 109-129.

COWARDICE AND TREACHERY

Attentive still to that maimed Stock we stood,
Thinking he might desire to tell us more,
When by a clamour we were startled, like
One who feels boar and chase approach his stand—
Who hears the beasts come crashing through the boughs.
And, lo, on the left hand, naked and torn,

[1] *Banquet*, Bk. iv, c. 28.

Were two, flying with haste impetuous
So that they broke each barrier in the Wood.
The foremost (one) ' Now hurry, hurry. Death! '
The other, seeming to himself too slow,
Cried: ' Lano, not so ready were thy legs
' When thou wert jousting on the Toppo even; '
And since his breath perhaps was failing him
He grouped himself (for refuge) with a Bush.
Behind them all the Wood was full of hounds,
Black, ravening and fleet, like grey-hounds that
Have slipped their leash. On him who squatted down
They set their teeth and hacked him piece by piece—
Then carried off those miserable limbs.

Talano
Adimari
runs away
from the
battle of
Campaldino.

Mercenary
soldiers in
headlong
assault.

In the Montefeltro episode, the effect of speed and ferocity
proper to a battlefield were sacrificed to the need for producing a deep moral impression. The real meaning of acts
of violence committed thoughtlessly in battle was to be
brought before the reader. The unsuspected truth that the
foes at which he hacked were no less human than himself, the
tragedy of exile and of slanderous calumny, all this is represented as flashing through the poet's mind. The hell framework too had to be accounted for, and deftly woven into the
allegorical sense of the imagery, so that the exiles, transformed
to poisonous stocks in the eyes of their foes, to be rooted out by
blood and fire, might appear in the more obvious narrative
to be damned souls suffering God's eternal judgments. But
now all this is effaced by a new and tempestuous scene. Suddenly Dante became witness of a new episode in the battle,
one in which he held the rôle of spectator rather than actor.
Roused by unusual clamour he turned to see two fugitives
tearing along in hot haste, forcing their way as they went
through the barriers framed of stakes with which the ground
had been prepared beforehand to check the charge of the
enemy cavalry. The two were being pursued by mercenary
soldiers familiarly known as ' *brache* ' or hounds of chase,
often men of foreign origin, paid to keep order in the city,
execute punishments ordered by the Podestà, and accompany
the army on expeditions of plunder or revenge. There were
hounds of this kind in both Guelf and Ghibelline armies; it
was their part to finish the business of the battle by dispatch-

ing those to whom no quarter was given and securing captives from whom ransom might be obtained.

The two fugitives were apparently Guelfs. They retained their human likeness which the Ghibellines, to him who opposed them, had lost. One led the way, shouting as he went to the other: 'Run now, haste, haste, Death'—an ejaculation which does not sound particularly valiant, however it may be interpreted. His comrade shouted to him as he disappeared in the distance: ' Lano, thy legs were not so ready (even) at the jousts of the Toppo.' What happened to Lano there is nothing more to show, but from this taunt, and from the fact that he did not stop to aid his comrade, he is plainly marked out for a coward. He is committing moral suicide in the act of saving his own skin. The use of his own name shows pretty clearly who he was. Lano is an obvious abbreviation of *Talano* and the allusion to the ' jousts of the Toppo ' at which Talano cut a queer figure, establishes his identity. A few months before the battle of Campaldino, the warriors of the Guelf Taglia, including many Florentines and a contingent from Siena, having taken several adjoining castles made a sortie against the city of Arezzo and besieged it in force. The Aretines, strongly fortified, remained behind their city walls, looking on, while the Florentines in the mocking spirit which was a feature of the times, contented themselves with running in full view of the enemy their national game, the *Pallio*, on the customary day, the Feast of John the Baptist. Then they retired, no blows having been struck on either side. But the contingent from Siena, fired with that vanity which Dante declared was a conspicuous trait in the Sienese,[1] refused to join the strongly-guarded retreat of the main force. Their camp had been damaged by a storm and they delayed some time behind. Buonconte da Montefeltro, having observed this, had time to lay an ambush for them at the ford of the Toppo on the Piave, a small stream which crossed the road a few miles from Arezzo. The Ghibelline ambush was completely successful. The Sienese, among whom was Talano Adimari, were surprised and thrown into wild disorder. They were outnumbered and outmanœuvred, and their only refuge lay in flight. This ignominious defeat, which turned the laugh against the Guelf Taglia in their audacious enterprise, is that with which one of these Guelf fugitives taunts the

[1] *Inf.*, xxix, 121. 'Now was there ever so vain a people as the Sienese?'

other at the moment when Dante caught sight of them. The Lano of the text is evidently Talano Adimari, and Dino Campagni strikes in with the missing link of evidence which connects Talano with the battle of Campaldino. For in Dino's graphic account of the battle there occurs the illuminating sentence: ' Messer Talano Adimari and his men returned in hot haste (*presto*) to their own home.' It is pretty evident that this was before the issue of the battle was decided, though Talano may have given to his precipitate return the colour of bearing tidings of victory to the expectant city. Putting the various pieces of evidence together, the identification of Talano seems conclusive. Dante plainly says that he saw Lano in the act of running away from the enemy, as he had done in the skirmish on the Toppo a few months before, and his reason for pillorying this ignominious coward seems to lie in the fact that the two incidents had stamped Lano as sufficiently notorious to be recognizable. His flight fixes the occasion and supplies a strong clue to the meaning of the strange events which took place in the Wood.

So far the only action which Dante has recorded of himself was one of sudden terror and cruelty. In recalling that tumultuous day, its changing panorama of dismay, assault, danger, and triumph, there was yet one more incident, an act this time, not of violence, but of mercy on his part, that he desired to put on record. It would seem that as Lano vanished, his comrade changed his own headlong advance into a violent attack. The Wood was by this time alive with the Aretine mercenaries depicted as fierce war-dogs. Eager for bloodshed, no longer restrained from plunder, these savage auxiliaries followed their masters like hounds of chase, wherever the enemy's ranks gave way. Hard in the path was the low-growing Bush, and on this Lano's comrade hurled himself, seemingly, so the verse suggests, turning on his foe for lack of breath to flee further. In an instant the Bush was the centre of a fierce hand-to-hand struggle, one of the writhing breathless ' groups ' into which medieval battlefields were apt to be resolved. Just as Dante a while ago had broken single-handed the bough from the Thorn-Tree, so now Lano's comrade, supported by savage war-dogs,[1] attempted to break down the dense low-growing human thicket. ' They

[1] Dante elsewhere calls the Aretines 'botoli' or savage dogs (*Purg.*, xiv, 46.)

set their teeth into that which crouched (*i.e.*, the Bush as contrasted with the lofty Thorn) and tore it piecemeal; then they dragged away the wretched limbs—elsewhere alluded to as ' fronde.'

Inf., XIII, 130-151.

THE BISHOP OF AREZZO EXCULPATES HIMSELF

Then did my Escort take me by the hand
And lead me to the Bush that was in vain
Lamenting o'er its bleeding injuries.
' O Giacomo ', it cried, ' da Sant' Andrea
' What hast thou gained by making me thy screen?
' How am *I* guilty for thine evil life? '
Then when my Master close beside it stopped,
He said: ' Who wast thou, that through many wounds
' Art breathing out with blood such dolorous speech? '
And he to us: ' O spirits that have come
' To see the slaughter treacherous through which
' My shoots have been thus vilely torn from me,
' Gather them at the foot of their sad plant.
' I of that city was that hath exchanged
' Its first protector, for the Florin.
' Hence with its craft will it for ever make
' The city sorrowful; and were it not
' That on the Arno's passage still remains
' Some vestige of him, would those citizens
' Who builded it again upon the ashes
' Attila left, have done their work in vain.
' I made a gallows for me of my Castles.'

The first protector of Florence was the Empire.

The incident, which is presented as a *chose vue*, exhibits certain very obscure features. Its treacherous character is twice implied, first in the mention that the chase advanced on the left side, and next in the complaint made by the Bush that the massacre was ' *disonesto* '. This was no straightforward deed of war such as Dante's assault upon the *Pruno*. Unless we are to take the ejaculation of the Bush, ' O Jacopo da Sant' Andrea ' as an invocation (an explanation which does not satisfy), it must be concluded that Jacopo was the name of Lano's comrade. The description ' da Sant' Andrea ' may imply that he was a member of the Conti Guidi family, for all the four branches of the Conti Guidi bore a Saint Andrew's cross on their shields, and there were many members of the family present at the battle, some as Guelfs, some as Ghibellines. He may, however, have been a descendant, son, or grandson, of the Jacopo della Capella di Sant' Andrea mentioned by some early commentators. From the indignant remonstrance ' What use has it been to thee to make a screen of me? ' it may be inferred that the ' Bush ' had fallen into a trap set for him by Jacopo with the design of covering his own malpractices. The assault upon the *Cespuglio* may possibly point to the following historical circumstances, though full particulars are lacking.

One of the most famous Florentines fighting against his own city in the battle of Campaldino was the Bishop of Arezzo, Guglielmino degli Ubertini. Like Guido da Montefeltro, he was there under a cloud of suspicion. Foreseeing the desperate nature of the struggle which lay before Arezzo, he had ventured on his own responsibility to enter upon negotiations with the Priors of Florence, with a view to peace. As Bishop he was one of the great territorial magnates in Arezzo, and owned certain castles which were of the utmost importance to the Florentines. It was these ' Case ' that he had proposed to make over for a final sum of money to the Florentine government as pledge of peaceful intentions on the part of Arezzo. His mistake was in undertaking such negotiations unknown to his Ghibelline colleagues. The circumstances leaked out and the Bishop was openly accused of selling his adopted city. Feeling grew so high in Arezzo that a conspiracy was formed to assassinate him. This plot was discovered by his nephew, Guglielmo de' Pazzi, in time to protect the Bishop, though men said the nephew openly regretted the deed had not been done before he came to hear about it. It was under such conditions that the unhappy Bishop took the field. His position was to the last degree precarious. On the one hand he was hated by the Florentines as a renegade, fighting against his native city. On the other hand he was feared and suspected by the soldiers he ostensibly commanded. From Villani's account there seems to have been a great slaughter round his banner. Not only was the Bishop killed, but Guglielmo de' Pazzi and his nephews also. There is grave reason to suspect that the Bishop was slain, not by the enemy, but by the angry Aretines.

He afforded a conspicuous example of one who flung his own life away. And it was his shifty dealings in connection with Bibbiena and his other dwellings which cost him his life and honour. He ' made a gibbet for himself out of his own houses '.

His allusion to Florence is entirely in keeping with the bitter sentiments of one slain fighting against her. He calls it the city ' which changed its first patron into the " Baptist " '. The first patron, so the commentators tell us, was Mars, and they point in support of this interpretation to a fragment of a statue of Mars on the bridge over the Arno. It is true this may have been the ostensible meaning. But it is likely that in the allegorical sense the first patron is intended for the Emperor in allusion to the days when the whole of Italy was the appanage of the Empire, and that the change to the ' Baptist ' is a sardonic reference to the Florentine florin which bore the figure of the Baptist [1] on the reverse side, and had become the new master of the city. Were it not that some Ghibelline blood still remained in the city in the quarter near the bridge, it could never have been raised up to glory, so the old Ghibelline maintained. If the words of Cacciaguida in which he tells over with pride the names of old Ghibelline families, be compared with this dying lament it will be seen that the same spirit animates them both. Florence might root out the old stocks. But it was on them after all that her fame rested. It would seem that the *Cespuglio* meant to draw a parallel between his own conduct and that of his native city. Both had forsaken their real patron and transferred their allegiance to the Florin.

Meantime Dante was performing an act of mercy, and since all Dante's actions in the poem are to be understood as things which he actually did in real life, it may be concluded that he was moved by gracious feelings of love and pity to come to the rescue of the fellow-citizen who was his foe. Possibly he brought together some of his scattered kindred [2] who might receive his last commands. When Dante turned away the voice of the *Cespuglio* was growing '*fiocco*' or faint, and it may be inferred that he was near his end. It is impossible to resist the conviction that a sharp contrast is intended to be drawn between Dante's act of violence in the first episode and his act of mercy in the second. Actual contact with bloodshed

---

[1] Cf. *Inf.*, xxx, 74.
[2] Cf. *Para.*, xv, 88. ' *O fronda mia-* ' for ' my descendant '.

had transformed the exiles for him from lifeless stocks into human beings and he acted accordingly. It is a unique instance of such intervention in the *Inferno*.

The narrative of the happenings in the Wood is curiously inadaptable to any notion of eternal punishment. The human stocks who by their own act had destroyed themselves are presented at the beginning, it is true, in a static condition. But this conception is speedily effaced by a diversity of incidents which could not recur, and were in no sense retributive since they were the direct consequences of Dante's action. The transition from rapid movement to long pauses of reflection when Virgil addresses the actors in the drama are in keeping with a reminiscence of the past, when sometimes a flash of memory awakens former impressions in vivid detail, while sometimes Reason calls a halt to summon up the motives of the unhappy victims and let them plead their own excuses.

THE REMAINDER OF THE JOURNEY

Freed from military service Dante depicted himself at the age of twenty-five in act to enter the *Arena* of public life. It lay stretched out before him in the likeness of those burning plains which the Prophet took as an image of an ill-governed State. The flames of ceaseless ecclesiastical malediction descended over all, scorned by hardened offenders; source of extreme apprehension to some; biting deep into certain Ghibellines, stripped naked of all they possessed; wholly innocuous to others beheld busily pursuing their illegal trade of usury. Of these latter Dante was to gain ' full experience ' for there is documentary record of the loans he procured during these years, not all repaid at the time of his death.

Thence he descended lower to gain first-hand knowledge of the Papal administrative system, under the figure of Leviathan, with which it would seem he connected himself during the brief reign of the Joachist Pope Celestine V. Thereupon we behold the great Leviathan taking a downward and retrograde course, while from his unsafe seat Dante could observe terror, confusion, and flames around.

In successive scenes he exposed the iniquities of the Papal system in Rome (Malebolge), under Boniface VIII, and described his own personal encounters with the Pope. He painted in vivid, often passionate language, his successive adventures among fraudulent statesmen, hypocrites, sacrilegious thieves, false counsellors, fomenters of discord and falsifiers.

Finally, in a specifically harsher vein, he depicted the scenes which passed before his eyes on a still lower level of brutal inhumanity among traitors guilty of betraying their kindred, their benefactors, their native country, their lawful Emperor Henry VII. Into this latter stage of the journey he wove an image of frozen age, ending with Death. Under the Satanic form of Dis he hid the detested Papal system to whose sinister machinations the Spirituals attributed the woes of mankind.

The narrative is punctuated with dates by means of which the course of Dante's own autobiography may be traced. These are partly indicated through the device of mentioning the hour. The journey started about 7 p.m., and Dante's life at the year 1265. Reckoning the average life of man at seventy-two years, the travellers must advance at the rate of three years to an hour in order to occupy the entire night and day allotted to the journey. The close is, however, indeterminate. For, although not without forebodings of his end, he could not know at what hour he should encounter Death.

Other dates were fixed by details supplied about well-known personages whom Dante had met, as, for instance, the description recorded above of Talano degli Adimari, in the act of running away at Campaldino, in 1289, taunted as he ran for having done the same at a recent skirmish. Another significant date was fixed by the allusion to Buiamonte (under description of his coat-of-arms) as the *Cavalier Sovrano*, with powers to execute justice on illegal usurers. Buiamonte was Gonfalonier of Justice in Florence during the year 1292, and was clearly holding that office when Dante overheard him invoked.

The key-date of the *Inferno* at 7 a.m., corresponding to the year 1300-1, has been already mentioned. One more instance must suffice. One of the Sowers of Discord in Canto xxviii, evidently meaning to impute heretical sympathies to Dante, bade him warn Dolcino, leader of the Apostolic Brethren against whom Clement V was leading a Crusade, that his stronghold at Novarese would shortly be taken and his followers starved out by stress of weather. This actually happened in 1306, and was followed by Dolcino's barbarous execution. The encounter with the personage, disguised under the figure of Mahomet, is therefore fixed for the period just before the perpetration of this crime.

Many of the enigmatic figures whom Dante either left unnamed, or presented under some character chosen from history or literature, as bearing an obvious analogy to men of his own time, yield up their identity when the particular *mise en scène* is laid side by side with the events then being enacted. In this way it is possible to get glimpses of Dante's actions in certain emergencies, no less than of his judgments on his contemporaries.

Perhaps at some future time there may be opportunity to develop further the theme of Dante's personal adventures in the *Inferno*.

PRINCIPAL WORKS USED OR CITED

ON THE LIFE AND WORKS OF DANTE

ANONIMO FIORENTINO. *La Commedia di D.A.* Comento.

EUGÈNE AROUX. *Dante Hérétique, Révolutionnaire, et Socialiste.* Paris. 1854.
Clef de la Comédie Anti-catholique de Dante Alighieri. Paris. 1856.

BRUNONE BIANCHI. *La Commedia di D.A.* Florence. 1886.

G. BOCCACCIO. *Comento sopra la Commedia, preceduto della vita di D.* 2 vols. Florence. 1895.

FRANCESCO DA BUTI. *La Commedia di D.A.* Comento.

DANTE. *The Banquet.* Translated by K. Hillard. 1859.

DURANTE. *Il Fiore.* Texte inédit publié par F. Castets. Paris. 1881.

PROFESSOR EARLE. *Dante's Vita Nuova. Quarterly Review.* July 1896.

G. M. FILELFO. *Vita di D.A.* 1828.

PIETRO FRATICELLI. *Storia della Vita di D.A.* 1861.

E. G. GARDNER. *Dante and the Mystics.* 1913.

GIOV. LIVI. *Dante, suoi primi Cultori, sue Gente in Bologna, con documenti inediti, etc.* Bologna. 1918.

ISIDORO DEL LUNGO. *Dante ne' Tempi di Dante.* Bologna. 1888.
Dal Secolo e dal Poema di Dante. Florence. 1898.

EDWARD MOORE. *Contributions to the Textual Criticism of the Divina Commedia.* 1889.
Studies in Dante. First, second, and third series.
Time References in the Divina Commedia. 1887.

MOORE AND PAGET TOYNBEE. *Le Opere di Dante Alighieri.* Oxford. 1924.

FRANCESCO D'OVIDIO. *Nuovi Studii Danteschi.* Milan. 1907.

A. F. OZANAM. *Dante et la Philosophie Catholique au 13ième Siècle.* Paris. 1872.

JULES PACHEN. *Psychologie des Mystiques Chrétiens. Dante et les Mystiques.* Paris. 1909.

GIOVANNI PAPANTI. *Dante secondo la Tradizione e i Novellatori.* Leghorn. 1873.

W. H. V. READE. *Moral System of Dante's Inferno.* 1919.

GABRIELE ROSSETTI. *La Divina Commedia con comento analitico.* 1826.

G. A. SCARTAZZINI. *Divina Commedia.* 4 vols. Florence. 1874-90.
Dantalogia. 1894.
Enciclopedia Dantesca. 1896.
Vocabolario Concordanza. 1905.

TEMPLE CLASSICS. *Inferno, Purgatorio, Paradiso.* Edited by H. Oelsner, translated by Thomas Okey.
Il Convivio. Translated by P. H. Wicksteed.
De Monarchia. Translated by P. H. Wicksteed.
Epistolae. Translated by P. H. Wicksteed.
Ecloghi. Translated by P. H. Wicksteed.
De Vulgari Eloquentia. Translated by A. G. F. Howell.

PAGET TOYNBEE. *Dante Alighieri, His Life and Works.* Fourth Edition. 1910.
Dantis Alegherii Epistolae. Oxford. 1920.

W. W. VERNON. *Readings on the Inferno of Dante.* 1899.

P. H. WICKSTEED. *Early lives of Dante translated.* 1904.
Dante and Aquinas. 1913.

P. H. WICKSTEED AND E. G. GARDNER. *Dante and Del Virgilio.* 1901.

NICOLA ZINGARELLI. *Dante. Storia Letteraria d'Italia.* Milan.

HISTORICAL

MICHELE AMARI. *Storia del Vespro Siciliano.* Paris. 1843.

FUNCK BRENTANO. *Caractère religieux de la Diplomatie.*

VITA COELESTINI PAPAE V. *Muratori Rer. Ital. Scrip.* Vol. iii.

DOMENICO COMPARETTI. *Virgilio nel medio evo.* 2 vols. Firenze. 1896.

ROBERT DAVIDSOHN. *Geschichte von Florenz.* Berlin. c. iv. 1927.

P. H. DENIFLE UND FRANZ EHRLE (editors). *Archiv für Litteratur und Kirchengeschichte des Mittelalters.* II, III. Berlin.
1. *Petrus J. Olivi.*

2. *Die Spirituelen.*
3. *Angelus de Clareno* and *Historia Tribulationum.*
CLAUDE FLEURY. *Histoire Ecclésiastique.* XVIII, XIX. Paris. 1758.
EMILE GEBHART. *Recherches Nouvelles sur l'Histoire du Joachinisme.*
Revue Historique. XXXI. 1886.
F. GREGOROVIUS. *The City of Rome in the Middle Ages.* V, VI. Translated by A. Hamilton.
CHARLES JOURDAIN. *Excursions Historiques et Philosophiques à travers le moyen âge.* Paris. 1880.
CRISTOFORO LANDINO. *Li Livri in Virgilii Allegories.* 1508.
C. V. LANGLOIS. *Questions d'Histoire et d'Enseignement.* Paris. 1902.
H. C. LEA. *History of Auricular Confession and Indulgences in the Latin Church.* 3 vols. 1876.
History of the Inquisition of the Middle Ages. 3 vols. 1888.
POMPEO LITTA. *Celebri Famiglie Italiane.* (Continued by L. Passerini.) Milan. 1852.
ISODORO DEL LUNGO. *Dino Compagni sua Cronaca.* Florence. 1879.
Una Vendetta in Firenze del 1295. *Arch. Stor. Ital.* 4S. C.18. 1886.
G. H. LUQUET. *Aristote et l'Université de Paris pendant le XIIIième Siècle.* Paris. 1904.
PIERRE MANDONNET. *Siger de Brabant et l'Averroïsme Latin.* Fribourg. 1899.
C. MINIERI-RICCIO (editor). *Charles of Anjou.* Letter book, 1273-1285.
CHARLES MOLINIER. *L'Inquisition dans le Midi de la France au 13ième et au 14ième Siècle.* Paris. 1880.
LODOVICO MURATORI. *Annali d'Italia.* VII, VIII. Monaco. 1763.
H. NETTLESHIP. *Ancient Lives of Vergil.* 1879.
F. T. PERRENS. *Histoire de Florence.* I, II, III, Paris 1877.
B. PLATINA. *Lives of the Popes.* Edited by W. Benham.
REGINALD POOLE. *Lectures on the History of the Papal Chancery.* Cambridge. 1915.
HASTINGS RASHDALL. *Universities of Europe in the Middle Ages.* I. Oxford. 1895.

PRINCIPAL WORKS USED OR CITED

ODERICUS RAYNALDUS. *Annales Ecclesiastici.* Lucca. 1747-56.

ERNEST RENAN. *Joachin de Flore et l'Evangile Eternel. Nouv. Ed. d'Hist. Relig.* Paris. 1884.

XAVIER ROUSSELOT. *Historie de l'Evangile Eternel.* Paris. 1861.

M. S. DE SISMONDI. *Histoire des Républiques Italiennes du Moyen Age.* Brussels. 1858.

SERGIO TERLIZZI. *Le Relazioni di Carlo d'Angio con la Toscana* 1265-1285. Rome. 1906.

PAGET TOYNBEE. *Dictionary of Proper Names and Notable Matters in Works of Dante.* Oxford. 1898.

A. S. TURBERVILLE. *Mediaeval Heresy and the Inquisition.* 1920.

FERRETUS VICENTINUS. *Hist. Rerum in Italia gestarum,* 1250-1318. *Rer. It. Ser.* t. 3.

J. M. VIDAL. *Bullaire de l'Inquisition Française au XIVième Siècle.* Paris. 1913.

PASQUALE VILLARI. *Two First Centuries of Florentine History.* Translated by Linda Villari. 1908.

LUCAS WADDING. *Annales minorum . . . Rome.* 1731-45.

JOHN K. WRIGHT. *Geographical Lore of the Times of the Crusades.* New York. 1925.

ON PHILOSOPHY AND RELIGION

ALBERTUS MAGNUS. *Opera.* Paris. 1591.

S. THOMAS AQUINAS. *Opera omnia.* Rome. 1882-99.

ARISTOTLE. *Nicomachean Ethics.* Translated by F. H. Peters. 1881.

S. AUGUSTINE. *Opera omnia.* Antwerp. 1700.

ROGER BACON. *Opera.* Edited by J. S. Brewer. Rolls Series, c. 1. 1859.

S. BERNARD. *De Consideratione.* Translated by George Lewis.

BIBLIA SACRA. *Vulgatae Editionio.* Paris. 1870.

BOETHIUS. *Consolations of Philosophy.* Various editions and translations.

S. BONAVENTURA. *Opera omnia.* Paris. 1874.

L. BOURGAIN. *La Chaire Française au XIIième Siècle.* Paris. 1879.

G. G. COULTON. *From S. Francis to Dante.* 1907.
Mediaeval Studies. Series I. 1915.
Infant Perdition in the Middle Ages. 1922.
Art and the Reformation. Oxford. 1928.
MARGARET DEANESLEY. *The Lollard Bible.* Cambridge. 1920.
EMILE GEBHART. *L'Italie Mystique.* 1893.
CHRISTOPH U. HAHN. *Geschichte der Ketzer im Mittelalter.* (Including extracts from *Joachim de Flore.*) Stuttgart. 1850.
ADOLPH HARNACK. *History of Dogma.* Translated by J. Miller. 1898.
J. B. HAURÉAU. *Histoire de la Philosophie Scolastique.* Paris. 1880.
RAMÓN LULL. *Blanquerna.* 1926.
Book of the Lover and the Beloved. 1923. Translated from Catalan by E. Allison Peers.
GUILLAUME DE LORRIS ET JEAN DE MEUNG. *Le Roman de la Rose.* Edition de Francisque Michel. Paris. 1864.
ALFRED MAUREY. *Croyance et Légendes du Moyen Age.* Paris. 1896.
E. R. OWST. *Preaching in Medieval England.* Cambridge. 1926.
W. H. V. READE. *Philosophy in the Middle Ages.* (Cambridge Medieval History. V.) Cambridge. 1926.
ERNEST RENAN. *Averroës et Averroïsme.* Paris. 1852.
GABRIELE ROSSETTI. *Il Mistero dell' Amor Platonico del Medio Evo.* 5 v.
Disquisitions on the Antipapal Spirit. Translated by G. Ward. 2 vols. 1834.
JOHN OF SALISBURY. *Opera omnia.* 5 v. 1848.
MICHELE SCHERILLO. *Alcuni Capitoli della Biografia di Dante.* Turin. 1890.
FELICE TOCCO. *L'Eresia nel Medio Evo.* Florence. 1884.
P. H. WICKSTEED. *Reactions between Dogma and Philosophy.* Series II. (Hibbert Lectures.) 1920.
NORMAN P. WILLIAMS. *The Ideas of the Fall and of Original Sin.* (Bampton Lectures.) 1924.
M. DE WULF. *Histoire de la Philosophie Médiévale 2ème édition.* Louvain and Paris.

PHILOLOGICAL

L. G. BLANC. *Vocabolario Dantesco.* Florence. 1890.

ADRIANO CAPELLI. *Dizionario di Abbreviature latine ed italiane.* Milan. 1912.

T. C. DONKIN. *Etymological Dictionary of the Romance Languages.* 1864.

C. DU F. DUCANGE. *Glossarium mediae et infimae Latinitatis.* Paris. 1846.

J. FACCIOLATI. *Lexicon.* 2 v. 1828.

W. W. SKEAT. *Etymological Dictionary.* Oxford.

F. D'ALBERTI DI VILLANOVA. *Grande Dizionario italiano-francese.* 2 v. Bassano. 1831.

Vocabolario degli Accademici Della Crusca Florence. 1863.

INDEX

Buiamonte, 264.
Buonconte (*see* Montefeltro, Buonconte da).

CACCIAGUIDA, 233, 262.
Caesar Augustus, 250.
Cain, 106, 107.
Calboli, Fulcieri da, 246.
Camilla, 40, 90.
Campaldino, battle of, 3, 79, 237, 238, 253, 254, 258, 264.
Casella, 210.
Cato, 118.
Cavalcanti, Guido, 15, 81, 177, 202, 207, 208, 209, 210, 211, 212.
Cecina, 246.
Celestine V, Pope, 22, 189, 193, 263.
Centaurs, 229, 230, 235, 236, 237, 238, 239, 241, 242.
Cerberus, 108, 116, 117, 118, 119, 188, 190, 191, 195, 196.
Cerchi, Vieri dei, 208.
Charles Martel, 193, 241, 242.
Charles of Anjou, 18, 23, 45, 70, 71, 73, 74, 76, 81, 82, 109, 110, 111, 112, 113, 114, 115, 123, 126, 127, 139, 140, 148, 149, 150, 151, 152, 153, 243.
Charles II of Naples, 23, 31, 193, 230, 237, 238, 243.
Charon, 57, 58, 59, 60, 61.
Charybdis, 132, 134.
Chaucer, 171.
Children of Dante, 3, 98.
Chiron, 235, 236, 239, 240, 241.
Ciacco, 108, 120, 121, 122, 123, 124, 125, 126, 134.
Cialuffi, Lapa (*see* Stepmother of Dante).
Cicero, 9, 65, 86, 205, 218, 228.
Ciris, 184.
City of Despair, 160.
Civil War, 141, 144.
Clement IV, Pope, 74, 110.
Clement V, Pope, 158, 264.
Clement VI, Pope, 66.
Cleopatra, 104.
Cocytus river, 64.
Compagni, Dino, 33, 208, 259.
Confession, 99, 101, 102.
Confirmation, 112.
Conradin, 70, 82, 109, 113, 251, 252, 253.
Constance, Queen, 140.
Constantinople, 68, 113.

Convivio, Il (see *Banquet, The*).
Cornelia, 90.
Corneto, 246.
Corradino (*see* Conradin).
Cowards and captives, vision of the, 74.
Cowardice and treachery, 256.
Crete, 231, 232.
Crosses, 168.
Crusade, 115, 233.
Cyclops, 162.

DANTE Alighieri:
allegorical form of writing, 2, 4, 10, 11, 18.
allegorical theme, 1, 2, 8.
allusion to Mother, 138, 149, 151.
autobiographical note, 25, 28, 35, 52, 92, 251, 264.
backsliding, etc., 29.
baptism, 83.
birth, 1, 80.
childhood and early education, 86.
childhood's early impressions, 80.
conception, 1, 67.
confession, 99.
confirmation, 99.
Dante myth, 17.
death, figure of, 1, 35.
deed of violence, 247, 262.
Divine Justice, conception of, 2.
early years, 28.
exile, 71, 210, 211, 215, 255, 256, 257.
exile and death sentences, 3, 25, 34.
Guild of Physicians and Druggists, 3, 30.
Inferno a parable, etc., 46.
Inferno a satire, 2, 8, 19.
life, 2, 3, 28, 34.
love, first thought of, 97.
military service, 2, 3, 248, 263.
monastic novitiate, 129, 146.
municipal labours, 3, 30.
opposition to Boniface VIII, 3, 19.
parentage, 2.
Prior, 3, 30, 32, 208.
Ptolemaic astronomy, 4.
religious principles, 1, 5.
school, grammar, 86, 129, 142.
secret history of his life and times, 2.
secret of his life, 25.